A Commentary upon the Creed of Imam al-Dardīr

Translation & Commentary
by Siddiq Adam Mitha

Forewords *by*
Shaykh Walead Mosaad &
Shaykh ʿAbd al-Raḥmān al-Shaʿʿār

Sunni Publications

First Edition, February 2019

ISBN 978-90-79294-40-4

A Commentary upon the Creed of Imam al-Dardir

Translation & Commentary by:
Siddiq Adam Mitha

Forewords by:
Shaykh Walead Mosaad &
Shaykh ʿAbd al-Rahman al-Shaʿʿar

Cover Design by:
A. Hiba

Printed by:
Bariet Ten Brink
Meppel, the Netherlands

Published by:
Sunni Publications
Rotterdam, the Netherlands
www.sunnipubs.com
info@sunnipubs.com

To my daughter Nur, my son Muhammad
and the future generations of Muslims
being raised in troublesome times—
may you be steadfast upon your faith always

Transliteration Table

ا/آ/ى	ā	ظ	ẓ
ب	b	ع	ʿ
ت	t	غ	gh
ث	th	ف	f
ج	j	ق	q
ح	ḥ	ك	k
خ	kh	ل	l
د	d	م	m
ذ	dh	ن	n
ر	r	ه	h
ز	z	و	w/ū
س	s	ي	y/ī
ش	sh	ة	a
ص	ṣ	ء	ʾ
ض	ḍ	أ	a/u
ط	ṭ	إ	i

Honorific Phrases

Exalted and Sublime is He

Allah's prayers and salutations be upon him

Peace be upon him

Peace be upon them

May Allah be pleased with him

May Allah be pleased with her

May Allah be pleased with them both

May Allah be pleased with them

TABLE OF CONTENTS

بسم الله الرحمن الرحيم

Foreword by Shaykh Walead Mosaad

Introduction to the Creed of Imam al-Dardīr

THE ISSUE OF THE REALITY OF THE UNIVERSE continues to provoke energetic discussion and debate. Scientists, philosophers, theologians, evolutionary biologists and the like have all offered their postulations and explanations for making meaning of our collective existence.

Indeed, these questions have intrigued humanity ever since recorded history began, and will continue to intrigue well beyond the lifespans of all living human beings today. Unlike our contemporary times, in the premodern era, roughly until the time of the European Enlightenment in the early eighteenth century, issues of the finer and technical points of theology were generally left to the theologians.

The emergence of the public intellectual in Europe during this time period posed a challenge to the hitherto monopoly of the clergy to issue pronouncements on the realities of the universe. Scientific inquiry began to steadily replace church doctrine as a means of ascertaining the truth about the nature of things, to the degree that religious doctrine ceased to be a means of knowledge, demoted to personal faith and private space, and consequently stripped of its ability to comment in the public space on the nature of the real and observed world.

Across the Mediterranean, in the Muslim majority world, similar developments were on the horizon. The rise of a theology based upon refutations of perceived deviant and heretic sects and doctrines came to define the genre of *ʿilm al-kalām* since the rise of sects within Islam after the period of the four righteous caliphs, and more intensely after the *Miḥna* (inquisition) driven by the *Muʿtazila* and their Abbasid patrons. As a result, the main focus of theological works in the time period from 500 H./1100 CE until 850 H./1450 CE was highly polemical, and the intended audience for such works were always the theologians themselves.

It was not until Ṣalāh al-Dīn's reassertion of Sunni control over Egypt, from the last Fatimid caliph, that the idea of a "theology for the masses" began to gain currency. The creed of the Fatimids, considered by the Sunni scholars as heterodox, was countered by reported readings of concise treatises of creed from Cairo's minarets. However, the formalization of this practice, coinciding with the Ayyubid Egypt, led to the popularization of the creedal text, characterized by the omission of philosophical and theological polemics of the earlier works.

One of the most famous of these creedal texts is the *Umm al-Barāhīn* of Muḥammad b. Yūsuf al-Sanūsī (d. 940 H./1490 CE), a North African scholar who was a theologian and pious Sufi. This work was quickly adopted by madrasas throughout North Africa, as well as Egypt and the Levant.

Similar works followed, such as Ibrāhīm al-Laqqānī's (d. 1041 H./1631 CE) *Jawhara al-Tawḥīd*, and al-Dardīr's longer work *al-Kharīda al-Bahiyya*. Commentaries were then penned on these short treatises as they were more akin to study aides than comprehensive self-explanatory works. Al-Dardīr wrote his own commentary on the *Kharīda*, but later penned a much shorter work, in prose, that succinctly summarized the essentials of the Islamic belief system. It would not be unreasonable to suggest that al-Dardīr had written this one page treatise with the average Muslim in mind, and not just the dedicated madrasa student.

Al-Dardīr was also a Sufi Shaykh, of the *Khalwatiyya*, a spiritual path that had enjoyed popular participation from students of the Sacred Law and the laity alike. The word revival would not be out of place of here, as some have suggested, as it is clear from al-Dardīr's methodology that he was concerned with the "average" Muslim, and his works in both jurisprudence and theology were distilled via the prism of Sufism, emphasizing the centrality of the servant's relationship with his Lord.

This venture into the practical ramifications of theology and jurisprudence acknowledged the uncertainty and instability of the early modern era in al-Dardīr's time, as if anticipating what was yet to come in the way of European domination and colonization.

Defining Islam via its core theology is essential to maintaining and preserving its normative practice. In an age where self-defined readings of Islam have begun to emerge, and perhaps even dominate, this wonderful translation and commentary is a welcome addition to the English language library of works on Islam. We pray that it serves as a continuous source of blessing for its original author, its translator and commentator, and all those who derive benefit from it.

Walead Mosaad—November 5, 2018

بسم الله الرحمن الرحيم

FOREWORD BY SHAYKH ʿABD AL-RAḤMĀN AL-SHAʿʿĀR

ALL PRAISE IS DUE TO ALLAH, Who declared Himself One in His essence, attributes and acts when He ﷻ said: ﴾*There is nothing like Him: He is the All-Hearing, the All-Seeing*﴿ [42:11], free from any partner or equal when He said: ﴾*Your God is the One God: there is no god except Him*﴿ [2:163] and to be in no need of a companion or child when He said: ﴾*...and that He—exalted be the glory of our Lord!—has neither spouse nor child.*﴿ [72:3]The One ﷻ Who sent Messengers by His pure grace and Who chose Islam as the religion for His servants when He said: ﴾*Today I have perfected your religion for you, completed My blessing upon you, and chosen as your religion Islam.*﴿ [5:3]

And may prayers and salutations be upon our master Muhammad ﷺ, a mercy sent to the whole universe, his family and companions. And I bare witness that there is no god but Allah ﷻ and that Muhammad ﷺ is His servant and Messenger.

Indeed, the science of theology is the most virtuous of the sciences. It is the primary obligation, and the foundation of all Islamic rulings due to its connection with the Divine essence. It is with this in mind that it is obligatory upon every Muslim to know that with which one's creed becomes sound. Allah ﷻ says in the Qurʾan: ﴾*I created jinn and mankind only to worship Me.*﴿ [51:56] Ibn Jurayj said: "...that is, to know Me." However, gnosis does not come except through knowledge. Allah ﷻ says: ﴾*So know, that there is no god but God.*﴿ [47:19]

In light of this, the theologians made the knowledge of Allah the first obligation upon the servant. Because of the importance of the science of theology, the scholars devoted their efforts to it. They wrote works in both prose and poetry, as is evident in the works of Imam al-Dardīr—may Allah sanctify his secret—"The Illuminous pearl" [*al-Kharīda al-Bahiyya*] and the text entitled, "The Creed of al-Dardīr" [*ʿAqīda al-Dardīr*].

Thus, our brother in faith, Dr. Siddiq Adam Mitha commendably set out in commentating upon this *Creed* in a simple and refined manner, a level appropriate for beginners in this field. I presented it to some knowledgeable brothers who have studied with this *faqīr* (poor one unto Allah), due to it being in the English language and they praised his commentary.

Therefore, may Allah ﷻ reward him with goodness and give him the ability to serve the great heritage of our nation even further. I ask Allah that He benefits with this commentary anyone who reads it or hears it in an all comprehensive manner.

Written by the lowly servant:
ʿAbd al-Raḥmān Muḥammad Rashīd al-Shaʿʿār
(19/12/18)

About the Author

Siddiq Adam Mitha comes from Bolton in the northwest of England. Whilst in Bolton he went through the traditional madrasa system where he developed an initial thirst for studying Islam. His enthusiasm and abilities were well noted by teachers and peers alike. Later as an adult, Siddiq left Bolton and went to study Medicine at the University of Liverpool. Here he was active in the Islamic Society. Through his role as president, he organised lessons and events for the Muslim student polity. He met inspiring teachers who further ignited his thirst for knowledge, and after completing Medical School and the subsequent training, he decided to answer his heart's call and follow his lifelong passion of studying and teaching the sacred sciences. He has since spent several years studying in Amman, Jordan. During this time, he has studied the Arabic language, *ʿaqīda* (creed), *manṭiq* (logic), Hadith sciences, *taṣawwuf* (Sufism) and is currently specializing in *Ḥanafī fiqh* (jurisprudence) under the tutelage and guidance of Shaykh Ṣalāḥ Abū al-Hāj. In addition, some of his other teachers include Shaykh ʿAlī Zayno, Shaykh Aḥmad al-Ḥasanāt, Shaykh ʿAbd al-Raḥmān al-Shaʿʿār, Shaykh ʿAlī Hānī, Shaykh Ismāʿīl al-Kurdī, Shaykh Muḥammad Nūr al-Ṣābirīn, Ustādh Maḥmūd al-Shūrbajī, and Dr. Muḥammad al-Najjār, amongst others. Siddiq's love for knowledge and the scholars has taken him to several countries to date, including Mauritania and Yemen. He currently resides with his family in Amman, Jordan where he is continuing his studies, as well as researching and writing, contributing to the corpus of Islamic literature in the English speaking world.

A COMMENTARY UPON THE CREED OF IMAM AL-DARDĪR

Translation & Commentary
by Siddiq Adam Mitha

Forewords *by*
Shaykh Walead Mosaad &
Shaykh ʿAbd al-Raḥmān al-Shaʿʿār

SUNNI PUBLICATIONS

بسم الله الرحمن الرحيم

PREFACE

Allah ﷻ says:
❴*So know, that there is no god but Allah.*❵ [47:19]

The Messenger of Allah ﷺ said:
"...say: 'I believe in Allah and then be steadfast.'"[1]

The Messenger of Allah ﷺ said: "...the people of Israel split into seventy-two sects and my nation will split into seventy-three sects: all of them are in the fire except one group. They asked: 'Who are they, O Messenger of Allah?' He ﷺ replied: 'What me and my companions are upon.'"[2]

Ibn ʿAṭāʾillah al-Iskandarī said: "Your reaching Him ﷻ,
is your reaching of knowledge of Him."[3]

The beliefs a person holds are of vital importance in the Islamic discourse, as one cannot be considered a Muslim until certain points of creed are accepted fully with both heart and mind. Once faith enters the heart, one must strive to keep steadfast upon it, protect it and nurture it.

Belief in Allah ﷻ is the pivot around which a Muslim's life revolves and the essence of his being, but most importantly, it is his key to Paradise and his protecting shield against Hellfire. It is with this understanding that the Prophets and Messengers strove tirelessly to make their people believe. They laboured and struggled to remove all types of abhorrent disbelief and to establish the word of God on earth. The Prophet Nūḥ عليه السلام is said to have called his people for nine hundred and fifty years[4] with little

---

[1] *Ṣaḥīḥ Muslim*, 1:65:38

[2] *Sunan al-Tirmidhī*, 5:26:2641

[3] *Al-Ḥikam* (Ibn ʿAṭāʾillah), Aphorism 203, p. 384

[4] Allah ﷻ says: ❴*We sent Nūḥ out to his people. He lived among them for fifty years short of a thousand; but when the Flood overwhelmed them, they were still doing evil.*❵ [29:14]

fruition; there is no doubt, however, that he did this because he understood the consequences of disbelieving which continued to fuel his concern for the fate of his people.

In the same manner, the final Messenger of Allah, our master Muhammad ﷺ, was sent as an eternal light to guide humanity towards the truth. His glorious life is ultimately a lesson that teaches us the magnitude of faith. Persecution, torture, war, abuse and emigration were the result of two powerful statements: the *shahādatayn*.[5] What the early generations endured, to protect and transmit this Message, is something that we will never be able to fully comprehend; however, what we can do is believe in the Message, understand it and be vehicles for its propagation.

In an age of uncertainty and confusion, having the *right* belief in Allah ﷻ is crucial, though once belief has been established, keeping steadfast upon it, as mentioned previously, is just as vital. As the ever-tightening grip of modernity and materialism grows stronger, we have seen the hold of religion weaken and loosen, to the point that many have started to question basic points of faith. This can either be due to their failure to reconcile modern thought with traditional orthodox theological views or because of their apathy and dislike for religion and tradition.

Learning about one's faith is not only necessary, it is a way to fortify the connection between the servant and his Creator. Theology is not—as is portrayed many a time—all about dispute, argumentation and rationalising, rather it is strongly tied to the science of spirituality. Learning, for example, about the necessary and impossible attributes of Allah ﷻ, not only protects one's outward faith but also consolidates one's relationship with Allah. How can one love one he does not know? Is not intimacy with God a result of having a deep connection and gnosis?

Throughout the ages there has been consensus with regards to what the basic tenets of faith are, like the oneness of Allah ﷻ, the finality of the Messenger of Allah ﷺ and the existence of an afterlife. However, there have always existed and still exist up to

[5] That is, the two testimonies of faith, which are: to testify that there is no god but God and that Muhammad ﷺ is the Messenger of God.

this day, everlasting debates concerning some of the finer points of creed, which ultimately materialise due to differences in understanding greater umbrella concepts like rationality and hermeneutics. Many a time, these finer points have no real significance to the general Muslim body polity, but nevertheless some of these creedal matters are of the utmost importance and cannot be ignored since "in the preservation of orthodoxy lies the preservation of Islam itself."[6]

Examples of these finer creedal matters are the vision of God, the nature of His ﷻ speech, the nature of the decree, destiny and the intended purport of some of the ambiguous verses in the Qurʾan. Yet, the ship of Sunni orthodoxy was kept afloat by stalwart Muslim theologians like Abū Ḥanīfa (d. 150 H.), al-Ṭaḥāwī (d. 331 H.), al-Ashʿarī (d. 324 H.), al-Māturīdī (d. 333 H.), al-Baqillānī (d. 403 H.), al-Ghazālī (d. 505 H.), al-Taftazānī (d. 793 H.), al-Sanūsī (d. 895 H.) and many others who sheltered the *umma* with the truth when the winds of falsehood and mendacity blew upon the Muslims. They sifted out the orthodox from the unorthodox, guarding the creed of Islam from innovation and preventing the laity from falling into dispute and disbelief.

These scholars wrote many a short treatise to help people understand their Lord and Creator in the correct manner. Texts like the famous *ʿAqīda* of Imam al-Ṭaḥāwī were free of lengthy prose and discussion, and only contained the basic tenets of faith. This meant that they were accessible to all, and many of them were memorised by children and adults alike.

The *ʿAqīda* or Creed of Imam al-Dardīr is one such text: it brings together with ease and succinctness most of the essential creed that every Muslim is obliged to have conviction in. The text is not as famous or as widespread as some of the other works in theology, like the Creed of Imam al-Ṭaḥāwī mentioned previously, the Creed of Imam al-Sanūsī or the Creed of Imam al-Nasafī (d. 537 H.); nonetheless, it is still taught widely and benefitted from by many teachers and students around the globe.

---

[6] *Aḥmad b. Ḥanbal and the Miḥna* (Patton), p. 2

A Note on the Translation and Commentary

I realised when I taught this text in 2016 that theology continues to baffle and perplex many students with its technical terms and rational arguments. It gives life to dormant areas in the brain and forces critical thinking, which many are unaccustomed to. This led me to write a commentary transmitting, relating and translating the words of the theologians with a view to unlock the text and help students to fully comprehend every single word of Imam al-Dardīr, which is the way of the Islamic scholarly tradition, so that the text can be confidently understood. It is an attempt to make theological concepts palatable to the modern reader, but at the same time staying true to the traditional model of the Islamic theologians. Although ideally the text should be studied with a teacher who can elucidate upon some of the harder concepts, the commentary has been written in a way that one can still find benefit even without a teacher.

I have tried to elaborate, where appropriate, on differences between the different schools of theology, especially between the *Ashʿarī* and *Māturīdī* schools and the *Muʿtazila*. However, it is important to note here that the basis of the text and commentary is according to the *Ashʿarī* school. The school of the *Muʿtazila* is more or less non-existent in the modern age, although their views and opinions are still alive and widespread. Therefore, I have decided to mention their stances in the commentary, firstly to understand the orthodox position better by understanding the opposite since "a person is unable to understand what he needs to except by learning that which he does not,"[7] and secondly, to allow one to strengthen one's capacity of reasoning in the theological arena.

I thought it appropriate to precede the commentary with some preliminary foundational topics related to theology. I have briefly discussed the name and definition of the science, its subject matter, its codifiers, Sunni orthodoxy and the *Muʿtazila*. They are in no way exhaustive in their content, but will hopefully provide a sufficient summary.

---

[7] *Al-Mabsūṭ* (al-Sarakhsī), 1:241

With regards to the translation, use has been made of the commentary and marginalia of Shaykh Muṣṭafā al-ʿAqabāwī on the *ʿAqīda al-Dardīr*, published by Muṣṭafā al-Bābī al-Ḥalabī, 1949 H. I have copied and reproduced the Arabic of the treatise from this edition. It is important to note that I came across four different, but similar, names for this treatise. In the aforementioned Muṣṭafā al-Bābī al-Ḥalabī edition, three different names appear: on the front page it is titled, *ʿAqīda al-Dardīr* (The Creed of al-Dardīr); on the third page, just above the actual treatise in Arabic, it is called *al-ʿAqīda al-Tawḥīdiyya* (The Creed of Oneness), and Muṣṭafā al-ʿAqabāwī himself, in his commentary, calls it *ʿAqīda Ahl al-Tawḥīd* (The Creed of the People of Oneness). Moreover, Shaykh Ismāʿīl al-Ḥāmidī in his commentary, published by Muṣṭafā al-Bābī al-Ḥalabī in 1939 CE, calls it *al-ʿAqīda al-Ṣughrā* (The Concise Creed).

There are no chapters or sections in the text as published in Arabic. The translator alone is responsible for the chapter divisions and headings as they appear in this work.

Generally, "*The Qurʾan: A New Translation*" by M. A. S. Abdel Haleem, published by Oxford University Press has been the translation of choice for verses of the Qurʾan translated in to English found throughout this text. Some minor edits have been made to certain verses; however, as a whole, the translations are of Professor Abdel Haleem.

ACKNOWLEDGEMENTS

First and foremost, I praise Allah ﷻ and show my utmost gratitude for His numerous blessings and countless bounties.

Secondly, there is no doubt that this work would not be possible if it was not for all the people who have supported me, and continue to do so, whether emotionally, financially, academically, or spiritually. I would like to extend my sincere gratitude to my parents, parents-in-law, family and friends for their love and continued support. I thank my wife especially, who gives me much needed confidence during depressing moments and provides comfort in times of hardship. I also thank a true friend, Talha Hafezi, for coordinating affairs and helping me achieve my dreams of learning and teaching.

And finally, my sincere gratitude to all my teachers, those who taught me and helped me understand this religion, and those who inspired me to seek knowledge and illuminated before me the way of the scholars.

Finding well-grounded teachers who possess not only knowledge but who also emulate the Prophetic way is becoming an increasingly difficult task. Here, I would like to briefly mention some of my teachers. Some of the inspiring individuals I have been blessed to study with include one of my childhood inspirations, Mawlānā Iqbāl Miṣbāḥī, who has dedicated his life to the service of religion. Another core teacher is Shaykh Ibrahim Osi Efa, who is an extremely charismatic teacher. I still remember the extraordinary theology classes where he taught *ʿAqīda al-Ṭaḥāwiyya* in Liverpool in 2006. There is no doubt that he watered within me the seed of pursuing the sacred sciences that had been planted by my childhood teachers. Also, Shaykh Haroon Hanif, a gifted teacher, who has had a great influence on my understanding of *Ḥanafī fiqh* and theology. In addition, during my stay in Amman, I have had the privilege to study theology with Shaykh Aḥmad al-Ḥasanāt, currently the general secretary of the *Dar al-Iftā* in Amman. He is a *Shāfiʿī* jurist of the highest caliber who benefitted me greatly with his deep insight in theology and *manṭiq* (logic). I had the opportunity to read *Sharḥ al-Kharīda al-Bahiyya* of Imam al-Dardīr with him in theology and the *Sullam* and *Īsāghūjī* in *manṭiq*. Also, Dr. Mohammad al-Najjār, a lecturer at the Hanafi Fiqh College at the World Islamic Sciences and Education University in Amman. He is another beautiful personality: a man of deep spirituality and wisdom who not only taught me *al-ʿAqāʾid al-Nasafiyya* but showed me how to inculcate theology in my spiritual development. I truly believe that he is a hidden gem who should be benefitted from. There is also Shaykh ʿAbd al-Raḥmān al-Shaʿʿār to mention. He is a young Syrian scholar from Damascus, currently residing in Amman. He is someone whom I studied theology with, and I still benefit from him tremendously. As a lover of all things spiritual and a specialist in *ʿaqīda*, he is a bright star with huge potential. He taught me the *Sharḥ Naẓm ʿAqīda Ahl al-Sunna* by Shaykh Muḥammad al- Hāshimī and *Umm al-Barāhīn* of Imam al-Sanūsī.

Before I finish, these acknowledgements would not be complete without mention of Dr. Ṣalāḥ Abū al-Ḥāj. Dr. Ṣalāh, whilst I have not studied theology with him, has been one of my greatest inspirations. He has been my primary mentor and directed me towards many of the teachers mentioned above. It is Dr. Ṣalāḥ who opened up before me the way of scholarship and instilled in me the seriousness and resolve one needs on the arduous path of knowledge. I have great love and admiration for him and pray Allah سبحانه وتعالى blesses his endeavours to revive the way of traditional Islam in Jordan and around the world.

All in all, I hope that both the beginner and advanced student and anyone interested in learning about the creed of Islam can benefit from this work, and that it can be a source of goodness to all in navigating the world in their journey towards God.

A Commentary upon the Creed of Imam al-Dardīr

Translation & Commentary
by Siddiq Adam Mitha

Forewords *by*
Shaykh Walead Mosaad &
Shaykh ʿAbd al-Raḥmān al-Shaʿʿār

Sunni Publications

بسم الله الرحمن الرحيم

INTRODUCTION

AHL AL-SUNNA WAL-JAMĀʿA

DURING THE TIME OF THE MESSENGER OF ALLAH ﷺ, there was no fixed term to define those who followed him, except the term *Muslim*. However, in later generations, after the demise of the Messenger of Allah, the creed of Islam was sullied with innovative thought and ideas—such as those of the *Muʿtazila* or *Khawārij* (Secessionists) and the like—which did not concur with the creed of the early generation [*salaf*].

In addition, during the fertile Abbasid period, there was a transmission of Hellenistic philosophy and many of the scholarly works of the Greeks were translated into Arabic in the pursuit of intellectual advancement. This, however, did not come without its challenges due to the many new "conflicting" ideas it presented. For this reason, it became important for people to distinguish themselves as being the true followers of Islam and the term *Ahl al-Sunna wal-Jamāʿa* (Sunni orthodoxy) was coined to define those who followed the Qurʾan, the Sunna and the way of the early generation [*salaf*]—as opposed to the people of innovation and heresy.[8]

The problem that has arisen in the current climate is lack of awareness with regards to what this term actually means when applying it to the vast array of sects, groups, ideologies and differences present within Islam: the term "has been so completely derailed in our times that few Muslims even know it is rolling down another track."[9]

According to al-Saffārīnī[10] and others, when this term is used it refers to *only* three[11] well known schools of theology:[12]

---

[8] *Ahl al-Sunna al-Ashāʿira* (al-Sinān & al-ʿAnjarī), p. 80

[9] *Kalam and Islam* (Keller), p. 1

[10] He is the erudite scholar and Imam, Muḥammad b. Aḥmad b. Sālim b. Sulaymān al-Saffārīnī, al-Nablusī al-Ḥanbalī. Born in the year 1114 H. in one of the villages of Nablus, Palestine, called Saffārīn. He travelled to Damascus in search of knowledge and studied with the famous Shaykh

I. The *Ash'arīs*
II. The *Māturīdīs*
III. The *Atharīs*[13]

There has been an overwhelming consensus in scholarly arenas, both historically and in the present time, that these are the only three schools of Sunni orthodox creed.[14] The majority of Muslims have either followed or follow one of these schools, which indicates their soundness and authenticity.

'Abd al-Ghani al-Nablusī, Shaykh al-Islam Muḥammad al-Ghazzī and many others. He died in the year 1188 H. in Nablus, leaving behind a plethora of works. [*Silk al-Ḍurar* (al-Murādī), 4:31]

[11] Some separate the people of *taṣawwuf* (Sufism or spirituality) into a fourth separate group; however, in reality, they do *not* have a creedal system that differs with the above three schools. The Sufis differ in their experience of theology, in that they look at creed from a variant angle. For example, rather than rationalising the existence of God, they endeavour to live and taste the oneness of God in their worldly life. Al-Hujwirī states: "*Ma'rifa* of God is of two kinds: one is discursive [*'ilmī*] and the other affective [*ḥālī*]." [*Kashf al-Maḥjūb*, Trans. from: *Islamic Theological Themes, A Primary Source Reader* (Renard), p. 421]

[12] *Lawāmi' al-Anwār al-Bahiyya* (al-Saffārīnī), 1:73

[13] *Athar* in Arabic is a tradition or narration. It is generally used as a synonym for the term Hadith. The term *Atharī* (scripturalist) is attributed to a group of scholars who emphasized reliance upon scripture to extrapolate creed, and restraint in rationally interpreting theological matters or extensively explaining them beyond the transmitted texts. Thus, they did not delve into discussions concerning the ambiguous verses [*mutashābihāt*] and relegated their meaning to Allah alone. Scholars such as Imam Aḥmad b. Ḥanbal and many of the scholars of Hadith like Imam al-Bukhārī have been attributed to this way of thought. [*Muqaddima Taqlīd al-Qalā'id* (al-Ḥamawī), p. 43-44]

It is crucial to note that the labelling of this group of scholars as the people of Hadith is not an indication that the *Ash'arīs* or *Māturīdīs* do not use Hadith or scripture. All three schools are from the people of Hadith, but what differs is their understanding of how to use scripture.

[14] Many Muslims may be unaware of the different schools of theology and their names and fear that their faith may be deficient. To know the name of these schools is not important, what is important is that the faith that one holds is in agreement with what the scholars of these schools have concurred upon.

As the Messenger of Allah ﷺ said: "Allah does not let my nation agree upon error;"[15] and so, it is inconceivable that the majority of Muslims have erred with regards to their creed.

It is worth mentioning that some restricted *Ahl al-Sunna* to only the *Ashʿarī* and *Māturīdī* schools. Al-Zabīdī states:

> If *Ahl al-Sunna wal-Jamāʿa* are mentioned, the intended meaning is: the *Ashʿarīs* and the *Māturīdīs*. Al-Khayālī states, in his marginalia upon *Sharḥ al-ʿAqāʾid*, that: "The *Ashʿarīs*, they are *Ahl al-Sunna wal-Jamāʿa*. This is what is well known in the lands of Khorasan, Iraq, the Levant and majority of places. And, in the lands beyond the river, it is used to mean the *Māturīdīs*, the followers of Imam Abū Manṣūr al-Māturīdī..."[16]

Moreover, when Ibn Ḥajar al-Haytamī, an Imam from the *Shāfiʿī* school, was asked about the people of innovation, he replied:

> The intended meaning of the people of innovation in it[17] is whoever contravenes *Ahl al-Sunna wal-Jamāʿa*, that is, the followers of Shaykh Abū al-Ḥasan al-Ashʿarī and Abū Manṣūr al-Māturīdī, the two Imams of *Ahl al-Sunna*.[18]

In a similar vein, the erudite scholar and polymath Shaykh Zāhid al-Kawtharī states: "Al-Ashʿarī and al-Māturīdī are the two Imams of *Ahl al-Sunna wal-Jamāʿa* in the lands of the east and west."[19]

Shaykh Abū Bakr al-Mullā, a famous twelfth century scholar from Aḥsāʾ likewise states: "One should know that *Ahl al-Sunna wal-Jamāʿa* are the followers of the two Imams: Imam Abū al-Ḥasan al-Ashʿarī and Imam al-Hudā Abū Manṣūr al-Māturīdī."[20]

---

[15] *Sunan al-Tirmidhī*, 4:466:2167

[16] *Itḥāf al-Sāda al-Muttaqīn* (al-Zabīdī), 2:6

[17] He is referring to a Hadith mentioned earlier in the text: "The worst of matters is the newly invented, and every innovation is misguidance."

[18] *Al-Fatāwā al-Ḥadīthiyya* (al-Haytamī), p. 280

[19] *Muqaddimāt al-Imam al-Kawtharī*, p. 51

[20] *Maslak al-Thiqāt* (al-Mullā), p. 19

It is worth noting that these schools differ very slightly and in reality, agree completely with regards to the basic and core tenets of faith. Al-Zabīdī states:

> Tāj al-Dīn al-Subkī said: "Know that *Ahl al-Sunna* have all agreed upon one creed with regards to what is necessary, possible and impossible, but they differed in the ways and principles that led to that."[21]

Similarly, Mullā ʿAlī al-Qārī al-Ḥanafī, was also of the opinion that the differences between the *Ashʿarīs* and *Māturīdīs* are speculative and "do not relate to creed built upon certainties."[22]

In summary, there is no doubt that the orthodox Sunni creed has been encapsulated by the aforementioned schools. The way is apparent for all who desire the truth and want to adopt the way of the vast majority of scholars, sages and theologians with regards to creed and belief. Orthodoxy in Islam is evident and manifest, the Prophet ﷺ is reported to have said that it is "a clear path whose night is like its day: no one deviates from it after me, except one who is damned."[23]

CODIFIERS OF THE SCIENCE

There are two main personalities who codified the creed of *Ahl al-Sunna wal-Jamāʿa* as we know it today:

I. Abū al-Ḥasan al-Ashʿarī[24]

He was the great Imam and theologian, ʿAlī b. Ismāʿīl b. Abū Bishr Isḥāq b. Sālim b. Ismāʿīl b. ʿAbdullah b. Mūsā, b. Bilāl b. Abū Burda b. Abī Musa ʿAbdullah b. Qays al-Ashʿarī (the companion of the Messenger of Allah ﷺ).

He was born in Basra in Iraq in the year 260 H. and resided in Baghdad until he passed away in the year 324 H.

---

[21] *Itḥāf al-Sāda al-Muttaqīn* (al-Zabīdī), 2:6
[22] *Mirqāt al-Mafātīḥ* (al-Qārī), 1:261
[23] *Sunan Ibn Mājah*, 1:29:43
[24] *Tabyīn Kadhib al-Muftarī* (Ibn ʿAsākir); *Ṭabaqāt al-Shāfiʿiyya* (al-Subkī), 3:347; *Ahl al-Sunna al-Ashāʿira* (al-Sinān, & al-ʿAnjarī), p. 39

In the beginning of his scholarly life, for approximately forty years, he followed the school of his stepfather,[25] the renowned *Muʿtazilī* scholar and head of the *Muʿtazila* in Basra, Abū ʿAlī al-Jubbāʾī. Under his tutelage, Abū al-Ḥasan al-Ashʿarī mastered the *Muʿtazilī* teachings and became one of the greatest proponents of the school.

However, later on in his theological career, the Imam started to realise the fallacies of the school and began his journey of doubt. He was regularly questioned regarding certain *Muʿtazilī* positions, prompting him to research and ask his teacher for guidance and answers, but the answers he received failed to satisfy him and gave little reassurance to his enquiring self.

It has been said that once he performed two units of prayer and asked Allah ﷻ to guide him to the straight path, after which he fell asleep. Whilst sleeping he had a dream in which he was blessed to see the Messenger of Allah. He complained to him ﷺ about some of his troubles, to which the Messenger of Allah said: "Hold fast to my Sunna." This, according to some, became one of the reasons for his abandonment of the *Muʿtazila* and his conversion to traditional Sunni orthodoxy.

Al-Ashʿarī was not ashamed to publicly declare his conversion. After having disappeared for fifteen days into his house, he reappeared and went to the mosque, ascended the minbar and shouted with the loudest of voices:

> O people, whoever knows me, knows me. Whoever does not know me then I will introduce myself to him: I am the son of so and so, the son of so and so. I used to say that the Qurʾan is created, that the [beatific] vision of Allah ﷻ [in the hereafter] is impossible, and that the actions of the servants [of God] are their own [creation]. And here, I stand repenting from the *Muʿtazilī* way...[26]

Imam Abū Bakr al-Ṣayrafī states:

[25] *Al-Mawāʿiẓ wal-Iʿtibār* (al-Maqrīzī), 4:193

[26] *Al-Fihrist* (Ibn al-Nadīm), p. 225

> The people of innovation before Imam Abū al-Ḥasan had raised their heads, but when he—may Allah have mercy upon him— appeared before them, he isolated them to the inside of a sesame seed.[27]

His Students

Some of his main students were:

I. Imam Abū al-Ḥasan al-Bāhilī[28]
II. Imam Abū ʿAbdullah b. Mujāhid
III. Imam Abū Muḥammad al-Ṭabarī, better known as al-ʿIrāqī

His Works

It has been said that he left over two to three hundred different works.

II. Abū Manṣūr al-Māturīdī[29]

He was the erudite scholar, theologian, *Ḥanafī* jurist and defender of the faith, Muḥammad b. Muḥammad b. Maḥmūd Abū Manṣūr al-Māturīdī.

The date of his birth is unknown, but his passing away has been recorded to be in the year 333 H. (944 CE), a short while after the demise of his contemporary, Abū al-Ḥasan al-Ashʿarī.

He was from an area called Māturīd in Samarqand, which is in present day Uzbekistan where he is also buried.

Abū Manṣūr was extremely wise, learned and intelligent and was one of the first (even before Abū al-Ḥasan al-Ashʿarī) to codify and expound the creed of *Ahl al-Sunna*, and specifically that of the great polymath and jurist Abū Ḥanīfa.

He studied under the tutelage of Abū Bakr Aḥmad al-Jūzjānī, Abū Naṣr al-ʿIyāḍī, and Naṣīr b. Yaḥyā al-Balkhī, who all took from Abū Sulaymān al-Jūzjānī. The latter's teachers were Qāḍī Abū

---

[27] *Ṭabaqāt al-Shāfiʿiyya* (al-Subkī), 3:349

[28] Abū Isḥāq al-Isfarāyīnī states: "I was next to Abū al-Ḥasan al-Bāhilī like a drop next to an ocean; and I heard al-Bāhilī say: 'I was next to al-Ashʿarī like a drop next to an ocean.'" [Ibid., 3:369]

[29] *Al-Fawāʾid al-Bahiyya* (al-Laknawī), p. 319; *Al-Jawāhir al-Muḍiyya* (Wafā al-Qurashī), p. 375; *Tāj al-Tarājim* (Ibn Quṭlubghā), p. 248

Yūsuf and Muḥammad b. al-Ḥasan al-Shaybānī, the two exceptional students of Abū Ḥanīfa. This direct chain of transmission to Imam Abū Ḥanīfa and his adherence to the school of Imam Abū Ḥanīfa may be the reason why so many of the followers of the *Māturīdī* school in theology are also *Ḥanafī* with regards to Islamic law.

Abū al-Muʿīn al-Nasafī states, in praise of al-Māturīdī:

> He is the one who was immersed in the seas of knowledge and extracted its pearls. He came to the proofs of religion, and with his eloquence, deep insight, and great talent beautified it, to the extent that Shaykh Abū al-Qāsim al-Ḥākim ordered that when he died it should be written on his grave that, "This is the grave of the one who attained the sciences with every breath of his, exhausted every possibility in its dissemination and acquisition and so his works in religion have been praised and the fruits from his life harvested."[30]

The *Muʿtazila*

The *Muʿtazila* (Withdrawers) are a group of Islamic speculative theologians whose school flourished in Basra and Baghdad between the 8th and 10th centuries CE. The school's origin is traced back to Wāṣil b. ʿAṭāʾ (d. 131 H.). Ḥasan al-Baṣrī (d. 110 H.), whilst teaching, is said to have been asked:

> O Imam of the religion, there is a group in our time which charges those who have committed major sins with disbelief: a major sin is disbelief according to them with which one exits the fold of Islam, they are the anathematizing *Khawārij*. Yet there is another group which defers judgement upon grave sinners: they say a major sin does not affect faith, just as an act of devotion is devoid of benefit without faith, and they are the Deferrers [*Murjiʾa*] of this nation. What is your judgement with regards to what should be believed in this matter?

[30] *Tabṣira al-Adilla* (Abū al-Muʿīn al-Nasafī), 1:471

Ḥasan al-Baṣrī begins to ponder. However, before he could reply, Wāṣil b. ʿAṭāʾ, one of Ḥasan al-Baṣrī's students, answered and said: "I do not say that the one who has committed a major sin is a complete believer or an outright disbeliever, but he is in a state between two states, neither a believer nor a disbeliever."

He is then reported to have withdrawn himself to a pillar in the mosque, relating his answer to others. To this, Ḥasan al-Baṣrī said: "Wāṣil has withdrawn [*iʿtazala*] from us." And so, he and his followers were the first ones who were termed as the *Muʿtazila* or the ones who withdrew.[31]

It is important to mention that it was their opponents who labelled them as the *Muʿtazila*, the name they chose for themselves was: *Ahl al-Tawḥīd wal-ʿAdl* (the People of Oneness and Justice).[32]

From thence, the school developed until it became the established doctrine in 827 CE in the reign of the Abbasid caliph Maʿmūn, which resulted in the great inquisition in the year 833 CE.

The *Muʿtazilī* school introduced Greek philosophical reasoning and gave the intellect a role beyond what can be rationally justified for it. They did not disregard scripture, but subjugated it to fit the limitations of their minds. This lead to the introduction of "a variety of abhorrent innovations"[33] in creed and caused them to deviate from the way of the early generations [*salaf*]. Many amongst the early *Muʿtazila* heavily occupied themselves with refuting Christians, Jews and atheists[34] and these "frequent close encounters with deviant groups"[35] may have been a cause of their downfall.

Their creed was summarized into five main principles [*al-uṣūl al-khamsa*] by the *Muʿtazilī* theologian and Qāḍī, ʿAbd al-Jabbār al-Hamadhānī:[36]

---

[31] *Al-Milal wal-Niḥal* (al-Shahrastānī), 1:62

[32] Ibid., p. 56

[33] *Ḥāshiya al-Kawtharī ʿalā al-Sayf al-Ṣaqīl li-Taqī al-Dīn al-Subkī*, p.21

[34] *Muqaddimāt al-Imam al-Kawtharī*, p. 44

[35] *Ḥāshiya ʿalā al-Sayf al-Ṣaqīl*, p.21

[36] *Sharḥ Uṣūl al-Khamsa* (al-Hamadhānī), p. 123

I. *Tawḥīd (Divine Oneness)*
II. *ʿAdl (Divine Justice)*[37]
III. *Al-Waʿd wal-Waʿīd (The Promise and the Threat)*[38]
IV. *Al-Manzila bayna al-Manzilatayn*
(The Intermediate Station)[39]
V. *Al-Amr bil-Maʿrūf wal-Nahiy ʿan al-Munkar*
(Commanding the Good and Forbidding Evil)

Most of the *Muʿtazilī* opinions mentioned throughout this work point back to one of these five principles.

THEOLOGY: DEFINITION AND NAMES

In this chapter, we will take a brief look at the definition of Islamic theology and some of its variant names in the Arabic language.

In the Arabic language, the science of theology is primarily called *ʿaqīda*. Linguistically, *ʿaqīda* means: to tighten, strengthen and to tie.[40]

---

[37] According to the *Muʿtazila*, all of God's actions are considered good, He ﷻ does not do any evil and does not desire it. By this they mean that Allah is obligated to do and will what is defined as "good" and impossible for Him to do the contrary of that; man is the originator of anything that is defined as "evil." This understanding of Divine justice led them to believe in the obligation upon Allah ﷻ to do that which is good or better for the servant, which in turn led them to believe in the necessity of sending Messengers and that disbelief is not willed by Allah ﷻ.

[38] According to the *Muʿtazila*, it is necessary for Allah ﷻ to keep His promises of reward for obedient servants because they are rightfully deserving of it, and it is necessary to keep His promises of punishment to disobedient servants because they are rightfully deserving of it. To rescind on His ﷻ promises is considered unjust, and therefore impossible for Allah.

[39] This is the *Muʿtazilī* belief, in opposition to the *Khawārij* and the *Murjiʾa*, which states that the one who commits a grave sin is neither a disbeliever nor a believer, but a *fāsiq*. [*Manhaj al-Ḥanafiyya fī Naqd al-Ḥadīth* (Khalīfa), p. 61]

[40] *Muʿjam Maqāyīs al-Lugha* (Ibn Fāris), 4:86

Al-Zabīdī states: "That which the scholars of morphological derivation have expressed is that the original meaning of *'aqd* is the opposite meaning of untying [*ḥal*]."[41]

Technically, the scholars define it as: the science through which religious doctrine is determined by bringing forth irrefutable proof and expelling uncertainty.[42]

Ibrāhīm al-Mārighnī al-Mālikī states: "...It is the science which researches Islamic creed that has been extrapolated from irrefutable evidence."[43]

Some of its other names are:[44]

I. *Al-Fiqh al-Akbar* (The Greatest Understanding)
II. *'Ilm al-Tawḥīd* (The Science of Monotheism)
III. *Uṣūl al-Dīn* (The Foundations of Religion)
IV. *'Ilm al-Dalīl wal-Burhān* (The Science of Evidences and Proofs)
V. *'Ilm al-Kalām* (Scholastic Theology)[45]

---

[41] *Tāj al-'Arūs* (al-Zabīdī), 8:394
[42] *Sharḥ al-Mawāqif* (al-Jurjānī), 1:40
[43] *Ṭāli' al-Bushrā* (al-Mārighnī), p. 66
[44] Ibid.
[45] *Kalām* linguistically means "speech." "At first, the term was used by pious believers in contempt of those who relied on logic and philosophy to give a rational explanation of their faith. Eventually, it came to mean scholastic theology." [*A Commentary on the Creed of Islam* (Evans & Elder), p. xiv]

There is a difference of opinion with regards to why it is employed as a name for the science of theology; some of the reasons that the scholars give are [as mentioned in *Sharḥ al-'Aqā'id al-Nasafiyya* (al-Taftazānī), p. 16]:

I. Because of the problem related to the speech [*kalām*] of God and the creation of the Qur'an, which became one of the most renowned of its issues, the most strongly disputed and the subject of the most controversy.
II. Because the subject of its investigations was their saying: "The discourse [*kalām*] about such-and-such."
III. Because of the ability it imparts in verbal debate and in compelling one's adversaries to submit.
IV. Because the theologians chose to speak about issues that the early generations chose to refrain from engaging.

Subject Matter

The topics addressed in traditional Islamic theology are three:

I. Pertaining to God [*Ilāhiyyāt*]
II. Pertaining to Prophethood [*Nubuwwāt*]
III. Eschatology or the Unseen [*Samʿiyyāt*]

Imam al-Dardīr deals with all three of these areas in his short treatise; however, he focuses mainly on God and His attributes, which is also the case in other theological tracts. This is because the crux of Islamic theology is related to God. Topics concerning Prophethood and eschatology are, in reality, ancillary, bearing no consequence theologically if one is devoid of faith in God.

Imam al-Dardīr

He is: Abū al-Barakāt, Aḥmad b. Muḥammad b. Aḥmad al-ʿAdawī al-Mālikī al-Khalwatī, famously known as Imam al-Dardīr.[46]

He was born in the year 1127 H. (1715 CE) and passed away on the 6th of *Rabīʿ al-Awwal*, in the year 1201 H. (1786 CE) in Cairo.

He had a thirst for the sacred sciences from a very young age, which led him to memorise the Qurʾan and enrol at the famous seminary of al-Azhar in Cairo. His proficiency and expertise in the *Mālikī* school made him one of the leading authorities of his time in *Mālikī* jurisprudence. Law, however, was not his sole interest. The Imam was a part of the Khalwatiyya Sufi order in which he excelled until he was given the mantle to lead the order and instruct others.

V. Because it is the most disputatious and controversial of the sciences, so speech was greatly needed for conversing with those of the opposite view and for refuting them.

[46] *Al-Aʿlām* (al-Zarkalī), 1:244; *Muʿjam al-Muʾallafīn* (Kaḥḥāla), 2:67; *Shajarāt al-Nūr al-Zakiyya* (Makhlūf), 1:516: bio no. 1446

Like many of the great scholars of the past, the Imam penned numerous works in various areas such Arabic rhetoric, *Mālikī fiqh* and spirituality. Some of his most well-known books are:

I. *Sharḥ al-Ṣaghīr* (The Concise Commentary)
II. *Sharḥ al-Kabīr* (The Great Commentary)[47]
III. *Al-Kharīda al-Bahiyya* (The Illuminous Pearl)
IV. *Sharḥ al-Kharīda al-Bahiyya*
(A Commentary of the Illuminous Pearl)
V. *Tuḥfa al-Ikhwān fī Ādāb Ahl al-ʿIrfān*
(A Gift for the Brethren Concerning the Conduct of the People of Gnosis)
VI. *Tuḥfa al-Ikhwān fī ʿIlm al-Bayān*
(A Gift for the Brethren: Concerning Rhetoric)
VII. *Aqrab al-Masālik li-Madhhab al-Imam Mālik*
(The Closest of Paths to the School of Imam Mālik)
VIII. *Fatḥ al-Qadīr fī Aḥādīth al-Bashīr al-Nadhīr* ﷺ
(Openings from the Almighty with regards to the Traditions of the Herald and Warner ﷺ)

The Imam left many students, his more well-known ones are:

I. Aḥmad b. Muḥammad al-Ṣāwī
II. Muḥammad b. Aḥmad b. ʿArafa al-Dasūqī
III. Ṣāliḥ b. Muḥammad al-Sibāʿī
IV. Muṣṭafā al-ʿAqabāwī

After his demise, some of the pious saw the Messenger of Allah ﷺ in a dream, giving them glad tidings that "Imam al-Dardīr had been bestowed with that which no eye has seen and no ear has heard." It is evident that the Imam was a true saint of Allah ﷻ, a sincere follower of the Muhammadan way, and an esteemed scholar whose knowledge still benefits today.

[47] The *Sharḥ al-Kabīr* and *al-Ṣaghīr* are commentaries upon the *Mukhtaṣar al-Khalīl* in *Mālikī fiqh*. They are two of the most important books of *fatwā* in the *Mālikī* school.

حاشيـــــة

علـــى

شرح عقيدة الدردير

تأليف

مصطفى بن أحمـد العقباوى

الطبعة الأخيرة

١٣٦٨ هـ – ١٩٤٩ م

مطبعة مصطفى البابي الحلبي وأولاده بمصر

العقيدة التوحيدية

للقطب الدردير رضى الله عنه

بسم الله الرحمن الرحيم

يَجِبُ عَلَى الْمُكَلَّفِ مَعْرِفَةُ مَا يَجِبُ لِلَّهِ تَعَالَى وَلِأَنْبِيَائِهِ وَمَلَائِكَتِهِ الْكِرَامِ ، فَيَجِبُ لِلَّهِ تَعَالَى عِشْرُونَ صِفَةً ، وَهِيَ : الْوُجُودُ ، وَالْقِدَمُ ، وَالْبَقَاءُ ، وَالْمُخَالَفَةُ لِلْحَوَادِثِ ، وَالْقِيَامُ بِالنَّفْسِ ، وَالْوَحْدَانِيَّةُ ، وَالْحَيَاةُ ، وَالْعِلْمُ ، وَالْإِرَادَةُ ، وَالْقُدْرَةُ ، وَالسَّمْعُ ، وَالْبَصَرُ ، وَالْكَلَامُ ، وَكَوْنُهُ تَعَالَى : حَيًّا ، وَعَلِيمًا ، وَمُرِيدًا ، وَقَادِرًا ، وَسَمِيعًا ، وَبَصِيرًا ، وَمُتَكَلِّمًا . فَهَذِهِ عِشْرُونَ صِفَةً الْأُولَى نَفْسِيَّةٌ ، وَالْخَمْسَةُ بَعْدَهَا سَلْبِيَّةٌ ، وَالسَّبْعَةُ بَعْدَهَا صِفَاتُ مَعَانٍ ، وَالَّتِي بَعْدَهَا مَعْنَوِيَّةٌ ؛ فَهُوَ سُبْحَانَهُ وَتَعَالَى : وَاجِبُ الْوُجُودِ ، قَدِيمٌ بَاقٍ ، مُخَالِفٌ فِي ذَاتِهِ لِجَمِيعِ الْخَلَائِقِ ، فَلَيْسَ بِجِسْمٍ ، وَلَا عَرَضٍ ، وَلَا يَتَّصِفُ بِالْمَكَانِ ، وَلَا بِالزَّمَانِ ، وَلَا بِالْيَمِينِ ، وَلَا بِالشِّمَالِ ، وَلَا بِالْخَلْفِ ، وَلَا بِالْأَمَامِ ، الْقَائِمُ بِنَفْسِهِ ، وَاحِدٌ فِي ذَاتِهِ وَصِفَاتِهِ وَأَفْعَالِهِ . حَيٌّ ، عَلِيمٌ بِكُلِّ شَيْءٍ مَاكَانَ ، وَمَا يَكُونُ ، وَمَا لَمْ يَكُنْ . مُرِيدٌ لِكُلِّ شَيْءٍ جَرَى وَبَرَزَ مِنَ الْعَوَالِمِ ، وَمَا لَمْ يَكُنْ مِنْهَا . قَادِرٌ عَلَى كُلِّ شَيْءٍ مِنَ الْمُمْكِنَاتِ وَعَلَى إِعْدَامِهَا ، لَا يُشَارِكُهُ فِي ذَلِكَ مُشَارِكٌ . سَمِيعٌ لِكُلِّ مَوْجُودٍ ، وَمُبْصِرٌ . مُتَكَلِّمٌ بِكَلَامٍ أَزَلِيٍّ مُنَزَّهٍ عَنِ الصَّوْتِ وَالْحَرْفِ . وَيَجِبُ لِلْأَنْبِيَاءِ عَلَيْهِمُ الصَّلَاةُ وَالسَّلَامُ الْعِصْمَةُ ، فَلَا يَقَعُ مِنْهُمْ مُخَالَفَةٌ لِلَّهِ فِي أَمْرِهِ وَنَهْيِهِ ، وَكَذَلِكَ الْمَلَائِكَةُ ؛ وَيَجِبُ لِلرُّسُلِ عَلَيْهِمُ الصَّلَاةُ وَالسَّلَامُ تَبْلِيغُ مَا أُمِرُوا بِتَبْلِيغِهِ لِلْخَلْقِ مِنَ الْأَحْكَامِ وَغَيْرِهَا ، كَالْيَوْمِ الْآخِرِ وَمَا فِيهِ : مِنَ الْحِسَابِ ، وَالْعِقَابِ ، وَالصِّرَاطِ ، وَالْمِيزَانِ ، وَالْجَنَّةِ ، وَالنَّارِ ؛ وَبِالْعَرْشِ ، وَبِالْكُرْسِيِّ ، وَبِالْكُتُبِ السَّمَاوِيَّةِ وَالرُّسُلِ وَمَا وَقَعَ لَهُمْ مِنْ أُمَمِهِمْ ، وَبِالْحُورِ الْعِينِ ، وَالْوِلْدَانِ ، وَالْأَوْلِيَاءِ ، وَبِإِسْرَائِهِ صَلَّى اللَّهُ عَلَيْهِ وَسَلَّمَ ، وَبِالْمِعْرَاجِ ، وَبِأَنَّ الشُّهَدَاءَ أَحْيَاءٌ عِنْدَ رَبِّهِمْ يُرْزَقُونَ ، وَبِشَفَاعَةِ نَبِيِّنَا مُحَمَّدٍ صَلَّى اللَّهُ عَلَيْهِ وَسَلَّمَ ، وَبِعَلَامَاتِ السَّاعَةِ ، وَتَجْدِيدِ التَّوْبَةِ مِنَ الذُّنُوبِ ، وَالرِّضَا بِالْقَضَاءِ وَالْقَدَرِ .

« فَاعْلَمْ أَنَّهُ لَا إِلَهَ إِلَّا اللَّهُ »
(قرآن كريم)

بسم الله الرحمن الرحيم

الحمد لله رب العالمين ، والصلاة والسلام على سيدنا محمد سيد المرسلين ، وعلى آله وصحبه أجمعين .
أما بعد ؛ فهذه حواش دقيقة وتحقيقات رقيقة جمعها شيخنا العالم العلامة الشيخ « مصطفى ابن أحمد العقباوى » على شرحه الذى ألفه على رسالة قطب الزمان شيخنا وأستاذنا وقدوتنا إلى الله تعالى العلامة سيدى الشيخ « أحمد الدردير » نفعنا الله به فى الدارين (قوله راجى) من الرجاء بالمد أما بالقصر فناحية البئر ، والممدود لغة : الأمل ؛ واصطلاحا تعلق القلب بمرغوب فى حصوله : أى فى المستقبل ، إذ المتعلق بالماضى تمنّ يحصل مع الأخذ فى الأسباب وهو ممدوح شرعا ، فإن لم يأخذ فى الأسباب فطمع وهو مذموم شرعا ، قال ابن الجوزى : إن مثل الراجى مع الإصرار على المعصية كمثل من رجا حصادا وما زرع ، وولدا وما نكح ، فنتوسل بسيدنا محمد صلى الله عليه وسلم أن يوفقنا لما يرضيه . قال سيدى عبد القاهر بن طاهر :

يا من أعد لى كل باب مرتج ... إنى لعفو منك ربى مرتجى
فامنن على بما يفيد سعادتى ... فسعادتى طوعا متى تأمر تجى

وقال الإمام الشافعى رضى الله عنه فى مرض موته لما سأله ابن مسكين كيف أصبحت يا أبا عبد الله ؟ قال : أصبحت من الدنيا راحلا ، وللإخوان مفارقا ، ولكأس المنية شاربا ، ولا أدرى إلى الجنة تصير روحى فأهنيها أم إلى النار فأعزيها . ثم قال :

ولما قسا قلبى وضاقت مذاهبى ... جعلت رجائى نحو عفوك سلما
تعاظمنى ذنبى فلما قرنته ... بعفوك ربى كان عفوك أعظما

(قوله عفو الخ) أى إسقاطها والتجاوز عنها ومحوها فيصير خالصا طالبا إنعام الله ، يقال عفا الله عنك : محا ذنبك ، وعفوت عن الحق : أسقطته ، وعافاه الله : محا عنه الأسقام ، وعفا الماء : لم تطأه شىء يكدره ، وعفوه وأعفيته : أتيت أطلب معروفه (قوله المساوى) أى النقائص والمعائب جمع مسوءة بوزن مفعلة (قوله مصطفى) علم شخص موافق لاسم أفضل الخلق صلى الله عليه وسلم . اللهم بجاهه صلى الله عليه وسلم اجعل له من اسمه نصيبا إذ هو من الصفوة بمعنى الخلوص من الكدر ، وأصله مصتفو قلبت التاء طاء والواو ألفا وتثنيته مصطفوان ، وجمعه على حد المثنى عند البصرى مصطفون فى الرفع ومصطفين فى غيره ، وأصله مصطفوون استثقلت الضمة على الواو الأولى فحذفت فسكنت الواو فحذفت لالتقاء الساكنين ، ولك أن تقول تحركت الواو وانفتح ما قبلها فقلبت ألفا ثم حذفت لالتقاء الساكنين (قوله ابن أحمد) وافق الاسم الشريف الذى ورد فى حقه « يوقف الله من اسمه أحمد بين يديه فيقول له ألم تفعل كذا فى يوم كذا ؟ فيقول بلى يارب فعلت ، فيقول الله غفرت لك لا أعذب من اسمه على اسم حبيبى أحمد » (قوله العقباوى) نسبة لمنية عقبة ، وسيدى عقبة مشهور فيها وله كرامات ظاهرة . قيل هو الصحابى المعلوم رضى الله عنه وعنا به ، والنسبة

بسم الله الرحمن الرحيم الحمد لله والصلاة والسلام على رسول الله سيدنا محمد صلى الله عليه وسلم .
وبعد فيقول راجى عفو المساوى مصطفى بن أحمد العقباوى :

لما أراد الله تعالى حصول الخير الكثير جلب القلب لعقيدة أهل التوحيد القطب الشهير الذى عم النفع به وهو شيخنا وأحمد بن محمد الدردير فكانت نفحا صرفا للكبير والصغير فكيف لا وهى بارزة عمن شغله ربه المعرض عن الدنيا بيده وقلبه

على غير قياس (قوله لما أراد الله الخ) معمول ليقول (قوله بحصول) أى ثبوته وتجمعه يقال حصل حصولا وتحصل تجمع وثبت (قوله الخير) هو خلاف الشر ، فهو ما به نفع ومسرة دنيا وأخرى جمعه خيور وخيار كفلوس وسهام ، ويقال رجل خير اسم تفضيل ، وعلامته وقوع من التفضيلية بعده وأصله أخير أى أفضل واسم فاعل أى ذو خير أى جامع له ومنه أى من الأول بدليل الصلاة خير من النوم ، والمرأة خيرة ، وتجمع على خيرات مثل بيضة وبيضات (قوله الكثير) كما وكيفا تقول كثره وأكثره واستكثره عده كثيرا إذا أكثرت فعله (قوله جلب) وجذب كل لغة بابه ضرب : أى سحبه وأماله . والقلب يطلق على اللحمة المعلومة وعلى العقل وهو المراد وجمعه قلوب (قوله لعقيدة أهل التوحيد) علم على الألفاظ الدالة على المعانى سماها بذلك المصنف أنعم الله عليه . واعلم أن أسماء التراجم والعلوم والكتب من قبيل أسماء الأجناس على ماحققه الإمام السبكى وولده وجماعة وقيل علم جنس نظرا لكونها موضوعة لماهية معهودة فى ذهن المخاطب وإن تعدد محل ذلك المعهود ، وقيل علم شخص نظرا لكون التعدد للمذكور يعد عرفا شيئا واحدا معينا فى الخارج كزيد يحل فى أمكنة متعددة ولا يخرجه ذلك عن كونه علم شخص وعند التأمل تجد الخلاف لفظيا ، فمن اعتبر التعدد بتعدد المحل جعلها أعلام أجناس ومن لم يعتبره جعلها أعلام أشخاص ، والتعدد بتعدد المحل لا خلاف فيه إنما الكلام هل يعتبر أم لا (قوله القطب) بوزن قفل مايدور عليه الشىء ويعتمد عليه ، ويطلق على كوكب بين الفرقدين ثابت ، ويطلق على من أمده الله بالأسرار والمعارف وأعطاه التصرف فى العالم بإذنه ومنهم الإمام على رضى الله تعالى عنه والأقطاب من ذريته ولا شك أن شيخنا المصنف بهذه الرتبة كما هو مشاهد لاينكره إلا محروم (قوله الشهير) أى المشهور الظاهر فى الخيرات ظهورا كثيرا الذى عم النفع به لحصول الخلق منه خير الدنيا والآخرة فترى مجالسه توحيدا خالصا بحيث يقوم من جالسه متقنا للعقائد خالصة بدون شبه ، إذ يقررها ويكررها فى أقل زمن فى المجلس فتثبت بأسرارها فى قلب متلقيها بقبول فلله الحمد الذى حشرنا فى زمرته وجعلنا من أهل محبته (قوله أحمد بن محمد) نعم الأصل والفرع وتقدم مايشهد لفضل التسمية بأحمد ، وقد قال صلى الله عليه وسلم فى فضل من اسمه محمد « من رزق بولد فسماه محمدا شوقا إلى كان هو وولده فى الجنة » وكان محمد والد المصنف مداوما على تلاوة القرآن وربما صوفيا ويكفيه بروز هذا الإمام من صلبه فرحمه الله رحمة واسعة (قوله فكانت) تفريع على كونها منسوبة لمن عم النفع به (قوله صرفا) أى خالصا مما يكدره فهى سهلة يحصل بها الخير لمن يتعاطاها كما يأتى (قوله الكبير) متعلق بنفعا والمراد به غير المبتدى فى الفن والصغير المبتدى فيه (قوله وهى بارزة) أى ظاهرة وناشئة يقال برز الشىء بروزا وبابه قعد : أى ظهر (قوله عمن شغله) أى عن شخص كامل فى العقل شغله بضم المعجمتين ، وقد تسكن الثانية تخفيفا أى اشتغاله وعادته التعلق بربه ذاكرا له متأملا فى كمالاته جل وعلا مقررا ومظهرا لشرع حبيبه المصطفى صلى الله عليه وسلم من تأمل فى حاله عرف ذلك ، فمن نعم الله على تلميذه الفقير أنه يراه عند ابتداء الدرس يهيم فى ربه مخلصا له فى عمله ، وفى قوله عند ابتداء الدرس ياواحد من الأسرار للمتأمل مالا يحصى ، وكذلك فى مجالسة الناس لقضاء حوائجهم ، وأما فى حالة الذكر فأمر عجيب فلله الحمد (قوله المعرض) من أعرض عن الشىء وولى عنه جانبا : أى لبس ملتفتا له وعند حصولها فى يده لايمسكها بل يصرفها فيما أمره به ربه ، فقد انطبق عليه قول الغزالى : القلب النير من طهر عن التعلق بالدنيا ثم صقل بالرياضة البالغة ثم نور بالذكر الصافى ثم غذى بالفكر الصائب ثم ترقى بالملازمة حدود الشرع ففاض عليه النور من

مشكاة .

THE CREED OF IMAM AL-DARDĪR

In the name of Allah,
the Lord of mercy [al-Raḥmān], the Giver of mercy [al-Raḥīm]

[Pertaining to God—*Ilāhiyyāt*]. It is necessary upon the legally responsible person [*mukallaf*] to know [*ma'rifa*] what is necessary for Allah Almighty, His Prophets and noble angels.

Twenty attributes are necessary for Allah Almighty, they are:

I. Existence [*Wujūd*]
II. Pre-eternality [*Qidam*]
III. Sempiternality [*Baqā'*]
IV. Otherness [*Mukhālafa lil-Ḥawādith*]
V. Self-Subsistence [*Qiyām bil-Nafs*]
VI. Oneness [*Waḥdāniyya*]
VII. Life [*Ḥayāt*]
VIII. Omniscience [*'Ilm*]
IX. Will [*Irāda*]
X. Omnipotence [*Qudra*]
XI. Hearing [*Sam'*]
XII. Sight [*Baṣar*]
XIII. Speech [*Kalām*]

And Him سبحانه وتعالى being:

I. Living [*Ḥayy*]
II. Omniscient [*'Alīm*]
III. Willing [*Murīd*]
IV. Omnipotent [Qādir]
V. All-Hearing [*Samī'*]
VI. All-Seeing [*Baṣīr*]
VII. Speaking [*Mutakallim*]

And so, these are the twenty attributes: the first is the essential attribute [*al-ṣifa al-nafsiyya*], the five following it are the negating attributes [*al-ṣifāt al-salbiyya*], the seven after that are the qualitative attributes [*al-ṣifāt al-ma'ānī*] and the ones after that are the predicative attributes [*al-ṣifāt al-ma'nawiyya*].

عقيدة الدردير

بسم الله الرحمن الرحيم

[الإلاهيات]

يجِبُ على المُكلَّفِ مَعْرِفَةُ ما يجِبُ لله تعالىٰ ولأنْبيائِهِ ومَلائِكتِهِ الكِرامِ.

فيجبُ لله تعالىٰ عشرُونَ صفةً وهِي: الوُجُودُ، والقِدَمُ، والبقاءُ، والمُخَالَفَةُ لِلْحَوادِثِ، والقِيامُ بِالنَّفْسِ، والوَحْدانيَّةُ، والحياةُ، والعلم، والإرادةُ، والقدرةُ، والسَّمْعُ، والبصرُ، والكلامُ.

وكونُه تعالى: حيًّا، وعليمًا، ومُرِيدًا، وقادِرًا، وسميعًا، وبصيرًا، ومُتكلِّمًا.

فهٰذِهِ عِشْرُونَ صِفةً الْأُوْلىٰ نَفْسِيّةٌ، والخمسةُ بعدَها سَلْبِيَّةٌ، والسَّبْعَةُ بَعْدَها صفاتُ معانٍ، والَّتِيْ بَعْدَها مَعْنَوِيَّةٌ.

And thus, He ﷻ is: Necessarily existent, Pre-eternal and Sempiternal, His Entity is dissimilar to all created beings and is therefore neither a body nor an accident. He is not characterised by place, time, being right, left, behind or in front. He is Self-subsistent [*Qā'im bil-nafs*], One in His essence, attributes and acts. He is Living, Omniscient of all things past, that which will be, and that which will not come to pass. He wills everything that happens, that which manifests itself in the worlds, and that which has not manifested in them.

He is Omnipotent over all possible things and their annihilation; no one shares with Him in that. He hears and sees all that exists. He speaks with an eternal speech that is free from sounds and letters.

[Pertaining to Prophethood—*Nubuwwāt*]

It is necessary for Prophets—prayers and salutations be upon them—to have infallibility [*'iṣma*]. Thus, they do not contravene Allah with regards to His commands and prohibitions; and likewise, the angels. It is necessary for Messengers—prayers and salutations be upon them—to convey to creation that which they have been commanded to convey from rulings and other matters...

فَهُوَ سُبْحانَهُ وتعالىٰ: واجِبُ الوُجُودِ، قَديمٌ باقٍ، مُخالِفٌ في ذاتِهِ لجميع الأخْلاقِ، فليس بجِسمٍ، ولا عَرَضٍ، ولا يَتَّصِفُ بالمَكانِ، ولا بالزَّمانِ، ولا بالْيمينِ، ولا بالشِّمالِ، ولا بالخَلْفِ، ولا بالأَمامِ، القائِمُ بنَفْسِهِ، واحِدٌ في ذاتِهِ وصفاتِهِ وأفعالِهِ. حَيٌّ، عَلِيْمٌ بكُلِّ شَيْءٍ ما كانَ وما يَكُوْنُ وما لم يَكُنْ، مُرِيْدٌ لِكُلِّ شيْءٍ جَرَى وبَرَزَ مِنَ الْعَوالِمِ، وما لم يكُنْ منها.

قادِرٌ على كلِّ شيْءٍ منَ المُمْكِناتِ وعَلىٰ إعدامِها، لا يُشارِكُهُ في ذلك مُشارِكٌ، سميعٌ لكلِّ مَوْجُودٍ ومُبْصِرٌ، مُتكَلِّمٌ بكلام أَزَليٍّ مُنَزَّهٌ عن الصَّوتِ والحرفِ.

[النبوات]

ويجِبُ للأنبياءِ عليهِمُ الصلاةُ والسلامُ العِصْمَةُ، فلا يَقَعُ منهم مُخالَفَةٌ لله في أمرِهِ ونَهيِهِ، وكذالكَ الملائِكةُ، ويجِبُ لِلرُّسُلِ عليهم الصلاةُ والسَّلامُ تبلِيغُ ما أُمِرُوْا بِتَبْلِيغِهِ لِلْخَلْقِ من الأحكامِ وغَيْرِها.

[Eschatology—*Samʿiyyāt*]

Such as: the Last Day [*al-Yawm al-Ākhir*] and that which occurs in it from the reckoning [*ḥisāb*], punishment [*ʿiqāb*], the bridge [*ṣirāṭ*], the scales [*mīzān*], Paradise [*Janna*] and Hellfire [*Jahannam*]. And [it is necessary to believe in:] the throne [*ʿarsh*], the chair [*kursī*], the heavenly books, the Messengers—prayers and salutations be upon them—and what their nations did to them, the maidens of Paradise, the everlasting youths, the saints, his ﷺ night journey, his ﷺ heavenly ascent, that martyrs are living, provided for by their Lord, the intercession of our Prophet Muhammad ﷺ, the signs of the Hour, the renewal of repentance from sins and contentment in *qaḍāʾ* and *qadar* (pre-destination).

[السَّمْعِيّات]

كالْيَومِ الأخِرِ وما فِيهِ: منَ الْحِسابِ، والعِقابِ، والصِّراطِ، والمِيزانِ، والجَنَّةِ، والنَّارِ، وبالْعَرْشِ، وبالكُرْسِيِّ، وبالكُتبِ السَّماوِيّةِ، والرُّسُلِ وما وَقَعَ لهم من أُمَمِهِم، وبالحُوْرِ العَيْن، والوِلْدانِ، والأولياءِ، وبإسراءِه صلى الله عليه وسلم، وبالمِعراجِ، وبأنَّ الشُّهَداءَ أحْياءٌ عند رَبِّهم يُرْزَقُوْن، وبشفاعَةِ نبيِّنا محمَّدٍ صلى الله عليه وسلّم، وبعلاماتِ السَّاعةِ، وتَجْديدِ التَّوبةِ من الذّنُوبِ، والرِّضاءِ بالقَضاءِ والقَدَرِ.

A Commentary upon the Creed of Imam al-Dardīr

Translation & Commentary
by Siddiq Adam Mitha

Forewords *by*
Shaykh Walead Mosaad &
Shaykh ʿAbd al-Raḥmān al-Shaʿʿār

Sunni Publications

THE COMMENTARY

بسم الله الرحمن الرحيم

PART I

MATTERS PERTAINING TO GOD [*ILĀHIYYĀT*]

بسم الله الرحمن الرحيم

In the name of Allah, the Lord of mercy [*al-Raḥmān*], the Giver of mercy [*al-Raḥīm*]

THE *BASMALA*

The statement, "In the name of Allah, the Lord of mercy, the Giver of mercy" [*bi-ism Allah al-Raḥmān al-Raḥīm*] is called the *basmala*.

It is from the way of the scholars to begin their treatises and works with the *basmala*, in accordance with the sequence of the Qur'an. Usually, the *basmala* is followed by the *ḥamdala*[48] and then salutations upon the Messenger of Allah ﷺ—this is what is known as the Divine order [*al-tartīb al-tawqīfī*].

The Messenger of Allah ﷺ is reported to have said: "Every act of the son of Ādam that does not begin with 'in the name of God the most Merciful, the Compassionate' is severed (from blessings)."[49]

---

[48] The phrase in Arabic is *al-ḥamdulillah* which means: "All praise is due to Allah."

[49] *Al-Jāmiʿ li-Akhlāq al-Rāwī wa-Ādāb al-Sāmiʿ* (al-Baghdādī), 2:69:1210; *Al-Arbaʿīn al-Buldāniyya li-Isḥāq b. Rāhawayh* according to al-Suyūṭī in *al-Jāmiʿ al-Ṣaghīr* [2:391]

Muṣṭafā al-ʿAqabāwī relates in his treatise that the first thing the pen wrote on the preserved tablet was: "In the name of Allah, the Lord of mercy and the Giver of mercy [the *basmala*]. Verily, I am Allah, there is no god but Me [and] Muhammad is My Messenger. Whoever submits to My decree, remains patient over My trials, is thankful for My blessings and content with My judgement, then I consider him utmost veracious and will raise him with the utmost veracious ones [*ṣiddīqūn*]."[50]

THE NAME ALLAH: DEFINITION AND DERIVATION

There are various definitions for the Divine name "Allah." According to al-Bājūrī it is: "A proper name for a Being Whose existence is necessary and is deserving of all praise."[51]

Al-Ghazālī defined it as: "A name for that which exists, the Real, Who encompasses all the attributes of divinity, is characterised by the qualities of Lordship and is alone with regards to real existence."[52]

What distinguishes this name from the other names of Allah سبحانه وتعالى is that it is said to incorporate the meanings of all the other names[53] and is thus comprehensive in signifying the Divine essence and attributes in all their types. This is why al-Ghazālī and many others considered it the greatest and supreme name of all the names of Allah, a mighty name whose meaning is not shared by anything else, "whether in a literal or metaphorical sense."[54]

---

[50] *Ḥāshiya al-ʿAqabāwī*, p. 6

[51] *Tuḥfa al-Murīd* (al-Bājūrī), p. 24;
Sharḥ al-Kharīda al-Bahiyya (al-Dardīr), p. 106

[52] *Al-Maqṣad al-Asnā* (al-Ghazālī), p. 61

[53] *Sharḥ Asmāʾ Allah al-Ḥusnā* (al-Zarrūq), p. 31;
Madārij al-Sālikīn (Ibn al-Qayyim), 1:32-33

[54] *Al-Maqṣad al-Asnā* (al-Ghazālī), p. 61

THE SUPREME NAME OF GOD [*ISM ALLAH AL-Aʿẓ̣AM*]

A great amount of consideration and thought has been given to the supreme name of Allah ﷻ, mostly due to a tradition in which the Messenger of Allah ﷺ describes it as the name which, "if used when supplicating to Allah, He answers, and if used to ask, He bestows."[55] A certain sense of mystery has always surrounded this topic because of the power it is said to contain, such that "it would be not be far off to say that everything from the heavens and earth could be rendered obedient by way of it."[56] Certain anecdotes related in the Qur'an of individuals who had knowledge of the supreme name are mentioned below. The scholars have always been keen to discover this name, many of whom believed the name "Allah" to be the supreme name of God[57] of which various traditions attest to. An example of this is the tradition from Jabir b. Zayd, who said: "The supreme name of God is Allah."[58]

Moreover, on the authority of Asmāʾ bt. Yazīd, who said: "The Messenger of Allah ﷺ said: 'The supreme name of God is in these two verses: ﴿*Your God is the One God, there is no god but Him, the Lord of mercy, the Giver of mercy,*﴾ [2:163] and in the beginning of *Āl-ʿImrān*: ﴿*Alif Lām Mīm. God: there is no god but Him, the Ever Living, the Ever Watchful.*﴾ [3:1-2]'"[59]

Numerous statements of scholars also seem to affirm the name Allah as the supreme name. The *Ḥanbalī* scholar Shams al-Dīn al-Saffārīnī states:

> Some of the people of *taṣawwuf* and others have said: "The supreme name of God is: '*In the name of Allah, the Lord of mercy, the Giver of mercy*'"—all of it. According to the majority of the people of knowledge, it is the majestic name:

[55] *Sunan al-Tirmidhī*, 5:515:3475
[56] *Sharḥ Asmāʾ Allah al-Ḥusnā* (al-Zarrūq), p. 149
[57] *Sharḥ al-Ṣāwī ʿalā Jawhara al-Tawḥīd*, p. 48;
ʿUmda al-Murīd (al-Laqqānī), 1:60
[58] *Muṣannaf Ibn Abī Shayba*, 6:47
[59] *Sunan al-Tirmidhī*, 5:517:3478

> Allah. There is no answer, for the majority of people, when used to supplicate with due to the absence of some pre-conditions from which sincerity and eating the lawful are from amongst the most important...[60]

Both Imam Abū Ḥanīfa and al-Ṭaḥāwī also seem to be of the same sentiment, as is related by Ibn Amīr Ḥāj al-Ḥanafī who states:

> On the authority of Muḥammad b. al-Ḥasan, who said: "I heard Abū Ḥanīfa say: 'The supreme name of God is Allah.'" This is what al-Ṭaḥāwī said too, and likewise, many of the learned and majority of the Gnostics.[61]

It is important to note, however, that there are other opinions with regards to this name. Imam al-Bayḍāwī mentions six:[62]

I. It is not a specific name. It is reported from some from the early generations that it is the name that the servant mentions when he is drowned in His gnosis and withdrawn from all other than Him ﷻ.

II. It is the name *Hū*.

III. It is a combination of the names *al-Ḥayy* and *al-Qayyūm*. This was the opinion of Imam al-Nawawī.[63]

IV. It is the statement, *Dhū al-Jalāl wal-Ikrām* (the possessor of glory and majesty).

V. It is mentioned in the letters mentioned at the start of certain chapters of the Qur'an, for example: *ḥā, mīm, ʿayn, sīn* and *qāf.*

VI. It is unknown to creation.

---

[60] *Lawāmiʿ al-Anwār al-Bahiyya* (al-Saffārīnī), 1:35
[61] *Al-Taqrīr wal-Taḥbīr* (Ibn Amīr Ḥāj), 1:11-12
[62] *Sharḥ al-Asmāʾ al-Ḥusnā* (al-Bayḍāwī), p. 143-147
[63] *Tuḥfa al-Murīd* (al-Bājūrī), p. 25

Those who had Knowledge of the Supreme Name

As mentioned previously, there is mention in the Qurʾan of certain individuals who were privy to the Supreme Name:[64]

I. Bulʿum b. Bāʿūrā[65]

Allah ﷻ says: ❨[O Muhammad,] tell them the story of the man to whom We gave Our Messages: he sloughed them off, so Satan took him as his follower and he went astray.❩ [7:175]

Abū Ḥayyān al-Andalusī in al-Baḥr al-Muḥīṭ states in explanation of the above verse that:

> The scholars differed with regards to this person whom Allah gave His Messages to [...] The majority said, it is a specific person, and thus it was said, it is Bulʿum or Bilʿām. He was a man from the Canaanites who had been given some of the books of Allah. It is said that he had knowledge of the supreme name of God.[66]

II. Āṣaf b. Barkhiyā

Allah ﷻ says: ❨Then he said: "Counsellors, which of you can bring me her throne before they come to me in submission?" A strong and crafty jinn replied: "I will bring it to you before you can even rise from your place. I am strong and trustworthy enough," but one of them who

---

[64] It is important to note that some considered Hārūt and Mārūt, the two angels that taught people witchcraft mentioned in Sūra al-Baqara [2:102], to have had knowledge of the supreme name of Allah ﷻ. However, the basis of various narrations mentioned in numerous books of tafsīr is most likely Israelite narrations [Isrāʾīliyyāt], and thus they cannot be given much attention. Abū al-Suʿūd states commentating upon these traditions: "As for what is related [...] 'when they entered the evening they would make remembrance of the supreme name of God and ascend to the heavens' [...] then it is from that which is not relied upon, because it is based upon Israelite narrations, in addition to what it contains that contradicts evidences from both reason and scripture."
[Irshād al-ʿAql al-Salīm (Abū al-Suʿūd), 1:138]
[65] There is a difference of opinion with regards to the name of Bulʿum's father. Ibn ʿAbbās ﵁ said that it was Bāʿūrā. However, Ibn Masʿūd ﵁ thought it was Abrah, and, al-Suddī and Mujāhid thought it was Baʿruwayh. [Al-Baḥr al-Muḥīṭ (Abū Ḥayyān), 5:221]
[66] Ibid.

had some knowledge of the Scripture said: "I will bring it to you in the twinkling of an eye.﴿ [27:38-40]

There are various opinions with regards to the identity of the person that was given knowledge of the scripture mentioned in the above verse. According to the majority of the scholars it was a veracious and pious man named Āṣaf the son of Barkhiyā, the scribe of the Prophet Sulaymān ﷺ.[67]

THE NAMES *AL-RAḤMĀN* AND *AL-RAḤĪM*

After the majestic name Allah ﷻ, there is mention of two other names in the *basmala*: *al-Raḥmān* (the Lord of mercy) and *al-Raḥīm* (the Giver of mercy). Both of these names are related to mercy; however, what is important to note is that their constructs in the Arabic language indicate some hyperbole in their intended meaning.[68]

Linguistically, mercy [*raḥma*] means: a gentleness of the heart, that is, its kindliness. This gentleness necessitates the bestowal of grace and generosity, which is the intended meaning when mercy is attributed to Allah,[69] as it is impossible to characterise Allah ﷻ with its literal meaning. As a general principle: *if the apparent meaning of an attribute is impossible for Allah Almighty, then, what is meant is its intended meaning.*[70]

The Difference between the Names al-Raḥīm and al-Raḥmān

It is commonly mentioned in the books of theology that *al-Raḥmān* signifies the bestowal of great and significant blessings [*jalā'il al-ni'am*] like: existence, faith, provision, health, intellect, hearing, sight and the like, whereas, *al-Raḥīm* is the bestowal of finer blessings [*daqā'iq al-ni'am*] like: beauty, an increase in faith, intelligence, an increase in one's provision and a sharpness of one's hearing and sight.[71]

---

[67] Ibid.
[68] *Sharḥ al-Kharīda al-Bahiyya* (al-Dardīr), p. 107
[69] Ibid.
[70] Ibid.
[71] *Sharḥ al-Kharīda al-Bahiyya* (al-Dardīr), p. 107-108; *Ḥāshiya al-'Aqabāwī*, p. 6-7

However, Abū Ḥayyān al-Andalusī, the notable exegete of the Qur᾿an, mentions that:

> It has been said that *al-Raḥmān* is the Bestower of those types of blessings which are inconceivable from man; [and] *al-Raḥīm* is the Bestower of those types of blessings that are conceivable from man. Abū ʿAlī al-Fārisī said: "*Al-Raḥmān* is a generic name that encompasses all types of mercy that Allah ﷾ is distinguished by, and *al-Raḥīm* is for the believers."[72]

Another important difference between the two names is that *al-Raḥmān* is a quality specific for Allah ﷾: nothing other than He, Mighty and Sublime, can be entitled with the name *al-Raḥmān*—and this may well be why it is given precedence over the name *al-Raḥīm* in the *basmala*.

يَجِبُ على المُكلَّفِ مَعْرِفَةُ ما يَجِبُ لله تعالىٰ ولأنْبيائِهِ ومَلائِكتِهِ الكِرامِ.

> It is necessary upon the legally responsible person [*mukallaf*] to know [*maʿrifa*] what is necessary for Allah Almighty,[73] His Prophets and noble angels.

The Necessity of Knowing Allah ﷾ and the Role of Revelation and Reason

Knowledge of Allah ﷾, that is, of His attributes and existence, is necessary as stated by Imam al-Dardīr without any dispute. What is disputed and a topic of discussion between the theologians, however, are the questions: who made it necessary? How was this ruling discovered? And, what is the role of scripture and intellect in that regard?

---

[72] *Al-Baḥr al-Muḥīṭ* (Abū Ḥayyān), 1:31

[73] Allah ﷾ says in the Qur᾿an: ﴾*Know that there is no god but Allah.*﴿ [47:19]

According to the school of Imam al-Ashʿarī, it is the Sacred Law or revelation that has made it incumbent upon the one deemed responsible [*mukallaf*] to know Allah ﷻ and His attributes. The *Ashʿarīs* believe that reason without revelation does not have the capacity to ascertain the ruling of a certain action. They believe there is no binding obligation of knowing something simply by way of the intellect or affirming a specific legal ruling for that thing. Therefore, according to this opinion, hypothetically speaking, one would not be rewarded if one came to know that there was a Creator in the absence of revelation merely using one's reason and intellect, as all rulings are ultimately only determined by revelation.[74]

In slight contrast, the *Māturīdīs* believe that the necessity of having faith in a Creator and His necessary attributes *can* be known solely through the process of reasoning. Their belief is that the One Who has made it necessary is Allah ﷻ, *but* by way of reason, since reason is a pre-condition for the necessity of having belief, similarly to how Allah has made certain things lawful and unlawful but through the Messenger of Allah ﷺ. In essence, reason, according to their understanding, is a tool that has the capacity to know and reveal certain Divine rulings. And therefore, in contrast to the *Ashʿarīs*, if Allah did not send any Messengers, reason can still be applied to know of the existence God by way of the signs in creation that indicate towards His existence.[75] Al-Bayāḍī states in *Ishārāt al-Marām* that:

> By the mere presence of reason during the period of deduction, it is necessary to have knowledge of His, the Almighty's, existence, His oneness, His omniscience, His omnipotence, His speech, His will [and] the contingency of the universe.[76]

---

[74] *Ḥāshiya al-ʿAqabāwī*, p. 7; *Sharḥ al-Kharīda al-Bahiyya* (al-Dardīr), p. 131; *Al-Mukhtaṣar al-Mufīd* (al-Quḍāt), p. 21;
[75] *Masāʾil al-Ikhtilāf Bayna al-Ashāʿira wal-Māturīdiyya* (Ibn Kamāl Pāshā), p. 41-48
[76] *Ishārāt al-Marām* (al-Bayāḍī), p. 54

It is important to clarify that both the *Ash'arīs* and *Māturīdīs* agree that it is only Allah ﷻ Who decides whether something is good or bad, and that all rulings come from Allah and not from the intellect in and of itself.

According to the *Mu'tazila*, it is solely through reason that one comes to know of the necessity of knowing the existence Allah ﷻ and His attributes. They considered revelation as simply an aid and confirmation for the findings of the intellect and therefore believe that it can never contradict reason. They believe that the intellect decides what is good and what is evil, and thus the necessity of belief is not made incumbent by revelation but by reason itself.[77]

THE LEGALLY RESPONSIBLE PERSON [*MUKALLAF*]

A legally responsible person [*mukallaf*] is: a sane, adult human with sound senses whom Divine teachings have reached.[78] To understand this definition properly, it is important to take a deeper look into each constituent of this definition:

I. Sane

The insane person who does not understand the words spoken to him is excused from learning the tenets of faith. Due to this, one will not be punished by Allah ﷻ if one reached adulthood whilst being insane and died in that state, without ever becoming sane.

II. Adult

According to the *Ash'arīs*, a child[79] is not legally responsible to learn the tenets of faith, as the mental capacity of a child is

---

[77] *Sharḥ al-Kharīda al-Bahiyya* (al-Dardīr), p. 131

[78] *Al-Mukhtaṣar al-Mufīd* (al-Quḍāt), p. 20-21;
Sharḥ Naẓm 'Aqīda Ahl al-Sunna (al-Hāshimī), p. 40

[79] According to the *Ḥanafī* school, a male or female child is considered an adult when they reach fifteen lunar years or from the moment a male child has a nocturnal emission and the female has her first menses.

deemed deficient. However, it is recommended for the legal guardian to teach the child about God, the Messengers and other creedal matters.[80]

According to the *Māturīdīs*, however, the cognisant and understanding child *is* responsible, like an adult, due to having an intellect that is capable of reasoning and understanding. Therefore, they believe that a cognisant child is rewarded and punished by actively believing or disbelieving. If, however, he has the capacity to decide and fails to either believe or disbelieve, then he would be punished for not believing.[81]

III. Reaching of Divine Teachings

This condition is stipulated by the *Ashʿarīs*. It is to be aware that Allah has sent a Messenger to the people whose name is Muhammad ﷺ, who possesses noble qualities and teaches that Allah is One and has no partners. If this Message has not reached a person, then he is not required to believe and would not be punished for his disbelief. Allah ﷻ says: ﴾*...Nor do We punish until We have sent a Messenger.*﴿ [17:15]

Distorted Divine Teachings

It is important to note that if Divine teachings have reached a person but in a distorted manner, then, according to the more correct opinion, they are not obligated to believe and will not be punished for their disbelief.[82]

The People of Primordiality [fiṭra]

The people of primordiality [*fiṭra*] who lived before the coming of a Messenger or in the time of a Messenger that was not sent to them—according to the more correct opinion—will not enter Hellfire *even if* they worshipped other than Allah ﷻ.[83]

---

[80] *Al-Mukhtaṣar al-Mufīd* (al-Quḍāt), p. 20
[81] *Tuḥfa al-Murīd* (al-Bājūrī), p. 67
[82] *Ḥāshiya al-ʿAqabāwī*, p. 7
[83] *Tuḥfa al-Murīd* (al-Bājūrī), p. 67;
Sharḥ Naẓm ʿAqīda Ahl al-Sunna (al-Hāshimī), p. 41

Al-ʿAqabāwī states that: "From the greatest of the people of *fiṭra* are the parents of the Messenger of Allah ﷺ: they are in the greatest everlasting felicity."[84]

It is worth mentioning here that there are those who were from the people of *fiṭra*, but whose abode is Hellfire. The Prophet ﷺ mentioned that ʿImru al-Qays, the famous poet from the pre-Islamic era, and Ḥātim al-Ṭāʾī, are two people who are destined for Hell even though they existed in a period between Prophets. These are, however, mere exceptions that have come to us on the tongue of Prophecy and we cannot use them to determine the fate of all the people of *fiṭra*.[85]

The Māturīdī Opinion

According to the *Māturīdīs*, however, the reaching of Divine teachings is not a pre-condition for one to be considered responsible. They considered it necessary for every person to employ the intellect to reflect, ponder and seek rational proof, until one realises that this world has one Creator—just like the people of the cave [*ahl al-kahf*] did when they said: ﴿*"Our Lord is the Lord of the skies and earth"*﴾ [18:14] and just like the Prophet Ibrāhīm did ﷺ.[86]

It has been reported that Imam Abū Ḥanīfa would say: "There is no excuse for anyone in creation to be ignorant of their Creator, due to what one can see in the creation of the skies and earth, in one's self and in all of creation."[87]

In some other narrations Imam Abū Ḥanīfa is reported to have said: "If Allah ﷻ did not send any Messengers it would still be necessary upon creation to know Allah by way of their intellects."[88]

In the same manner, Imam al-Māturīdī is also reported to have said: "The way to the Sacred Law is by revelation; as for faith, the way to it is through the intellect."[89]

---

[84] *Ḥāshiya al-ʿAqabāwī*, p. 7
[85] Ibid.
[86] *Baḥr al-Kalām* (Abū al-Muʿīn al-Nasafī), p. 85. Al-Kāsānī also narrates a similar statement in his *Badāʾi al-Ṣanāʾi*, 7:132
[87] *Talkhīṣ al-Adilla* (Ṣaffār al-Bukhārī), p. 132
[88] Ibid.
[89] Ibid.

IV. Sound Senses

The one who is both deaf and dumb, and thus does not have the capacity to comprehend information, is exempted and excused. However, if he is deaf only or dumb only then he is still considered to be responsible.[90]

THE FIRST OBLIGATION: TO KNOW ALLAH

The first obligation with regards to belief is to actively know and have gnosis of the existence of Allah, and to know what is necessary, impossible and possible for Allah ﷻ.[91]

Imam al-Laqqānī states:[92]

Be certain that the first requirement is to know...

In a similar vein, al-Sūdānī states:

> The people of truth are in consensus, without exception, that the first necessary act is to have knowledge of Allah ﷻ: they all agree upon the invalidity of the worship of the one who does not know who he is worshipping.[93]

It is worth noting, however, that there is some debate with regards to this issue: Imam al-Bājūrī mentions twelve different opinions with regards to the first obligation. One other major opinion is of Abū Isḥāq al-Isfarāyīnī who states that the first obligation is the actual contemplation or reflection that would lead one to the knowledge of the existence of Allah ﷻ and His attributes.[94]

---

[90] *Al-Mukhtaṣar al-Mufīd* (al-Quḍāt), p. 20; *Tuḥfa al-Murīd* (al-Bājūrī), p. 68; *Sharḥ Naẓm ʿAqīda Ahl al-Sunna* (al-Hāshimī), p. 41

[91] *Ḥāshiya al-ʿAqabāwī*, p. 8; *Sharḥ al-Kharīda al-Bahiyya* (al-Dardīr), p. 133

[92] *Jawhara al-Tawḥīd* (al-Laqqānī), p. 15, verse, 14

[93] *Zubad al-ʿAqāʾid* (al-Sūdānī), p. 35

[94] *Tuḥfa al-Murīd* (al-Bājūrī), p. 82

What does it Mean to Know?

Knowing or having gnosis in Arabic is called *maʿrifa*. It is commonly defined as: an absolute certain belief, which agrees with reality and is supported by evidence.[95] Below, we will take a deeper look into each constituent of this definition:

I. *Absolute certain belief*

This is to have total conviction in something. The presence of even a little doubt is not considered *maʿrifa*. Therefore, having an iota of doubt in the existence of Allah ﷻ is considered disbelief.

II. *In Agreement with Reality*

This is to have total conviction in something that is not inaccurate or erroneous like, the pre-eternality of the world or the existence of more than one God; having this type of belief would not be considered *maʿrifa*.

III. *Supported by Evidence*

That means evidence that has been attained either rationally [*ʿaqlī*], through the physical senses [*ḥawās*], true reports [*al-khabar al-ṣādiq*] or the illumination of the soul [*ishrāq al-rūḥ*].[96]

It is sufficient for the common believer to be certain in the existence of Allah ﷻ by way of general and nonspecific evidence. For example, he may deduce that there is a God by concluding that there is a world and that the world is contingent and therefore the world must have a Creator. He is not required to prove that theory in detail—this is the role of the theologians.[97]

Blind Following [*Taqlīd*] in Matters of Faith

The above discussions bring us to the very important issue of blind following in matters of faith. If someone possessed certain belief in the existence of Allah ﷻ and His attributes based on the statement of another person without any evidence or proof, then

---

[95] *Sharḥ al-Kharīda al-Bahiyya* (al-Dardīr), p. 131;
Sharḥ Naẓm ʿAqīda Ahl al-Sunna (al-Hāshimī), p. 38
[96] *Al-ʿAqīda al-Islāmiyya wa-Ususuhā* (Ḥabannaka), p. 49
[97] *Sharḥ al-Kharīda al-Bahiyya* (al-Dardīr), p. 132;
Sharḥ Naẓm ʿAqīda Ahl al-Sunna, p. 39

this person is termed a blind follower [*muqallid*]. There is a difference of opinion with regards to his status, that is, with regards to whether he is considered a believer or not?

The most correct and reliable opinion is that his belief is sound, as long as he would not retract from his faith if the person he was following was to do so. He is, however, required to ponder and seek evidence if he has the capacity to do so. Failure to do this would not make him a disbeliever but it would be considered sinful.[98]

فيجبُ لله تعالىٰ عشرُونَ صفةً وهِي: الوُجودُ، والقِدَمُ، والبقاءُ، والمُخالَفَةُ لِلْحَوادِثِ، والقِيامُ بِالنَّفْسِ، والوَحْدانِيَّةُ، والحياةُ، والعلم، والإرادةُ، والقدرةُ، والسَّمْعُ، والبصرُ، والكلامُ.

> Twenty attributes are necessary for Allah Almighty, they are: [I] existence [*wujūd*], [II] pre-eternality [*qidam*], [III] sempiternality [*baqā'*], [IV] otherness [*mukhālafa lil-ḥawādith*], [V] self-subsistence [*qiyām bil-nafs*], [VI] oneness [*waḥdāniyya*], [VII] life [*ḥayāt*], [VIII] omniscience [*ʿilm*], [IX] will [*irāda*], [X] omnipotence [*qudra*], [XI] hearing [*samʿ*], [XII] sight [*baṣar*] and [XIII] speech [*kalām*].

IS ALLAH ﷻ QUALIFIED BY A SPECIFIC NUMBER OF ATTRIBUTES?

Allah ﷻ is characterised by perfection that cannot be quantified by a specific number of attributes; however, there are some attributes that are necessary for a believer to recognise and have conviction in.[99]

There is a difference of opinion within the school of Imam al-Ashʿarī with regards to whether the attributes one must have conviction in are twenty or thirteen in number. According to the

---

[98] *Tuḥfa al-Murīd* (al-Bājūrī), p. 133

[99] *Ḥāshiya al-ʿAqabāwī*, p. 11; *Sharḥ al-Kharīda al-Bahiyya* (al-Dardīr), p. 147

more correct opinion, only the first thirteen attributes mentioned by the author are necessary to specifically believe in; the last seven attributes (Him ﷻ being Living, Omniscient, Willing, Omnipotent, All-Hearing, All-Seeing and Speaking) are not considered independent attributes, but in reality, only exist by virtue of the qualitative attributes, and therefore they do not provide any additional meaning.[100]

THE *MĀTURĪDĪS* AND THE ATTRIBUTE OF *TAKWĪN* (TO BRING INTO BEING)

According to the *Māturīdīs*, the attribute of *takwīn* (bringing into being) is an additional pre-eternal qualitative attribute within the Divine essence similar to omniscience or omnipotence. Therefore, they consider it necessary to specifically believe in fourteen attributes and not thirteen.[101]

The *Māturīdīs* considered this attribute to be the source of all Divine acts; hence, it can be described in differing ways according to what the act is. For example, giving life is called *iḥyā'*, giving death is called *imāta*, giving provision is called *irzāq* and so on.[102]

THE TYPES OF DIVINE ATTRIBUTES

The *Ash'arī* theologians divide the attributes of Allah ﷻ into two categories:[103]

I. The Attributes of Divine Essence [*Ṣifāt al-Dhāt*]

According to the *Ash'arīs*, these are the attributes that when negated necessitate its opposite.[104]

---

[100] *Sharḥ al-Kharīda al-Bahiyya* (al-Dardīr), p. 147

[101] *Masā'il al-Ikhtilāf Bayna al-Ashā'ira wal-Māturīdiyya* (Ibn Kamāl Pāshā), p. 20-21; *Tabṣira al-Adilla* (Abū al-Mu'īn al-Nasafī), p. 402

[102] *Al-'Aqīda al-Islāmiyya* (Ḥabannaka), p. 371

[103] *Ḍaw' al-Ma'ālī* (al-Qārī), p. 50; *Al-Mukhtaṣar al-Mufīd* (al-Quḍāt), p. 79; *Al-Ikhtiyār* (al-Mawṣilī), 3:390; *Al-Shi'ār fī al-'Aqā'id* (Foudah), p. 137-138; *Baḥr al-Kalām* (Abū al-Mu'īn al-Nasafī), p. 104

For example, the negation of life [*ḥayāt*] necessitates death, the negation of omnipotence [*qudra*] necessitates incapacity, the negation of hearing [*sam*ʿ] necessitates deafness and so on.[105]

Others defined them as those attributes that are within the Divine essence (that is, they are necessary attributes of Allah ﷻ) or derived from an attribute that is not external to the Divine essence. For example, omniscience [*ʿilm*] is an attribute of the Divine essence and being Omniscient [*ʿAlīm*] likewise, as is it is derived from omniscience which is not external to the Divine essence.[106]

It is important to note that there is consensus that all the attributes of Divine essence are pre-eternal [*qadīm*].

II. The Attributes of Divine Acts [*Ṣifāt al-Fʿil*]

According to the *Ashʿarīs* these are those attributes when negated do not necessitate its opposite. Thus, if one negated the attribute of giving life [*iḥyāʾ*] or giving death [*imāta*] it does not necessitate that Allah ﷻ must be characterised with its opposite.[107]

Others defined it as, "any attribute of which both itself and its opposite are permissible to attribute to Allah ﷻ, such as: mercy [*raḥma*], compassion [*rāʾfa*], wrath [*sakhaṭ*] and anger [*ghaḍab*]."[108] A similar definition has also been mentioned by Mullā ʿAlī al-Qārī.[109]

It has also been defined as: those attributes that are derived from a meaning external to the Divine essence. For example, the attribute of being a "Creator:" this attribute is derived from the meaning of creation which is a meaning external to the Divine essence.[110]

---

[104] *Ḍawʾ al-Maʿālī* (al-Qārī), p. 50; *Minaḥ al-Rawḍ al-Azhar* (al-Qārī), p. 83
[105] *Minaḥ al-Rawḍ al-Azhar* (al-Qārī), p. 83
[106] *Al-Mukhtaṣar al-Mufīd* (al-Quḍāt), p. 79
[107] *Minaḥ al-Rawḍ al-Azhar* (al-Qārī), p. 83
[108] *Al-Ikhtiyār* (al-Mawṣilī), 3:390
[109] *Minaḥ al-Rawḍ al-Azhar* (al-Qārī), p. 83
[110] *Al-Mukhtaṣar al-Mufīd* (al-Quḍāt), p. 80

According to the *Ash'arīs*, giving life, giving provision, giving death, bringing into being [*takwīn*] and other such actions are all considered attributes of Divine acts. However, according to the *Māturīdīs* these are the effects of the attribute of *takwīn* itself as mentioned previously.[111]

Are the attributes of Divine acts pre-eternal [qadīm] like the attributes of Divine essence?

There is consensus between the theologians that the attributes of Divine essence are pre-eternal; however, they differed with regards to the attributes of Divine acts. The *Ash'arīs* do not consider the attributes of Divine acts pre-eternal, in that, they deem them to be the effect of Divine omnipotence [*qudra*].[112] The purport of this is that they do not deem God can be "called" a Creator until after He تعالى has created.

The *Māturīdīs*, however, consider both these types of attributes pre-eternal and thus did not see the "need to do distinguish between them,"[113] or categorise the attributes into attributes of Divine essence and attributes of Divine acts. As a result, the *Māturīdīs* believe God can be called a Creator in pre-eternity as the "establishment of the attribute of creating, which is *takwīn*, is in His تعالى essence in pre-eternity."[114]

JUDGEMENTS

Here we take a deeper look at what is meant when the theologians declare that a certain number of attributes are "necessary" for Allah تعالى. What do the theologians mean by this statement? Is it necessary because it has come in scripture and revelation? Or do they mean that these attributes are rationally necessary? Firstly, it is important to understand that judgements are of three types:[115]

---

[111] *Tuḥfa al-Murīd* (al-Bājūrī), p. 153
[112] *Al-Mukhtaṣar al-Mufīd* (al-Quḍāt), p. 80; *Ḍaw' al-Ma'ālī* (al-Qārī), p. 51; *Al-Iqtiṣād fī al-I'tiqād* (al-Ghazālī), p. 296
[113] *Tabṣira al-Adilla* (Abū al-Mu'īn al-Nasafī), p. 405
[114] Ibid., p. 403
[115] *Sharḥ al-Kharīda al-Bahiyya* (al-Dardīr), p. 124

I. Legal [*Sharʿī*]

This is the address of Allah ﷻ to those considered legally responsible that commands one to perform or to refrain, or makes something permissible to do. For example, prayer is obligatory and we know of that ruling through revelation.

II. Customary [*ʿĀda*]

This is to affirm or negate an effect between two things by way of repetition, for example: fire burning and water quenching thirst.

III. Rational [*ʿAqlī*]

This is to affirm or negate an effect between two things not by way of repetition or revelation, for example: 1+1=2

The answer to the questions posed above is that these twenty attributes mentioned by the author are *rationally* necessary. This means that anyone with a sound intellect should be able to come to the conclusion that the existence of God is necessary, without having access to scripture. It is impossible for a person to deny a rational judgement as these are based upon rational truths. No one can deny that 1+1=2, or that 4÷2=2. Islamic theology is only concerned with rational judgements and therefore it is paramount that we study the concept of rational judgements in more detail.

RATIONAL JUDGEMENTS

Rational judgements are of three types:[116]

I. *Necessary* [*Wājib*]

This is something of which the non-existence cannot be accepted by the intellect, for example: the existence of God. Rationally, it is inconceivable for there to be a world without a Creator.

---

116 *Tuḥfa al-Murīd* (al-Bājūrī), p. 73;
Sharḥ al-Kharīda al-Bahiyya (al-Dardīr), p. 135-137;
Sharḥ Umm al-Barāhīn (al-Sanūsī), p. 18-24

II. *Impossible* [*Mustaḥīl*]

This is something of which the existence can never be accepted by the intellect, for example: the non-existence of God, or a vehicle simultaneously moving and stayiwng stationary.

III. *Possible* [*Jā'iz*]

This is something which has both the capacity of existence and non-existence, for example: fire burning or food relieving hunger; it is rationally possible that fire may not burn, or food may not relieve one's hunger.

Each one of the above categories of rational judgements can be further sub-categorised into two types:[117]

IV. *A Priori* [*Ḍarūrī*]

This is something that does not depend upon deduction, proof or reflection, for example: the necessity of an object to occupy space, the impossibility of something to be stationary and mobile at the same time, or the possibility of something to be either mobile or stationary.

IV *A Posteriori* [*Naẓarī*]

This is something that depends upon proof, reflection and contemplation. For example, that it is necessary for Allah ﷻ to be Pre-eternal, that it is impossible for Allah to have a partner or the possibility of Allah rewarding the obedient and punishing the disobedient.

Having sufficient understanding of these categories is of utmost importance as it is incumbent upon every legally responsible person to know what is rationally necessary, impossible and possible with regards to Allah ﷻ and His Prophets, as elucidated by al-Dardīr in his other work, *al-Kharīda al-Bahiyya*, where he states:[118]

[117] *Sharḥ al-Kharīda al-Bahiyya* (al-Dardīr), p. 135-137

[118] *Al-Kharīda al-Bahiyya* (al-Dardīr), p. 94

It is necessary upon the one deemed legally responsible,
To know Allah the Lofty, so know
That is, know the necessary and impossible,
In addition to the possible for Him Almighty
And the like for the Messengers of Allah,
Upon them be the salutations of Allah

[I] EXISTENCE [*WUJŪD*]

Imam al-Dardīr now begins to list the attributes of Allah ﷻ that one must have knowledge of. He starts with existence [*wujūd*], which with regards to Allah ﷻ signifies the existence of the Divine essence itself. Strictly speaking, it is not an external attribute that describes the essence like the human whose existence is separate to the existence of his body,[119] but rather it is a term merely used to describe the presence of a Creator.

This attribute is considered the most important attribute of God, as all the other attributes of God exist by virtue of it. It is considered rationally necessary because, as described previously, the intellect can never fathom the non-existence of Allah ﷻ.[120]

Rational Evidence

How does one prove that God exists? This critical but somewhat simple question that many fail to find an answer to has been discussed thoroughly in many of the classical works of theology. The Muslim theologians provided a simple but sufficient answer to this question. Below, I have related two arguments to rationally prove the existence of God: the first is oft-mentioned in many of the books of Islamic theology to rationally prove the existence of God.

The First Argument: the Contingency [Ḥudūth] of the World

This argument is an example of syllogistic logic or Aristotelian syllogism [*qiyās al-manṭiq*], where arguments are systematically

[119] *Tuḥfa al-Murīd* (al-Bājūrī), p. 105-107

[120] *Sharḥ al-Kharīda al-Bahiyya* (al-Dardīr), p. 147; *Tuḥfa al-Murīd* (al-Bājūrī), p. 104

formulated to arrive at a certain truth. They normally involve two premises followed by a conclusion based upon those premises.

1. The First Premise: The world[121] is contingent [*ḥādith*].[122] By the constant change we witness in the world, we can conclude that the world is contingent. The theologians consider the world to be comprised of atoms and accidents. These atoms and accidents are constantly in a state of change and thus they conclude that the world by extension is necessarily changing and thus contingent.

2. The Second Premise: Anything that is contingent must have a Creator. If we presuppose that the world came into existence without a Creator, then this would mean that it came into being by itself. The theologians refute this idea as it would mean that between the two equal possibilities of existence and non-existence, one of them has outweighed the other one without any cause, which is impossible.[123]

3. Conclusion: The world must have a Creator.

The Second Argument: Intelligent Design

Allah ﷻ says: ﴾*Do they not gaze at the camel and how it was created?*﴿ [88:17]

This argument is also known as the "William Paley's watchmaker argument" or the "teleological argument." Paley argued that just as the function and complexity of a watch implied a watch-maker, likewise the function and complexity of the universe must imply the existence of a universe-maker. He said:

---

[121] "The world" is defined as: everything other than Allah ﷻ in existence. [*Tabṣira al-Adilla* (Abū al-Muʿīn al-Nasafī), p. 62]

[122] Contingent [*ḥādith*] means: something that was not in existence and is then brought into existence; that is, it has a beginning. [*Mawsūʿa Muṣṭalaḥāt ʿIlm al-Kalām* (Dughaym), 1:40]

[123] *Al-ʿAqīda al-Islāmiyya* (Ḥabannaka), p. 281

> If I stumbled on a stone and asked how it came to be there, it would be difficult to show that the answer, "it has lain there forever," is absurd. Yet this is not true if the stone were to be a watch.[124]

[II] PRE-ETERNALITY [*QIDAM*]

Pre-eternality [*qidam*] means: the negation of a beginning, that is, the existence of Allah ﷻ is not preceded by a period of non-existence.[125] Allah always was and will always be.[126]

It is important to know that Allah ﷻ and all His names and attributes of Divine essence are all considered pre-eternal. There is a dispute with regards to the attributes of Divine acts as has been mentioned previously.

There is a common misconception that the attribute *qadīm* is from the names of Allah; however, in reality it is a term coined by the theologians to make the name "the First" [*al-Awwal*] mentioned in the Qur'an comprehensible. Allah ﷻ says: ﴿*He is the First* [*al-Awwal*] *and the Last, the Outer and the Inner; He has knowledge of all things.*﴾ [57:3][127]

Rational Evidence

If we pre-suppose that Allah ﷻ was not pre-eternal, then He would have to have been brought into existence. This would, however, necessitate a creator who brings something into existence, making Him dependent upon a creator. This creator would also need a creator who would also need a creator and so on, resulting in an unbreakable cycle [*dawr*] or infinite chain [*tasalsul*],[128] which is an indication of the fallacy of the initial pre-supposition.

---

124 Philosophy.lander.edu, "*William Paley, 'The Teological Argument'*"
125 *Al-Musāyara* (Ibn al-Humām), p. 33
126 *Sharḥ al-Kharīda al-Bahiyya* (al-Dardīr), p. 154; *Ḥāshiya al-'Aqabāwī*, p. 12
127 *Shaykh 'Abd al-Fattāḥ Abū Ghudda's Addendum to Risāla al-Mustarshidīn*, p. 249
128 *Tuḥfa al-Murīd* (al-Bājūrī), p. 107; *Al-Musāmara* (Ibn Abī Sharīf), p. 33-34

It may be difficult for some to comprehend and conceptualise this attribute, as our experience of life tells us that everything has a beginning and an end. However, this does not mean in any way that it cannot exist: the philosophers have a statement which states that "the inability to comprehend something does not necessitate its inexistence in reality."[129]

[III] SEMPITERNALITY [*BAQĀ'*]

Sempiternality [*baqā'*] means: the everlastingness of Allah ﷻ, that is, there is no end to His existence, therefore He can never be characterised by non-existence.[130]

Allah ﷻ says in the Qur'an: ﴾*Everyone on earth perishes; all that remains is the Face of your Lord.*﴿ [55:26-27]

Rational Evidence

If pre-eternality is established for something, then sempiternality is a necessary consequence. It is impossible for something to have no beginning but to have an end. And so, the rational proof of this attribute is the same as that which has been provided for the attribute of pre-eternality.

[IV] OTHERNESS [*MUKHĀLAFA LIL-ḤAWĀDITH*]

Otherness [*mukhālafa lil-ḥawādith*] means: the complete dissimilarity of Allah ﷻ—that is, His ﷻ essence, attributes and acts—to anything in creation[131] and vice versa, regardless of whether that creation is in existence or not.[132]

Allah ﷻ states: ﴾*There is nothing like Him...*﴿ [42:11]

---

[129] *Kubrā al-Yaqīniyyāt al-Kawniyya* (al-Būṭī), p. 114
[130] *Sharḥ al-Kharīda al-Bahiyya* (al-Dardīr), p. 155;
Al-ʿAqīda al-Islāmiyya (Ḥabannaka), p. 344
[131] *Ṭāliʿ al-Bushrā* (al-Mārighnī), p. 75
[132] *Al-ʿAqīda al-Islāmiyya*, p. 345

This attribute is critical in gaining a proper understanding of God, especially in the current age where many, due to a plethora of reasons, have fallen into the arena of blasphemy, and due to this stand on the brinks of disbelief. Many preachers either inadvertently or intentionally carry on describing God in ways that is not befitting for Him, but because the study of classical theology is more or less non-existent, these unorthodox and blasphemous winds have, unfortunately, battered many a Muslim mind.

Therefore, it is vital to have a good grasp of what this attribute signifies, its necessary consequences, and specific beliefs that must be negated from Allah ﷻ:[133]

I. *Being a Substance [Jawhar]*[134]

In theology, a substance [*jawhar*] is a contingent thing which occupies space. This means that one can physically point towards it and state that it is here or there.[135] If this substance cannot be divided then it is termed as the indivisible particle (atom) [*al-jawhar al-fard*].

Every substance is confined to a specific area of space. For example, a ball takes up a certain amount of space, in which nothing else except the ball can exist. Allah ﷻ is not in need of any space to exist in, and thus cannot be a substance.

II. *Corporeality [Jismiyya]*

A body [*jism*] according to al-Ashʿarī means: that which is composed of two parts or more.[136] The *Muʿtazila*, however, defined a *jism* as being three dimensional, meaning that it has length, width and depth.[137] In reality, once "it is established that He ﷻ is not a substance, then it necessitates that He is not corporeal."[138]

---

[133] *Al-ʿAqīda al-Islāmiyya* (Ḥabannaka), p. 347-352; *Ghāya al-Marām* (al-Āmidī), p. 159; *Al-ʿAqāʾid al-Nasafiyya*, p. 68

[134] *Al-Musāyara* (Ibn al-Humām), p. 37; *Ghāya al-Marām* (al-Āmidī), p. 159

[135] *Mawsūʿa Kashāf* (al-Thānwī), p. 602

[136] *Al-Māturīdī and the Development of Sunni Theology* (Rudolph), p. 244; *Sharḥ al-ʿAqāʾid al-Nasafiyya* (al-Saʿdī), p. 47

[137] *Sharḥ al-ʿAqāʾid al-Nasafiyya*, p. 47

[138] *Ghāya al-Marām* (al-Āmidī), p. 164

III. *Being an Accident* [*ʿAraḍ*]

An accident is that which cannot subsist by itself but only in a body or substance [*jawhar*]. Colours, tastes, smells and movements are all examples of accidents.[139]

Accidents have the opposite qualities to a substance in that they cannot occupy space and can only reside in another thing, "thus, they constantly require a substrate [*maḥall*], and this substrate by definition can only be a corporeal substance [*jism*]."[140]

Because accidents are dependent upon a substrate, the substrate would logically have to precede the accident for the accident to exist. This entails that if Allah ﷻ was an accident, something would have to exist before Him. Allah would thus be dependent upon something else, and in addition necessitate the impossibility of attributing pre-eternality to Him.

IV. *Being Characterised by Shape, Colour, Smell, Physical Sensations or Emotions.*

These are attributes that are specific for bodies and thus impossible for Allah ﷻ to be characterised with.[141]

V. *Being Confined by Place*

Abū al-Muʿīn al-Nasafī states:

> If we say that He ﷻ is confined by place [*makān*] then this will lead to an ugly conclusion, for it entails that He is either in His entirety in every place, or in every place divided in parts, or in a place but not in another.
>
> It is false to say that He ﷻ is in His entirety in every place as this would necessitate the presence of two [or more] gods, and not one God—and God is One. It is [also] false for Him to be in parts, and whoever describes Allah ﷻ with parts has committed disbelief. And, it is impossible for Him to be in one place but not in another, as He would be in

---

139 Rahman, F., "ʿAraḍ" in: *Encyclopaedia of Islam, second edition*; *Al-ʿAqāʾid al-Nasafiyya*, p. 33

140 *Al-Māturīdī and the Development of Sunni Theology* (Rudolph), p. 244

141 *Sharḥ al-ʿAqāʾid al-Nasafiyya* (al-Taftazānī), p. 48

> need of moving, which is from the attributes of the created, and the characteristics of that which has been brought into existence—and Allah ﷻ is transcendent beyond that.[142]

ʿAlī b. Abī Ṭālib is reported to have been asked: "Where was our Lord before He created the throne?" He replied: "*Where*, is a question regarding place, and Allah Almighty was when there was no place or time and He is now as He was."[143]

A result of negating "place" from Allah ﷻ is that it is impermissible to describe Allah as being in every place or everywhere, unless one intends by it that His signs are everywhere.

VI. *Being Confined by Direction*

Allah ﷻ cannot be characterised as being, above, below, to the right, left, behind or in front. If Allah was characterised by being in a specific direction [*jiha*], then this would necessitate the pre-eternality of that direction which is impossible. Direction is also specific for things that occupy space, namely bodies or substances, and since that is impossible for Allah, so too is direction.

A question that arises often is that if Allah ﷻ cannot be confined by a direction then why do we raise our hands towards the sky when supplicating?

Al-Ghaznawī in his *Uṣūl al-Dīn* answers this question by stating:

> The hands are raised because it is the direction [*qibla*] for supplication [*duʿā*] just like the *Kaʿba* is the *qibla* for the prayer [*ṣalāt*], and placing the face on the ground when prostrating, even though Allah ﷻ is neither in the *Kaʿba* nor beneath the ground.[144]

---

142 *Baḥr al-Kalām* (Abū al-Muʿīn al-Nasafī), p. 130
143 Ibid. p. 127
144 *Uṣūl al-Dīn* (al-Ghaznawī), p. 71. Al-Ghazālī provides a similar answer in *al-Iqtiṣād fī al-Iʿtiqād.*

VII. *Being Confined by Time*

Imam al-Nasafī states: "Time does not affect Him."[145] And thus, there is no present, past or future for Allah ﷻ.[146]

VIII. *Physical Size*

It is impermissible to characterise Allah as being physically large or small. Al-Ghaznawī states:

> It cannot be said that Allah ﷻ is large with regards to His essence, because largeness in an entity is not possible except through a great number of parts; and He ﷻ is One, He cannot be divided or separated.[147]

IX. *Being Still or Moving*

Ibrāhīm al-Bukhārī states:

> Know that Allah ﷻ cannot be described with movement or stillness, and it cannot be said He is moving or still, because movement is the transfer from one place to another and stillness is to remain in a place, and it is impermissible to describe Allah as being in [both] every place, or in one place and not in another.[148]

X. *The Divine Essence being Connected or Disconnected to Creation.*

Allah is not part of this world or anything from His creation. Imam al-Jazūlī states:

> If a questioner asks you: "Is He ﷻ inside things or outside?" If you say, "inside things," then He would be a part of the world and if you say, "outside of them," then He would be in a known direction. The answer is to say to him: "He is not inside nor outside of things [...] but He ﷻ encompasses [*muḥīṭ*] them."[149]

---

[145] *Al-ʿAqāʾid al-Nasafiyya*, p. 34

[146] *Sharḥ al-ʿAqāʾid al-Nasafiyya* (Ramaḍān Effendī), p. 250

[147] *Uṣūl al-Dīn* (al-Ghaznawī), p. 111

[148] *Talkhīṣ al-Adilla* (Ṣaffār al-Bukhārī), 2:659

[149] *ʿAqīda al-Jazūlī*, p. 90

XI. *The Indwelling of the Divine Essence* [*Ḥulūl*] *or its Union* [*Ittiḥād*] *with another Being*

Shaykh ʿAbd al-Qādir ʿĪsā explains:

> Indwelling [*ḥulūl*] and union [*ittiḥād*] can only take place between things of the same genus, while Allah ﷻ is not a genus that would enable union between Him and other genera; so how can the Pre-eternal subsist within the contingent, the Creator within the creation? If it is the subsistence of an accident [ʿ*araḍ*] within a substance, then, Allah ﷻ is not an accident. If it is the subsistence of a substance [*jawhar*] within another substance, then, Allah is not a substance. Since indwelling between the creation itself is impossible—hence, a person cannot make two men into one because of their separate essences—the disparity between the Creator and the creation, the Maker and the made, between the Necessary cause of existence and the contingently existent, is even greater *a fortiori* due to the ultimate dissimilarity between the two realities.[150]

Ambiguous Verses in the Qurʾan [*Mutashābihāt*]

There are numerous verses in the Qurʾan that are called ambiguous [*mutashābihāt*] whose meanings are differed upon, as opposed to definite [*muḥkam*] verses whose meanings are apparent and unambiguous. This is a Qurʾanic dichotomy. Allah ﷻ says: ❮*It is He Who has sent this Scripture down to you* [O *Muhammad*]. *Some of its verses are* ***definite*** *in meaning—these are the cornerstone of the Scripture—and others are* ***ambiguous...***❯ [3:7]

These verses have an important connection to the attribute of "otherness," as they, at face value, contradict the above understanding; that is, with regards to Allah ﷻ being dissimilar to creation in any way shape or form. Some examples of these verses are:

I. ❮*They fear their Lord* ***above*** *them, and they do as they are commanded.*❯ [16:50]

II. ❮*The Lord of Mercy,* ***ascended over*** *the throne.*❯ [20:5]

[150] *Ḥaqāʾiq ʿan al-Taṣawwuf* (ʿĪsā), p. 435. Adapted from the English translation: *Realities of Sufism*, p. 356.

III. ﴾*...God's **hand** is placed on theirs.*﴿ [48:10]
IV. ﴾*All that remains is the **Face** of your Lord.*﴿ [55:27]

As is evident, these verses seem to allude to Allah تعالى being defined by physical direction or possessing certain human-like qualities.

Whether it is possible to ascertain the intended meaning of these verses or not is where the problem arises.[151] Allah تعالى says: ﴾*The perverse at heart eagerly pursue the ambiguities in their attempt to cause trouble and to pin down a specific meaning of their own: only God knows the true meaning. Those firmly grounded in knowledge say: "We believe in it: it is all from our Lord"—only those with real perception will take heed.*﴿ [3:7] It is also possible however to read the verse as: ﴾*...only God and those firmly grounded in knowledge know the true meaning. Say: "We believe..."*﴿ If the verse is read in this manner then this means it is possible to know the meaning of these verses, however if read in the former manner, it is not.[152]

And so, the scholars differed with regards to these verses. Some took a more conservative approach, whereas others saw the need to interpret them in a way befitting for Allah تعالى. Below, I have outlined the three schools of thought with regards to these verses as mentioned by Ibn al-Jawzī and many others.[153] The first two are considered orthodox Sunni opinions, whereas the third has no place in orthodox Sunni belief:

I. *The Salaf and Relegation* [*Tafwīḍ*]

The first school of thought with regards to these verses is of the *salaf*.[154] This means the likes of Mālik, Ibn ʿUyayna,

---

[151] *ʿUlūm al-Qurʾān al-Karīm* (ʿItr), p. 122

[152] According to Shaykh Abū Bakr al-Mullā, the majority of the companions read the verse stopping at ﴾*only God knows the true meaning.*﴿ He also mentions, however, that a few from the early generations like al-Ḍaḥḥāk and al-Mujāhid did read it as ﴾*those firmly grounded in knowledge know the true meaning.*﴿ [*Maslak al-Thiqāt*, p. 45]

[153] *Dafʿ Shubha al-Tashbīh* (Ibn al-Jawzī), p. 264;
Sharḥ al-Kharīda al-Bahiyya (al-Dardīr), p. 171

[154] The *salaf* are usually considered to be the companions, the followers [*tābiʿīn*], the followers of the followers [*atbaʿ al-tābiʿīn*] and the early well-known and reliable Imams. [*Lawāmiʿ al-Anwār al-Bahiyya* (al-Saffārīnī),

Abū Ḥanīfa, Ibn al-Mubārak, and Sufyān al-Thawrī. They adhered to the methodology of *tafwīḍ*, which is to completely "relegate the knowledge of the reality of the meaning of these verses to Allah alone,"[155] and to negate any understanding that could allude to Allah ﷻ being similar to creation.

In reality, the way of the *salaf* is one of complete submission. They refused to interpret these verses at all, but rather insisted on accepting them at face value without pondering over their meaning.

Many of them would say: "Let them pass as they came."[156] That is, believe that these verses are from Allah ﷻ and abstain from explaining them, whether literally or figuratively.

In an oft-mentioned narration, Imam Mālik was asked about the term "to ascend" [*istiwā'*] in the following verse: ﴾*...the Lord of Mercy, ascended over the throne* [*'alā al-'arsh istawā*]*...*﴿ [20:5] When asked this question, the Imam is said to have lowered his head until he was completely soaked in sweat and then said: "To ascend" [*istiwā'*] is not unknown [*ghayr majhūl*],[157] its modality is inconceivable [*ghayr ma'qūl*], to believe in it is necessary, to ask about it is an innovation and I do not see you except as an innovator."[158]

A similar statement has also been related from Muḥammad b. al-Ḥasan al-Shaybānī, who said:

> We believe in what has come from Allah ﷻ and do not delve into "how;" [we believe in] what Allah has intended with it, and in what the Messenger of Allah ﷺ has come with, and in what the Messenger of Allah intended with it.[159]

1:20]. However, it has also been said that they are the people from the first five decades after the *Hijra*. [*Tuḥfa al-Murīd* (al-Bājūrī), p. 156]

155 *'Ulūm al-Qur'ān al-Karīm* ('Itr), p. 125

156 *Al-'Aqīda al-Islāmiyya* (Ḥabannaka), p. 353

157 That is, its meaning is known to the scholars of language. [*Daf'u Shubah man Shabbaha wa-Tamarrada* (al-Huṣnī), p. 301]

158 *Al-Asmā' wal-Ṣifāt* (al-Bayhaqī), 2:305

159 *Baḥr al-Kalām* (Abū al-Mu'īn al-Nasafī), p. 128

These are just a selection of narrations that affirm the position of the *salaf* with regards to these verses. It is clear that the early generation of scholars, theologians and jurists chose the way of *tafwīḍ* and distanced themselves from attributing any type of human form or behaviour to Allah ﷻ.

II. *Interpreting Figuratively* [*Tā'wīl*]

The second orthodox Sunni school with regards to these verses is the school of the later generations [*khalaf*]. This school came into existence as a solution to stave off the threat posed by an increasing number of anthropomorphists.[160] It considered it appropriate to interpret the verses figuratively in a way that was in keeping with the usage of the Arabic language and in a manner befitting for Allah ﷻ.[161]

Al-Bājūrī states:

> If there is anything in the Qur'an that gives the perception of there being a direction, body, form or limbs [to Allah ﷻ], then the people of truth and other than them—except the *Mujassima* and *Mushabbiha*—are in consensus that that they should be interpreted figuratively.[162]

Therefore, proponents of this school understand the word "hand" as an example when ascribed to Allah ﷻ to mean omnipotence, and the word "Face" to mean the Divine essence and so on.[163]

From the scholars who seem to have preferred this method was 'Izz al-Dīn b. 'Abd al-Salām. He is reported to have said in some of his legal verdicts, that:

---

[160] See: Footnotes of Shaykh Muḥammad Zāhid al-Kawtharī in *Daf' Shubha al-Tashbīh* (Ibn al-Jawzī), p. 265

[161] *'Ulūm al-Qur'ān al-Karīm* ('Itr), p. 126

[162] *Tuḥfa al-Murīd* (al-Bājūrī), p. 157

[163] *Sharḥ al-Kharīda al-Bahiyya* (al-Dardīr), p. 171

> The way of figuratively interpreting, with its condition, is the closest to the truth. Its condition being that the meanings are in accordance with the requirements of the Arabic language.[164]

Ultimately, the way of relegation and the way of interpretation are both orthodox opinions; both schools negate the possibility of Allah ﷻ being similar to creation, and thus there is no blame upon followers of either way. However, it has been said that: "The way of the *salaf* is safer whereas the way of the *khalaf* is more precise."[165]

It is worth noting here that the *khalaf* do not intend to act in contrary to their predecessors and one must be careful not to entertain those types of thoughts.

III. *Anthropomorphism* [*Tajsīm*]

The anthropomorphists [*Mujassima*] are those who liken Allah ﷻ to creation by affirming a literal meaning to the ambiguous verses that they feel is befitting for Allah.[166] For example, Allah has a hand but not like any hand we know of. They attribute a limb to Allah but relegate its modality [*kayfiyya*] to Allah.[167] This is different to the way of the *salaf* who relegated the intended meaning [*murād*] of the word itself to Allah ﷻ.

One who holds this type of view holds the door open for Satan who could say: "If His hand is not like yours then what does it look like?" Imagination can easily run wild and characterise Allah ﷻ with qualities that are not befitting Him, inevitably leading to disbelief.

There is complete agreement amongst the Sunni jurists from all four schools of thought that anyone who holds the view that Allah ﷻ has a body or likens Him to creation in any way, has disbelieved.

---

[164] *Al-Musāmara* (Ibn Abī Sharīf), p. 49

[165] *Sharḥ al-Kharīda al-Bahiyya* (al-Dardīr), p. 171; *Tuḥfa al-Murīd* (al-Bājūrī), p. 156

[166] *'Ulūm al-Qur'ān al-Karīm* ('Itr), p. 129

[167] *'Aqīda al-Salaf al-Ṣāliḥ* (al-Kayyālī), p. 16

The *Ḥanafī* scholar al-Shalabī states: "If the anthropomorphist states, 'He Almighty has a hand or a foot like man,' then he is a disbeliever and is accursed."[168]

[V] SELF-SUBSISTENCE [*QIYĀM BIL-NAFS*]

The fifth necessary attribute of Allah ﷻ is self-subsistence or *qiyām bil-nafs*, which is to declare the:[169]

I. Absolute non-dependency of Allah upon an essence or substance to subsist in.

II. And, His absolute non-dependency upon an originator or creator.

Numerous verses in the Qur'an attest to the above understanding. Allah ﷻ says: ﴾*O People, it is you who stand in need of God—God needs nothing and is worthy of all praise...*﴿ [35:15] And, in another verse He ﷻ says: ﴾*God, the self-sufficient.*﴿ [112:2]

Rational Evidence

Imam al-Dardīr states:

> If He ﷻ was dependent upon that[170] then He would be an attribute and not an essence, as an essence does not subsist in an essence. However, for Him to be an attribute is impossible because, if He was an attribute the subsistence of permanent attributes would be impossible for Him, like, omniscience and omnipotence as an attribute cannot allow another attribute to subsist within it.[171]

---

[168] *Ḥāshiya al-Shalabī ʿalā Tabyīn al-Ḥaqāʾiq*, 1:347
[169] *Tuḥfa al-Murīd* (al-Bājūrī), p. 113
[170] That is, an essence or a substance.
[171] *Sharḥ al-Kharīda al-Bahiyya* (al-Dardīr), p. 155

[VI] Oneness [*Waḥdāniyya*]

Oneness [*waḥdāniyya*] is to negate any type of multiplicity in the Divine essence, attributes and acts.[172]

Elaborating further upon the aforementioned definition, the theologians derived five things or quantities [*kumūm*] that must be negated from Allah ﷻ as a consequence of the attribute of oneness.

The Five Quantities [*al-Kumūm al-Khamsa*] and their Negation[173]

I. *Negating Multiplicity in the Divine Essence*

1. *Connected Quantity* [*al-Kam al-Muttaṣil*]

This is to negate any composition; that is, to negate that Allah ﷻ is composed of multiple parts.

2. *Disconnected Quantity* [*al-Kam al-Munfaṣil*]

This is to negate multiplicity in the Divine essence, which means to negate the possibility of more than one God.

II. *Negating Multiplicity in the Divine Attributes*

1. *Connected Quantity*

This is to negate the multiplicity of an attribute from the same class or category, for example: having two or more attributes of omnipotence [*qudra*] or two or more attributes of omniscience [*'ilm*].

2. *Disconnected Quantity*

This is to negate the presence of an attribute of God in other than God, for example: a man being characterised with the attribute of knowledge like the omniscience of Allah ﷻ.

[172] Ibid., p. 158; *Ḥāshiya al-'Aqabāwī*, p. 17

[173] *Tuḥfa al-Murīd* (al-Bājūrī), p. 114;
Sharḥ al-Kharīda al-Bahiyya (al-Dardīr), p. 158

III. *Negating Multiplicity in the Divine Acts*

1. *Connected Quantity*

This is to know that all actions are God's; that is, they are created by God whilst the actions of others have no intrinsic effect. Nothing of our volitional actions is brought into existence by our own power: we and everything that we do are created by Allah without any intermediary. Allah ﷻ says: ﴾*Allah created you and all that you do.*﴿ [37:96][174]

The Theory of *Kasb* (Acquisition) and the Problem of Free Will vs. Pre-destination

A question that normally arises at this point is that if every action of ours is created by Allah then how can those acts be ascribed to man? And, why would Allah command us to act in the Qur'an and then hold us responsible for that which we have no control over?

The answer lies in the theory of *kasb* (acquisition). When a person desires to speak, cough, eat, sit and so on, he has no power over these willed acts in terms of bringing them into existence—Allah ﷻ is the only One Who creates our actions without any intermediary. However, we are held accountable for our actions due to the power of *kasb* that Allah has instilled and created in us. This theory states that when we desire to perform a certain act, Allah creates it for us, and it is this desire and volition that we are being held accountable for.

Allah ﷻ says: ﴾*...each acquires whatever good it has done, and suffers its bad.*﴿ [2:286] If Allah did not create within us the power to acquire acts, we would be considered coerced and not legally responsible for our actions, like the mentally ill or undiscerning child.[175]

Imam al-Laqqānī states:[176]

According to us the servant has acquisition,
Through which he is legally responsible,
And know that he did not have any effect therein

[174] *Sharḥ al-Kharīda al-Bahiyya*, p. 160
[175] Ibid., p. 161
[176] *Jawhara al-Tawḥīd* (al-Laqqānī), p. 175

Shaykh Muḥammad Saʿīd Ramaḍān al-Būṭī states: "The intent, resolve and acquisition are from you, and this being with the secret of volition that He ﷻ has placed within you."[177]

Imam al-Nasafī states:

> The servant has voluntary acts through which he is rewarded or punished, the good from them is with the pleasure of Allah ﷻ, and the evil from them is without His, the Almighty's, pleasure.[178]

In summary, the servant has a choice and he has the capacity to either perform an act or not perform it; however, it is only Allah ﷻ Who is able to create that act and not the servant.[179]

It is important to note here that even though all actions, whether good or evil, are created by Allah ﷻ, one should by way of respect only ascribe that which is good to Allah—the evil should be ascribed to the self even if Allah is the actual Creator of that act. Allah ﷻ says: ﴾*Whatever misfortune befalls you [people], it is because of what your own hands have done.*﴿ [42:30]

Deniers of the Theory of *Kasb*

There were some sects that refuted the above argument and denied the ability of man to acquire acts. Below we will take a look at some of these alternative ideologies in detail.

I. *The Determinists [Jabriyya]*

It is said that the originators of this school of thought were: Jaʿd[180] b. Dirham and Jahm[181] b. Ṣafwān al-Rāsibī.[182]

---

[177] *Kubrā al-Yaqīniyāt al-Kawniyya* (al-Būṭī), p. 163

[178] *Al-ʿAqāʾid al-Nasafiyya*, p. 34

[179] *Baḥr al-Kalām* (Abū al-Muʿīn al-Nasafī), p. 146

[180] Jaʿd was an Umayyad era heretic who originated from either Khorasan or Harran and later took residence in Damascus. It is said that he was the first person to say the Qurʾan was created, that Allah ﷻ did not take Ibrāhīm ﷺ as a close friend [*khalīl*] and that Allah did not speak to Mūsā ﷺ. These views made him a fugitive and eventually led him to flee to Kufa where he was to become the teacher of Jahm b. Ṣafwān. [*Tārīkh Dimashq* (Ibn ʿAsākir), 72:99:9788; *Siyar al-Aʿlām al-Nubalāʾ* (al-Dhahabī), 5:433]

From the erroneous beliefs of this school was the belief that man is compelled in all his actions, meaning that he has no volition or choice over his actions just like a feather has no choice in the wind. This theory led them to conclude that man is compelled to either believe or disbelieve.[183]

Al-Ghazālī rejected the determinist position on the grounds that it cannot account for the difference between a deliberate human action and an involuntary one, such as a bodily tremor."[184] A similar argument is also mentioned by al-Nasafī in his creed.

There is no doubt that anyone who holds this belief is an outright disbeliever as he has negated the concept of man being responsible, which is what the Prophets came with[185] and this is affirmed by clear verses of the Qur'an.

II. *Those that Assert Man's Creative Free Will* [*Qadariyya*]
This is the creed of the *Mu'tazila*:[186]

> ... [The *Mu'tazila*] consider humanity to have the power to produce its own actions, whether these are thoughts, volitions or bodily movements. They see this position as a requirement of Divine justice.[187]

According to this doctrine, it is man who creates his actions with a power that Allah ﷻ has created in him. They negate the relationship of the omnipotence of Allah with the actions of men

---

[181] A student of Ja'd b. Dirham, Jahm was likewise another Umayyad era heretic. It is said that he originated from Samarqand and was an astute and good debater. From his many freethinking beliefs were the created nature of the Qur'an and that Allah ﷻ is in all places.
[*Siyar al-A'lām al-Nubalā'*, 8:27]

[182] *Al-'Aqīda al-Islāmiyya wa-Madhāhibuhā* (al-Dūrī), p. 420

[183] *Al-Mukhtaṣar al-Mufīd* (al-Quḍāt), p. 103; *Baḥr al-Kalām* (Abū al-Mu'īn al-Nasafī), p. 146

[184] *"Causation in Arabic and Islamic Thought," The Stanford Encyclopaedia of Philosophy*

[185] *Sharḥ al-Kharīda al-Bahiyya* (al-Dardīr), p. 163

[186] *Tuḥfa al-Murīd* (al-Bājūrī), p. 168

[187] *"Causation in Arabic and Islamic Thought," The Stanford Encyclopaedia of Philosophy*

and believe that everything that emits from man is from the innovation and creation of man.[188]

There is some disagreement with regards to the validity of belief of someone who holds this opinion, with the more correct position being that one has not disbelieved.[189]

In sum:

> *Muʿtazilī* theologians appealed to Divine justice to show that the circle of agents include God and humanity, whereas al-Ashʿarī and his followers appealed to Divine omnipotence to limit agency to God alone. Generally speaking, *Ashʿarī* theologians seem to endorse occasionalism, this being the view that God is the only true cause.[190]

Customary Acts: Between Cause and Effect

In the following discussion we will look at some differing opinions with regards to customary acts and who or what causes the effect that we witness repeatedly. For example, when there is a flame, what causes the burning? And when there is water, what causes the quenching of thirst?

I. *Natural causation* [*ṭabīʿa*][191]

This theory states that things cause an effect by their very intrinsic nature, thereby implying the non-existence of an external causative agent. For example, fire burns or water quenches due to the intrinsic nature of fire or water. Anyone who holds this belief is considered a disbeliever.

---

188 *Al-Iqtiṣād fī al-Iʿtiqād* (al-Ghazālī), p. 212;
Al-Mukhtaṣar al-Mufīd (al-Quḍāt), p. 103

189 *Sharḥ al-Kharīda al-Bahiyya* (al-Dardīr), p. 163

190 *"Causation in Arabic and Islamic Thought," The Stanford Encyclopaedia of Philosophy.* "All natural beings are completely inert, and the true and sole agent in nature is God. Causes do not logically necessitate their effects and the relation between what we take to be causes and effects is merely one of correlation and is purely contingent, the one real, productive cause of all things is God." [*Occasionalism* (Hasker), 1998]

191 *Sharḥ al-Kharīda al-Bahiyya* (al-Dardīr), p. 164;
Miftāḥ al-Janna (al-Hāshimī), p. 175

II. *Mechanical Causation* [*ʿilla*][192]

This is to believe that a thing necessarily causes an effect in another thing. For example, moving one's finger is the cause for a ring worn on that finger to move also. This belief is also tantamount to disbelief.

It is important to note that the difference between what can be termed natural and mechanical causation is that natural causation occurs upon the existence of pre-conditions and the negation of preventatives, as can be seen in the example of burning—for "fire to burn" there must be contact and the absence of moisture. However, mechanical causation differs in that it does not rest upon the aforementioned—each time the cause exists, the effect also exists. Therefore, in mechanical causation the cause and effect are necessarily connected to each other, whereas in natural causation they are not.

III. *Potency* [*quwwa*][193]

This is the belief that customary acts cause an effect by a "potency" that God has placed within it. The consequence being that fire burns due to a potency God has created within it. This was the position of the *Muʿtazila*.

This belief is tantamount to heresy, but not disbelief. Shaykh Muḥammad al-Hāshimī states:

> The correct position is to not incur upon them disbelief as they do not make the 'creative power' of the servant like the creative power of God Almighty, in that, they made the servant dependent upon causes and means, as opposed to Him Almighty. The scholars of Transoxiana, however, considered them disbelievers and even considered the Magians in a better state than them because they do not associate with Allah ﷻ except one partner, whereas they have associated with Allah many partners.[194]

---

[192] Ibid.

[193] Ibid.

[194] *Miftāḥ al-Janna* (al-Hāshimī), p. 175-176

IV. *The Orthodox View*

The Sunni orthodox creed with regards to causation in customary acts is to believe that Allah ﷻ alone is the sole Creator and agent of all things and therefore, "natural causes do not have any influence upon their effects."[195]

Ibrāhīm al-Mārighnī al-Mālikī explains:

> Rather, Allah ﷻ has made it from His way, with full volition, to bring into existence the effects when the causes are present, that is, simultaneously with them and not by virtue of them. And so, the cause may be present but not the effect contrary to the norm, like fire without the burning.[196]

Al-Ghazālī states in *Incoherence of the Philosophers* that:

> The connection between what is customarily considered to be a cause and what is habitually believed to be an effect is not necessary, according to us. But [with] any two things, where "this" is not "that" and "that" is not "this" and where neither the affirmation of the one entails the affirmation of the other, nor the negation of the one entails negation of the other, it is not a necessity of the existence of the one that the other should exist, and it is not a necessity of the non-existence of the one that the other should not exist—for example, the quenching of thirst and drinking, satiety and eating, burning and contact with fire, light and the appearance of the sun, death and decapitation [...] and so on to [include] all [that is] observable among connected things in medicine, astronomy, arts and crafts. Their connection is due to the prior decree of God, Who creates them side by side, not to it being necessary in itself, incapable of separation.[197]

---

195 *Ṭāliʿ al-Bushrā* (al-Mārighnī), p.99

196 Ibid.

197 Richardson, Kara, *"Causation in Arabic and Islamic Thought," The Stanford Encyclopaedia of Philosophy*

[VII] Life [Ḥayāt]

The first of the qualitative attributes is life [*ḥayāt*]. In the science of theology, life is defined as: a pre-eternal attribute which necessitates the verity of omniscience, will and the other qualitative attributes.[198]

Allah ﷻ says: ﴾*God, there is no god but Him, the Ever* ***Living****, the Self-subsistent.*﴿ [3:2]

It is important to note that this attribute does not signify the life that created beings are characterized with which involves movement, sensation, hunger, thirst and the like.[199] Nor does it mean the presence of a soul [*rūḥ*] which is a creation of Allah ﷻ through which man is given life.[200]

Rational Evidence

I. Life is considered a perfect quality and its opposite, death, is considered an imperfect quality. Because Allah ﷻ is free from all imperfections, Allah is necessarily Living.[201]

II. If Allah ﷻ was not Living, it would be impossible for Him to grant life to other created beings, as "the one who does not have cannot bestow."[202]

Its Connections [*Ta'alluqāt*][203]

The attribute of life has no external connections and thus does not require any additional matter apart from being within the Divine essence.[204]

---

[198] *Sharḥ al-Kharīda al-Bahiyya* (al-Dardīr), p. 174
[199] *Al-Musāmara* (Ibn Abī Sharīf), p. 71
[200] *Al-Mukhtaṣar al-Mufīd* (al-Quḍāt), p. 67
[201] *Ḥāshiya 'alā al-Musāyara* (Ibn Quṭlūbghā), p. 71
[202] *Al-'Aqīda al-Islāmiyya wa-Madhāhibuhā* (al-Dūrī), p. 404
[203] See: "The Qualitative Attributes" on p. 98-99 for a discussion regarding "connections."
[204] *Al-Mukhtaṣar al-Mufīd*, p. 80; *Sharḥ Umm al-Barāhīn* (al-Sanūsī), p. 48

[VIII] Omniscience ['Ilm]

In the science of theology, omniscience is defined as: a pre-eternal attribute within the Divine essence that is related to the necessary, possible and impossible in an all-encompassing manner, as they really are, without any prior obscurity.[205] Allah ﷻ says: ﴾*And it is He Who has knowledge of all things.*﴿ [2:29]

And He says: ﴾*He has the keys to the unseen: no one knows them but Him. He knows all that is in the land and sea. No leaf falls without His knowledge, nor is there a single grain in the darkness of the earth, or anything, fresh or withered, that is not written in a clear record.*﴿ [6:59]

Rational Evidence

If Allah ﷻ was not Omniscient, it would necessitate characterizing Him with ignorance. However, ignorance is an imperfection, which is impossible for Allah.[206]

Allah's acts are perfect and wise, which is evident for anyone who gazes at the skies and upon his own self. When one's actions are perfect and wise it necessitates omniscience, just like if one saw a letter which involved words with deep meaning, he would automatically assume the writer to be knowledgeable.[207]

Its Connections

Every possible, impossible and necessary thing,

The omniscience of Allah ﷻ is considered *tanjīzī qadīm* (pre-eternally actualised), meaning that Allah knows all things pre-eternally, without acquisition, in all of its detail, regardless of whether it happened in the past, present or future. His knowledge is not *ṣulūḥī* (potential to be actualised) or *tanjīzī ḥādith* (temporal actualisation) as this would imply that there was a period where Allah was ignorant.[208]

---

205 *Al-Mukhtaṣar al-Mufīd*, p. 65; *Tuḥfa al-Murīd* (al-Bājūrī), p. 126

206 *Al-'Aqīda al-Islāmiyya wa-Madhāhibuhā* (al-Dūrī), p. 392

207 *Tuḥfa al-Murīd* (al-Bājūrī), p. 127

208 *Al-Mukhtaṣar al-Mufīd* (al-Quḍāt), p. 65

[IX] WILL [*IRĀDA*]

The ninth necessary attribute is *irāda* (will). Allah ﷻ says: ﴾*When He wills something to be, His way is to say, "Be" and it is!*﴿ [36:82] In theology, *irāda* is defined as: a pre-eternal attribute which specifies from the possible some of which is permissible for it.

The theologians describe that which is permissible from the possible, as the six mutually incompatible possibilities [*al-mumkināt al-mutaqābilāt al-sitta*]. These are: existence and non-existence, attributes, quantities, times, places and directions. The first possibility is with regards to existence [*wujūd*] and non-existence [*ʿadam*], that is: the existence of a thing negates its non-existence. The second possibility is with regards to attributes [*ṣifāt*], for example: the attribute of being white negates it being black and so forth. The third possibility is with regards to quantities [*maqādīr*], for example: tallness negates shortness. The fourth possibility is with regards to times [*azmina*], that is, being in a certain time period. For example, being in the time of the Prophet ʿĪsā ﷺ negates being in another time, like the time of the Prophet Ādam ﷺ. The fifth possibility relates to places [*amkina*], for example: being in Egypt negates being in England. And the sixth and final possibility is concerned with directions [*jihāt*], for example: being in the east negates being in the west.[209]

Rational Evidence

If Allah ﷻ was not characterised with will, He would be considered coerced. If He was coerced, then He would be considered powerless. And if He was powerless, then He would be incapable of creating anything.[210]

Will vs. Command [*Amr*]

Everything that exists has been willed by Allah ﷻ, and thus anything that does not exist has not been willed by Him.

[209] *Sharḥ al-Kharīda al-Bahiyya* (al-Dardīr), p. 174, *Ḥāshiya al-ʿAqabāwī*, p. 13; *Tuḥfa al-Murīd* (al-Bājūrī), p. 122

[210] *Al-ʿAqīda al-Islāmiyya wa-Madhāhibuhā* (al-Dūrī), p. 384

Although Allah may will something and also command its performance, He may also will something and forbid its performance. This interplay between will and command[211] results in four possible scenarios:[212]

I. *Commanded and Willed*

For example, the faith of Abū Bakr رضي الله عنه. Allah تعالى commanded Abū Bakr to believe and He also willed his belief.

II. *Not Commanded and not Willed*

For example, the disbelief of Abū Bakr رضي الله عنه. Allah تعالى did not command him to disbelieve and neither did He will it.

III. *Commanded and not Willed*

For example, the faith of Abū Jahl. Allah تعالى commanded him to believe but did not will it.

IV. *Not Commanded but Willed*

For example, the disbelief of Abū Jahl. Allah تعالى did not command Abū Jahl to disbelieve but willed it.

It is important to note here that the will of Allah does not automatically necessitate the contentment of Allah.[213]

Its Connections

"Will" only associates with the possible, both good and bad. The *Muʿtazila*, however, disagree and believe that Allah's تعالى will only associates with the good and not the bad, meaning that it is associated with only those things that Allah has commanded.[214]

---

[211] In explanation of what the command is, Mullā ʿAlī al-Qārī states: "An order [*ṭalab*] from Allah تعالى is of two types: an order to the legally responsible person [*mukallaf*] with the option to choose, this is what is known as the command [*amr*] and it does not necessitate that it must exist because of its dependence upon the choice of the legally responsible person." [*Minaḥ al-Rawḍ al-Azhar*, p. 79]

[212] *Sharḥ al-Kharīda al-Bahiyya*, p. 177

[213] *Tuḥfa al-Murīd* (al-Bājūrī), p. 125

[214] Ibid., p. 123; *Sharḥ Umm al-Barāhīn* (al-Sanūsī), p. 45

It has been reported that Qāḍī ʿAbd al-Jabbār al-Hamadhānī, one of the *Muʿtazilī* theologians, came to Ṣāḥib b. ʿAbbād whilst the learned Abū Isḥāq al-Isfarāyīnī—one of the Imams of *Ahl al-Sunna*—sat with him. When he (ʿAbd al-Jabbār) saw Abū Isḥāq, he proclaimed: "Sublime is He ﷻ Who is free from all obscenity." Abū Isḥāq replied immediately: "Sublime is He ﷻ in Whose kingdom nothing happens except that which He has willed."

Qāḍī ʿAbd al-Jabbār said: "Does our Lord will that He be disobeyed?" Abū Isḥāq replied: "Is our Lord disobeyed by compulsion?" The Qāḍī replied: "Do you not see if He prevented me from guidance and then judged upon me destruction, has He then been good towards me or has He mistreated me?"

Abū Isḥāq said: "If He prevented you from that which was yours then He has mistreated you, but if He prevented you from that which is His ﷻ then He specifies for His mercy whomsoever He ﷻ wills!"[215]

With regards to actualisation and potentiality, the will of Allah ﷻ is either:[216]

I. *Ṣulūḥī Qadīm* (*Pre-eternal Potentiality*)

This is the pre-eternal will that may specify that which is possible with existence or non-existence in pre-eternality.

II. *Tanjīzī Qadīm* (*Pre-eternal Actualisation*)

This is the pre-eternal will that is associated with specifying with the time at which a finite being will appear, and the attributes it will possess. Thus, Allah ﷻ willed in pre-eternity that our master Muhammad ﷺ would exist and that he would be a Messenger.

---

[215] Ibid., p. 124

[216] *Kubrā al-Yaqīniyāt al-Kawniyya* (al-Būṭī), p. 11

[X] Omnipotence [*Qudra*]

Omnipotence is defined as: a pre-eternal attribute upon which the existence and non-existence of the possible is dependant.[217]

Allah ﷻ says: ❴*He has power over all things.*❵ [2:109]

The role of omnipotence is to bring into existence that which He Almighty has willed.[218] However, it is it is crucial to understand that the omnipotence of Allah cannot bring into existence that which is rationally impossible, for example: the creation of an object that is simultaneously large and small, the creation of a square circle or the creation of another god, thus rejecting the idea of an irrational understanding of omnipotence.

Rational Evidence

If Allah ﷻ was not Omnipotent He would have to be attributed with incapacity, which would mean the non-existence of all that we witness from creation.[219]

Its Connections[220]

As mentioned above, this attribute is only associated with the possible; that is, His ﷻ omnipotence only affects that which can be brought into existence or made non-existent, and so it is considered either:

I. *Ṣulūḥī Qadīm* (*Pre-eternal Potentiality*)

This is the ability to bring things into existence or non-existence in pre-eternity.

II. *Tanjīzī Ḥādith* (*Temporal Actualisation*)

This is when Allah ﷻ actually brings something into existence or non-existence. According to the *Ashʿarīs*, this is the source of the attributes of Divine acts as mentioned previously.

---

[217] *Sharḥ al-Kharīda al-Bahiyya* (al-Dardīr), p. 174
[218] *Al-Musāmara* (Ibn Abī Sharīf), p. 68
[219] *Uṣūl al-Dīn* (al-Ghaznawī), p. 96
[220] *Sharḥ al-Kharīda al-Bahiyya* (al-Dardīr), p. 184

[XI] Hearing [*Sam*ʿ] and [XII] Sight [*Baṣar*]

Hearing [*sam*ʿ] is defined as: a pre-eternal attribute that comprehends all things that are heard [*masmūʿāt*] or exist [*mawjūdāt*][221] without the need of any hearing organ.[222]

Both hearing and sight can be deduced rationally.[223] However, both attributes have been mainly affirmed because of scripture.[224] Allah ﷻ says: ﴾*Verily, Allah is All-Hearing and All-Seeing.*﴿ [22:75] Thus, it is impermissible to attribute to Allah any other similar attributes like taste, smell and the like as they have not been affirmed by scripture.[225]

It is crucial to understand that the hearing and sight of Allah ﷻ bears no similarity to the way creation hears or sees. Ultimately, we are unaware of the reality of this attribute; however, what we do know is that Allah is not in need of hearing tools like an ear or intermediaries like sound waves to hear.[226]

It is also important to note here that these two attributes are not the same as the attribute of omniscience, as is claimed by the "philosophers [*falāsifa*], al-Kaʿbī[227] and Abū al-Ḥusayn[228]

---

[221] It is important to note that some, like al-Taftazānī, were of the view that this attribute only associates with those things that are heard or seen. Whereas others, like al-Sanūsī, al-Dardīr and al-Bājūrī, considered it to include all existent entities, meaning all sounds and all essences, and this seems to be the more well-known opinion. [*Tuḥfa al-Murīd* (al-Bājūrī), p. 132; *Kubrā al-Yaqīniyāt al-Kawniyya* (al-Būṭī), p. 123]

[222] *Kubrā Yaqīniyāt al-Kawniyya*, p. 122

[223] Both hearing and sight are considered to be attributes of completeness or perfection [*kamāl*] which creation has been characterized with, and Allah ﷻ is more deserving to be characterized with them than His creation. [*Al-Musāmara* (Ibn Abī Sharīf), p. 75]

[224] *Miftāḥ al-Janna* (al-Hāshimī), p. 111

[225] *Talkhīṣ al-Muḥaṣṣil* (al-Ṭūsī), p. 124

[226] *Al-Musāmara*, p. 74

[227] He is ʿAbdullah b. Aḥmad b. Maḥmūd al-Kaʿbī al-Balkhī al-Khorasānī. He was born in Balkh and died in the year 317 H. or 329 H. He was one of the Imams of the *Muʿtazilī* school and author of multiple works. His views included that Allah ﷻ does not possess will, and that all His actions take

al-Baṣrī;"[229] rather, they are additional attributes to omniscience according to most of the scholars from *Ahl al-Sunna* and the *Muʿtazila*.[230]

Its Connections

If we understand this attribute to be related to all that exists, then this attribute has three connections:[231]

I. *Tanjīzī Qadīm* (*Pre-eternal Actualisation*)

This is its connection with the essence of Allah ﷻ and His attributes.

II. *Ṣulūḥī Qadīm* (*Pre-eternal Potentiality*)

This is its connection with us, creation, before our existence.

III. *Tanjīzī Ḥādith* (*Temporal Actualisation*)

This is its connection with us after our existence.

Sight [*Baṣar*]

Sight is defined as: a pre-eternal attribute that comprehends all things that are seen or exist without the need of any visual tools or aides.[232] The attribute of sight follows the same rulings as the attribute of hearing.

---

place without the need for Him to will them. [*Wafayāt al-Aʿyān* (Ibn Khallikān), 3:45; *Siyar al-Aʿlām al-Nubalāʾ* (al-Dhahabī), 14:313]

[228] He is Abū al-Ḥusayn Muḥammad b. ʿAlī b. al-Ṭayyib al-Baṣrī, the Shaykh of the *Muʿtazila* and author of multiple works in the science of theology. He died in Baghdad in the year 436 H.
[*Siyar Aʿlām al-Nubalāʾ*, 17:587]

[229] *Muḥassil Afkār al-Mutaqaddimīn* (al-Rāzī), p. 124

[230] Ibid.

[231] *Ḥāshiya al-Bājūrī ʿalā Umm al-Barāhīn*, p. 115-116;
Sharḥ ʿAqīda al-Dardīr, p. 19

[232] *Kubrā al-Yaqīniyāt al-Kawniyya* (al-Būṭī), p. 122

[XIII] Speech [*Kalām*]

Kalām (speech) is defined as: a pre-eternal attribute within the Divine essence that is not comprised of letters or sounds and is free from any syntactic precedence, delay, grammar and morphology.[233]

Allah ﷻ says: ﴾*To Mūsā God spoke directly.*﴿ [4:164]

Rational Evidence

If Allah ﷻ was not attributed with speech, then it necessitates that He is attributed with dumbness which is a deficiency and thus impossible for Allah.[234]

Its Connections

The attribute of speech has the same connections as the attribute of omniscience, in that it associates with the impossible, possible and necessary.[235] However, the difference between them is that the attribute of speech connects to them in an indicative [*dilāla*] manner and not in a revelatory [*inkishāf*] way like the attribute of omniscience.[236]

All of the connections of the attribute of speech are considered *tanjīzī qadīm* according to the *Ash'arīs* except the command [*amr*] and prohibition [*nahiy*] which are considered *ṣulūḥī qadīm* before the existence of the legally responsible person and *tanjīzī ḥādith* after their existence.[237]

The Speech of Allah: Created or Uncreated?

There is no disagreement within the different schools of theology with regards to Allah ﷻ being characterised by the

[233] *Sharḥ al-Kharīda al-Bahiyya* (al-Dardīr), p. 177; *Tuḥfa al-Murīd* (al-Bājūrī), p. 130
[234] *Sharḥ 'Aqīda al-Dardīr*, p. 19
[235] *Kubra al-Yaqīniyyāt al-Kawniyya*, p. 131; *Ḥāshiya al-Bājūrī 'alā Umm al-Barāhīn*, p. 116
[236] *Ḥāshiya al-Bājūrī 'alā Umm al-Barāhīn*, p. 116
[237] Ibid.

attribute of speech; however, what is debated is the actual nature of the attribute—is it created or uncreated? Below is a summary of some of the main opinions with regards to this attribute:[238]

I. *The Orthodox View*

According to the orthodox Sunni schools of theology, the speech of Allah ﷻ is a term that describes two realities:

1. *Perceptible Speech* [*Kalām Ḥissī* or *Lafẓī*]

This comprises of written letters and words that are heard as sounds when the Qur'an is recited. This speech is **created** and is not within the Divine essence. It is *not* the pre-eternal speech of Allah ﷻ that we consider as one of His attributes.

However, the meanings of the words in the Qur'an that command, forbid or inform, indicate towards some of the pre-eternal speech of Allah which is within the Divine essence.

One may ask, how do we then understand the statement of 'Ā'isha: "Whatever is between the two covers of the Qur'an is the speech of Allah Almighty." Many of the theologians believe that the intended meaning of 'Ā'isha was the pre-eternal speech of God that is indicated by the meanings of the words that are present between the two covers of the Qur'an and not the actual created words and letters.

It is crucial to understand that even though this category of the speech of Allah ﷻ is created, it should not be publicly declared so. This is a topic that should be restricted to the circles of learning and theological debate, as it could be understood as a negation of one of the pre-eternal attributes of God.[239]

2. *Self-Speech* [*Kalām Nafsī*]

The second type of speech is called self-speech [*kalām nafsī*]. This speech is understood as the meanings within the Divine essence that are normally expressed as speech. This is the attribute of God that every Muslim must believe in.

---

[238] From the editor's notes to *Sharḥ al-Kharīda al-Bahiyya* (al-Dardīr), p. 177; *Tuḥfa al-Murīd* (al-Bājūrī), p. 130; *Al-Mukhtaṣar al-Mufīd* (al-Quḍāt), p. 69-70; *Kubrā al-Yaqīniyāt al-Kawniyya* (al-Būṭī), p. 124; *Al-Musāmara* (Ibn Abī Sharīf), p. 81

[239] *Tuḥfa al-Murīd* (al-Bājūrī), p. 130

It is not comprised of letters, sounds, grammar, morphology or the like: it is completely dissimilar to the speech of creation in every way and pre-eternal like all the other attributes of God.

It is with this speech, according to the *Ashʿarīs*, that Allah ﷻ spoke to Musa, without any sounds or letters.

The Qurʾan

Based upon this understanding of the speech of Allah ﷻ, *Ahl al-Sunna* consider the term Qurʾan to represent four realities:[240]

I. The actual sounds of the letters that are emitted when the Qurʾan is recited.
II. The written words and letters of the Qurʾan.
III. The actual book [*muṣḥaf*] and its pages.
IV. And, the meanings that the words indicate towards [*kalām nafsī*].

The orthodox position with regards to the Qurʾan is that the first three categories are created, and it is only the self-speech of Allah ﷻ that is His pre-eternal and uncreated word. However, as mentioned above, this should not be stated except in the arena of learning and teaching.[241]

Imam Abū Ḥanīfa states:

> We affirm that the Qurʾan is the speech of Allah ﷻ *uncreated* in its revelation and descent. It is neither He nor other than He, but it is His attribute according to the correct opinion. It is written on pages, recited on tongues recited, memorised in hearts but is not situated [*ghayr ḥāllin*] within them. The ink, paper and writing are all *created* as they are from the actions of man, and the speech of Allah, transcendent be He, is uncreated because the written form, letters, words and verses are a representation of the Qurʾan, due to the need of man for it.
>
> The speech of Allah Almighty subsists in His essence, whose meaning is understood through these things. Whoever states that the speech of Allah Almighty is created

[240] *Al-Mukhtaṣar al-Mufīd* (al-Quḍāt), p. 69
[241] Ibid.

> is a disbeliever in Allah the Great. Allah the Exalted is worshipped and He is as He was. His speech is recited, written and preserved without it being disconnected from Him ﷻ.[242]

II. *The Muʿtazila*

The *Muʿtazila* believe that the speech of Allah ﷻ is comprised of letters and sounds that are *not* within the Divine essence, but rather they are created by Allah in other than Him, like in the preserved tablet, in Jibrīl ﷺ or in a tree which then spoke to Mūsā ﷺ. They deny the presence of a pre-eternal attribute within the Divine essence and believe that the meanings present in the heavenly books [*al-kutub al-samawiyya*], in reality, return back to either the attribute of omniscience or the attribute of will. It would return back to omniscience [*ʿilm*] when related to the subject of informing, or will [*irāda*] when the meanings are related to the subject of commanding or forbidding.

Their belief that all speech must comprise of letters and sounds, which are created, led them to the understanding that the Qurʾan must also be created as it is composed of letters and sounds.

The Miḥna

The *Miḥna* (inquisition) was a direct consequence of the aforementioned debate between *Ahl al-Sunna* and the *Muʿtazila* regarding the created and uncreated nature of the Qurʾan. In the year 833 CE (218 H.) the Abbasid caliph al-Maʿmūn, who favoured the heterodox teachings of the *Muʿtazila*, initiated the religious persecution of any scholar who disagreed with the *Muʿtazilī* doctrine of the created nature of the Qurʾan. This policy lasted for a period of approximately fifteen years, both in the reign of al-Muʿtaṣim and al-Wāthiq, the two caliphs that succeeded al-Maʿmūn. One of the most notable scholars of *Ahl al-Sunna* that was persecuted was Imam Aḥmad b. Ḥanbal, who was sent to prison and tortured severely for refusing to call the Qurʾan created.[243]

---

242 *Al-Waṣiyya* (Abū Ḥanīfa), p. 53

243 *Aḥmad b. Ḥanbal and the Miḥna* (Patton), p.2

III. *The Innovators from amongst the Ḥanābila*

There is no doubt that Imam Aḥmad b. Ḥanbal and his true followers were upon Sunni orthodoxy with regards to this issue. However, there were those from amongst his followers who strayed from his school and held unorthodox and deviant beliefs with regards to the speech of Allah ﷻ. These innovators from amongst his so-called followers believed that the speech of Allah is comprised of sounds [*aṣwāṭ*] and letters [*ḥurūf*], within the pre-eternal Divine essence. This led them to believe that the sounds and letters of the Qur'an are also from the pre-eternal speech of God and, in turn, uncreated. Some went even further and stated that even the paper and cover of the Qur'an are pre-eternal and uncreated, which is without a doubt incorrect[244] and "falsehood by necessity" [*bāṭil bil-ḍarūra*].[245]

وكونُه تعالى: حيًّا، وعليمًا، ومُرِيدًا، وقادِرًا، وسميعًا، وبصيرًا، ومُتَكلِّمًا.

فهٰذِهِ عِشْرُونَ صِفةً الْأُوْلٰى نَفْسِيّةٌ، والخمسةُ بعدَها سَلْبِيَّةٌ، والسَّبْعَةُ بَعْدَها صفاتُ معانٍ، والَّتِيْ بَعْدَها مَعْنَوِيَّةٌ.

And Him ﷻ being: [XIV] Living [*Ḥayy*], [XV] Omniscient [*ʿAlīm*], [XVI] Willing [*Murīd*], [XVII] Omnipotent [*Qādir*], [XVIII] All-Hearing [*Samīʿ*], [XIX] All-Seeing [*Baṣīr*] and [XX] Speaking [*Mutakallim*].

And so, these are the twenty attributes: the first one is the essential attribute [*al-ṣifa al-nafsiyya*], the five after it are the negating attributes [*al-ṣifāt al-salbiyya*], the seven after that are the qualitative attributes [*al-ṣifāt al-maʿānī*] and the ones after that are the predicative attributes [*al-ṣifāt al-maʿnawiyya*].

[244] *Kubrā al-Yaqīniyāt al-Kawniyya* (al-Būṭī), p. 126

[245] *Al-Musāmara* (Ibn Abī Sharīf), p. 81

Understanding the Attributes of Allah ﷻ

According to *Ahl al-Sunna*, the attributes of Allah ﷻ, are not the Divine essence itself, but they subsist within the Divine essence and do not subsist on their own. This means that they do not have their own existence outside of the Divine essence. They are also not considered separate from the Divine essence, meaning that they can never exist independently without the Divine essence, as opposed to the attributes of created beings.[246]

'Allāma al-Ūshī states:[247]

The attributes of Allah ﷻ are not the Divine essence itself,
Nor other than it such that they can be separated

The Qualitative Attributes [*al-Ṣifāt al-Maʿānī*]

These attributes are called such because they relate to the existence of *meanings* within the Divine essence. In the science of theology, however, they are defined as: any attribute that is established within the essence of the one being characterised by it, but additional to this essence, necessitating a judgment [*ḥukm*][248] for this essence.[249]

They are sometimes also called:[250]

I. *Al-Ṣifāt al-Dhātiyya* (*Essential Attributes*)
Called thus as they cannot be separated from the essence.

---

[246] *Al-ʿAqīda al-Islāmiyya wa-Madhāhibuhā* (al-Dūrī), p. 372; *Ḍaw' al-Maʿālī* (al-Qārī), p. 49; *Al-Musāmara* (Ibn Abī Sharīf), p. 70

[247] *Bad' al-Amālī* (al-Ūshī), p. 49

[248] In the case of Allah ﷻ these judgements would be the *ṣifāt al-maʿnawiyya*, for example: the qualitative attribute *ʿilm* is the cause [*ʿilla*] for us to deem Allah ﷻ Omniscient, and so forth. [*Sharḥ al-ʿAqīda al-Kubrā* (al-Sanūsī), p. 165]

[249] From the editor's notes to *Sharḥ al-Kharīda al-Bahiyya* (al-Dardīr) p. 173

[250] Ibid.; *Al-ʿAqīda al-Islāmiyya wa-Madhāhibuhā* (al-Dūrī), p. 371

II. *Al-Ṣifāt al-Wujūdiyya* (*Existential Attributes*)

Called thus because of their existence in and of itself, either pre-eternal like the knowledge of Allah, or contingent like the knowledge of man.

The Qualitative Attributes and their Connections [*Taʿalluqāt*]

A "connection" is the requirement of a qualitative attribute to something additional to its subsiding within the Divine essence. The attribute of omniscience, as an example, requires that "which can be known," and the attribute of will requires the existence of "things that are willed" and so on.[251]

It is important to note that knowledge of these connections is not necessary for the legally responsible person, as it is from the finer and more complicated concepts of theology.

Denying the Qualitative Attributes of God [*Taʿṭīl*]

It is worth mentioning here that the *Muʿtazila* negated the existence of any pre-eternal qualitative attributes as additions to the Divine essence, meaning that they considered the attributes of Allah to be the Divine essence itself. They believed that the Divine essence has the attribute of being Omniscient when there is a connection with that which is known, or the attribute of being All-Hearing when there is a connection with that which is heard, and so on. They feared that by affirming the presence of pre-eternal attributes, this would corrupt the meaning of the oneness of Allah, as—according to them— it would lead to numerous pre-eternal entities.[252]

The Predicative Attributes [*al-Ṣifāt al-Maʿnawiyya*]

The predicative attributes do not add any extra meaning to the qualitative attributes: they are merely the result of the affirmation of the qualitative attributes. For example, if we affirm that Allah is characterised by speech, then He necessarily has to be characterised as being Speaking, and so on.

---

[251] *Sharḥ al-Kharīda al-Bahiyya* (al-Dardīr), p. 181; *Al-Mukhtaṣar al-Mufīd* (al-Quḍāt), p. 80

[252] *Ḍaw' al-Maʿālī* (al-Qārī), p. 49; *Al-Mukhtaṣar al-Mufīd* (al-Quḍāt), p. 78

فَهُوَ سُبْحانَهُ وتعالىٰ: واجِبُ الوُجُودِ، قَديمٌ باقٍ، مُخالِفٌ في ذاتِهِ لجميع الأخْلاقِ، فليس بجِسمٍ، ولا عَرَضٍ، ولا يَتَّصِفُ بالمَكانِ، ولا بالزَّمانِ، ولا باليمينِ، ولا بالشِّمالِ، ولا بالخَلْفِ، ولا بالأمامِ، القائِمُ بنَفْسِهِ، واحِدٌ في ذاتِهِ وصفاتِهِ وأفعالِهِ. حَيٌّ، عَلِيْمٌ بكُلِّ شَيْءٍ ما كانَ وما يَكُوْنُ وما لم يَكُنْ، مُرِيْدٌ لِكُلِّ شيْءٍ جَرَى وبَرَزَ مِنَ الْعَوالِمِ، وما لم يكُنْ منها.

> And thus, He ﷻ is: Necessarily existent, Pre-eternal and Sempiternal, His Entity is dissimilar to all created beings and is therefore neither a body nor an accident. He is not characterised by place, time, being right, left, behind or in front. He is Self-subsistent [*Qāʾim bil-nafs*], One in His essence, attributes and acts. He is Living, Omniscient of all things past, that which will be, and that which will not come to pass. He wills everything that happens, that which manifests itself in the worlds, and that which has not manifested in them.

It is crucial to believe that Allah ﷻ wills everything, good and evil, as has been mentioned previously. It has been related that ʿAmr b. ʿAbdullah, a *Muʿtazilī*, was on a boat with a Magian. ʿAmr told the Magian to believe, but the Magian said: "Allah has not willed my Islam," to which ʿAmr replied: "He ﷻ has willed it, but Satan does not leave you." The Magian then said: "I am therefore with the stronger one." ʿAmr repented to Allah after hearing that answer and came to the belief that Allah's will encompasses everything—even sin.[253]

[253] *Ḥāshiya al-ʿAqabāwī*, p. 14

قادِرٌ على كلِّ شيْءٍ منَ المُمْكِناتِ وعَلىٰ إعدامِها، لا يُشارِكُهُ في ذلك مُشارِكٌ. سميعٌ لكلِّ مَوْجُودٍ ومُبْصِرٌ، مُتكَلِّمٌ بكلام أَزَليٍّ مُنَزَّهٌ عن الصَّوتِ والحرفِ.

He is Omnipotent over all possible things and their annihilation; no one shares with Him in that. He hears and sees all that exists. He speaks with an eternal speech that is free from sounds and letters.[254]

UNDERSTANDING THE MEANING OF THE OMNIPOTENCE OF ALLAH ﷾

With regards to the omnipotence of Allah ﷾, one must believe that Allah can choose to bring or not bring into existence, from that what is possible [*jāʾiz*], whatever He wills. A consequence of this understanding is that Allah creates both belief and disbelief. He is not obliged to send any Messengers, or to allow us to see His blessed countenance, or to reward the obedient and punish the disobedient.[255] Below is a more detailed discussion with regards to some of these issues.

I. The Creation of Good [*Ḥasan*] and Evil [*Qabīḥ*]: Belief and Disbelief

As has been mentioned previously, it is possible for Allah ﷾ to create both the good and the evil, and He wills both the good[256] and the evil[257] that He creates. From this category of creating good and evil is the creation of belief and disbelief.

---

[254] For a detailed discussion regarding the hearing, sight and speech of Allah ﷾, see the chapters relating to these attributes on p. 91-97.

[255] *Sharḥ al-Kharīda al-Bahiyya* (al-Dardīr), p. 195

[256] That which does not necessitate punishment or blame. [*Al-Mukhtaṣar al-Mufīd* (al-Quḍāt), p. 108]

[257] That which necessitates punishment or blame. [Ibid.]

The position of *Ahl al-Sunna* is that it is Allah Who wills and creates belief and disbelief in a person; however, it is the person who acquires such a state. Shaykh Nūḥ al-Quḍāt states:

> If a person chooses faith, then Allah ﷾ creates within him faith and is content with that for him; and if a person chooses disbelief and ignorance, then Allah creates within him ignorance and disbelief and is not content with that for him.[258]

The *Muʿtazila* differed with *Ahl al-Sunna* with regards to this. They agreed that Allah ﷾ wills the good, but they disagreed with the notion that Allah wills evil. They believed that willing evil is evil, which is an imperfection, and because Allah is free from all imperfections He cannot will or create evil. The result of this whole theory is that Allah does not create disbelief which, as mentioned above, is contrary to the orthodox understanding.

II. Felicity [*Saʿāda*] and Damnation [*Shaqāwa*]: Shifting or Constant States?

The theologians, when discussing the matter of the creation of belief and disbelief, normally discuss another related topic which is the issue of felicity and damnation and whether they are constant or shifting states.

According to the *Ashʿarīs*, Allah ﷾ knows in pre-eternity who will be from the felicitous and from the damned, that is, those who will die upon faith and those who will die upon disbelief. However, Allah chooses not to punish anyone until what is meant to come to pass comes to pass. He gives every single person the opportunity to believe or disbelieve. Therefore, based upon this opinion, the states of felicity and damnation do not change; even a disbeliever is considered felicitous *if* he was destined to die upon faith and vice versa.

However, the *Māturīdī* theologians differed with the *Ashʿarīs* in that they considered them to be interchangeable realities. Therefore, a current believer is felicitous, and a current

[258] Ibid., p. 107

disbeliever is damned. If in the future the disbeliever would become a believer, then his state would change from damnation to felicity and vice versa.[259]

III. The Good [*Ṣalāḥ*] vs. the Better [*Aṣlaḥ*]

According to *Ahl al-Sunna*, it is not necessary for Allah ﷻ to do that which is good or better; rather, Allah is free to do whatever He wills.[260] If, however, He does do that which is good or better for the servant, then it is out of His pure grace and mercy. The existence of children being punished on earth, the creation of poor disbelievers,[261] or death through natural disasters and the like is enough of an indication that Allah is not obliged to do the "good" or the "better." Ibn Quṭlūbghā states: "If the better was necessary upon Allah, then there would be no such thing as gratitude, as giving that which is necessary is not considered benevolence."[262]

The majority of the *Muʿtazila*, especially those from Baghdad, did believe that it is necessary upon Allah ﷻ to choose that which is good for the servant or that which is better in this world and the next.[263] Some of the *Muʿtazila* considered it necessary for Allah to take into consideration that which is beneficial [*maṣlaḥa*] for the servant and not what is better.[264] What is meant by good here is the preference of good between good and evil, for example: to choose belief over disbelief; whereas better here means choosing the better between two things that are both considered good in their own right, although one is better than the other, such as the differing degrees of Paradise.

A famous conversation between al-Ashʿarī and his initial teacher al-Jubbāʾī brings to light the error of the *Muʿtazilī* stance. It has been related that Abū al-Ḥasan al-Ashʿarī asked his teacher, Abū ʿAlī al-Jubbāʾī, a *Muʿtazilī*, the opinion that it is necessary

---

[259] *Al-Mukhtaṣar al-Mufīd* (al-Quḍāt), p. 99-10;
Sharḥ al-Kharīda al-Bahiyya (al-Dardīr), p. 195
[260] *Ḍawʾ al-Maʿālī* (al-Qārī), p. 80
[261] *Sharḥ al-ʿAqāʾid al-Nasafiyya* (Ramaḍān Effendī), p. 437
[262] *Ḥāshiya ʿalā al-Musāyara* (Ibn Quṭlūbghā), p. 149
[263] *Ḍawʾ al-Maʿālī* (al-Qārī), p. 80; *Sharḥ al-Maqāṣid* (al-Taftazānī), 5:329
[264] Ibid.

upon Allah ﷻ to do good. He asked: "What do you have to say regarding three brothers: one who died in obedience, the other [who died] in disobedience and the third [who died] as a child?"

Al-Jubbāʾī replied: "The first will be rewarded with Paradise, the second will be punished in Hell, and the third will neither be rewarded nor punished."

Al-Ashʿarī then further asked: "What if the third one said: 'O Lord! Why did you make me die as a child and not let me stay until adulthood so that I could have obeyed you and be rewarded with Paradise?'"

Al-Jubbāʾī replied: "God will say: 'I know that if you were left to become an adult you would have sinned and then entered Hellfire, and so it was better for you to die as a child.'"

Al-Ashaʿrī then said: "What if the second said: 'O Lord! Why did you not let me die as a child, so that I could not have sinned and not enter into Hellfire?' What will God say?"

Al-Jubbāʾī was stunned, and it is related that he said to al-Ashʿarī: "Are you mad?"

Al-Ashʿarī said: "No! But, the Shaykh's donkey has stopped[265] in front of an obstacle."[266]

IV. Necessity of Sending Messengers

According to *Ahl al-Sunna*, "sending Prophets is possible, and not impossible or necessary."[267] Rather, it is kindness and mercy from Allah ﷻ because of the enumerable goodness that it contains—which He chooses for whomsoever He wills from His servants, without it being necessary upon Him, contrary to [the beliefs of] the *Muʿtazila*.[268]

The *Muʿtazila* considered it necessary for Allah ﷻ to send Messengers.[269] This notion, in reality, is a continuum of their

---

265 This is a literal translation of an idiomatic Arabic phrase which in English means similar to the expression, "the Shaykh has hit a brick wall."

266 *Sharḥ al-Kharīda al-Bahiyya* (al-Dardīr), p. 199;
Al-Iqtiṣād fī al-Iʿtiqād (al-Ghazālī), p. 332

267 *Al-Iqtiṣād fī al-Iʿtiqād* (al-Ghazālī), p. 344

268 *Sharḥ al-Maqāṣid* (al-Taftazānī), 6:8

269 Ibid., 6:6-7

belief that doing that which is better [*aṣlaḥ*] is necessary upon Allah, because He is aware that man's rectification is contingent upon the existence of Messengers.[270]

V. Reward and Punishment

The position of *Ahl al-Sunna* with regards to reward and punishment is that Allah ﷻ is in no way obliged to reward the obedient or punish the disobedient. Moreover, If He wishes, He can reward the disobedient and punish the obedient. Nevertheless, because Allah has promised, through various verses in the Qur'an, to reward the obedient and punish the disobedient, then it is deemed necessary upon Him by way of His own promise but not by way of the servant having an inherent right, as the servant in and of himself is not deserving of anything from Allah.

In short, if Allah ﷻ promises believers Paradise then *Ahl al-Sunna* believe that He will fulfil His promise, as failing to fulfil His promise would be a deficiency and imperfection which Allah is completely devoid of.[271] Shaykh Muḥammad al-Ṭāḥirī states:[272]

He ﷻ can reward the sinners, just as He can punish the obedient
However, that is legally [shar'an] impossible,
As there is no change to His statement

The *Mu'tazila*, however, because of their principle of the necessity of doing the good and the better, considered it necessary upon Allah ﷻ to reward the obedient and punish the disobedient.[273]

VI. The Beatific Vision

An issue that has been discussed at length by the theologians is whether man will be able to gaze at the blessed countenance of God in the hereafter. According to *Ahl al-Sunna*, those who are in Paradise will be able to gaze upon the countenance of Allah but not with a gaze that limits Allah or encompasses Him ﷻ. One will

---

[270] *Tuḥfa al-Murīd* (al-Bājūrī), p. 198
[271] Ibid., p. 181
[272] *Wasīla al-'Abīd* (al-Ṭāḥirī), p. 137
[273] *Al-Qawl al-Mufīd* (al-Muṭī'ī), p. 137

not see Him in a place or in a certain direction; neither will there be a matter of distance between the person and Allah, as these are issues specific for created beings. Ultimately, the vision will be created in the person in a manner that only Allah has knowledge of. *Ahl al-Sunna* affirm this vision due to numerous verses of the Qur'an and traditions that confirm its possibility, but also because there is no rational evidence that proves its impossibility.[274]

Allah ﷻ says: ﴾*On that Day there will be radiant faces, looking towards their Lord.*﴿ [75:22-23]

And He ﷻ says: ﴾*When Mūsā came for the appointment, and his Lord spoke to him, he said: "My Lord, show Yourself to me: let me see You!" He said: "You will never see Me, but look at that mountain: if it remains standing firm, you will see Me."*﴿ [7:143]

The beatific vision has also been affirmed in various Hadith. In one Hadith, narrated by Abū Hurayra ؓ, the Messenger of Allah ﷺ is reported to have said: "Do you dispute with each other in seeing the full moon on a cloudless night, or in seeing the sun?" They said: "No." He ﷺ said: "You will see your Lord just as you see the moon on a cloudless night, you will not dispute with each other in seeing Him."[275]

Similar to the topics mentioned previously, the *Muʿtazila* disagree with *Ahl al-Sunna* regarding the possibility of the beatific vision. Their understanding is that for something to have the ability of being seen, it has to be a substance, body or an accident; since Allah ﷻ is neither of those things, the beatific vision is impossible. Another one of their arguments is that if Allah could be seen, He would have to be in an opposite position to the one seeing Him, which would necessitate place, distance, direction and the like which are all impossible for Allah. However, *Ahl al-Sunna* consider these requirements as customary, that is, this is merely how vision occurs on this earth; therefore, it does not negate the fact that vision can occur in another way that does not require any of the above conditions.[276]

---

[274] *Al-Qawl al-Mufīd*, p. 113

[275] *Sunan al-Tirmidhī*, 4:688:2554. Similar traditions are related in *Ṣaḥīḥ al-Bukhārī*, 6:2704:7000 and *Ṣaḥīḥ Muslim*, 5:134:633.

[276] *Al-Qawl al-Mufīd* (al-Muṭīʿī), p. 113

بسم الله الرحمن الرحيم

PART II

MATTERS PERTAINING TO PROPHETHOOD [*NUBUWWĀT*]

وَيَجِبُ للأنبياءِ عليهِمُ الصلاةُ والسلامُ العِصْمَةُ، فلا يَقَعُ منهم مُخالَفَةٌ لله في أمرِهِ ونَهيِهِ.

It is necessary for Prophets—prayers and salutations be upon them—to have infallibility [*ʿiṣma*]. Thus, they do not contravene Allah with regards to His commands and prohibitions.

DEFINING A PROPHET

A Prophet in Arabic is called *Nabī*. There is a difference of opinion with regards to the linguistic root of the word *Nabī*. Some scholars thought it was derived from the word *nabwa*, which means "high ground," or from *naba'* which means "news" or "information." In reality, both meanings are considered appropriate for a Prophet as a Prophet is of an exalted status and informs his people of Divine teachings as well.[277]

Technically, in Islam, a Prophet [*Nabī*] is defined as: a free, male, human being, who is devoid of any repulsive traits and upon whom Allah ﷻ has revealed His teachings. If he has been ordered to convey these teachings then he is also a Messenger [*Rasūl*]; if he has not, then he is only considered a Prophet.[278]

Imam al-Bayḍāwī states:

[277] *Ḥāshiya al-ʿAqabāwī*, p. 9; *Qāmūs al-Muḥīṭ*, 1:53; *Tuḥfa al-Murīd* (al-Bājūrī), p. 33; *Muʿjam Maqāyīs al-Lugha* (Ibn Fāris), 5:385

[278] *Ḥāshiya al-ʿAqabāwī*, p. 10; *Al-Jawāhir al-Kalāmiyya* (al-Jazāʾirī), p. 41; *Sharḥ al-Kharīda al-Bahiyya* (al-Dardīr), p. 111

A Messenger [*Rasūl*] is the one who Allah ﷻ has sent with new Divine teachings and calls people towards it, whereas a Prophet is the one who is sent to affirm and uphold previous Divine teachings, like the Prophets of the people of Israel [*Banū Isrā'īl*] that came between Mūsā and 'Īsā ﷺ.[279]

The Definition Explained

Here, we will take a more detailed look at the definition of a Prophet mentioned above.

I. *Being Human* [*Bashariyya*]

Prophets and Messengers are sent by Allah ﷻ as guides to other human beings and thus it is necessary for them to also be human beings such that those they are guiding can follow their guidance and be instructed by them.[280]

When the polytheists asked that Messengers be sent as angels, Allah ﷻ says: ﴾*Indeed, if We had sent an angel as a Messenger, We would still have sent him in the form of a man, increasing their confusion.*﴿ [6:9]

II. *Being Free* [*Ḥurriyya*]

A slave does not have legal ownership of himself, meaning that he can be bought and sold. Thus, it is inconceivable that a Prophet, whose role is to lead his people and guide humanity, be a slave.[281]

III. *Being Male* [*Dhukūra*]

There is a clear verse in the Qur'an which states that the Messengers were all men. Allah ﷻ says: ﴾*All the Messengers We sent before you were men to whom We gave revelations, men chosen from the people of their towns.*﴿ [12:109]

---

279 *Anwār al-Tanzīl wa-Asrār al-Tā'wīl* (al-Bayḍāwī), 4:75
280 *Al-Mukhtaṣar al-Mufīd* (al-Quḍāt), p. 126
281 Ibid.

As a result of this verse there is an agreement between the theologians that all Messengers were male. As for Prophets, there is some disagreement regarding that. The school of Imam al-Māturīdī stipulates the condition of being male for a Prophet, whereas Imam al-Ashʿarī differed and did not consider being male a condition for being a Prophet. However, both agreed that a Messenger [*Rasūl*] must be male.[282]

Al-Ūshī states:[283]

There was never a Prophet who was female,
And neither a slave nor a person of foul character

Mullā ʿAlī al-Qārī states in commentary of this line of poetry that Ibn Jamāʿa said: 'The way of the people of scholastic verification [*ahl al-taḥqīq*] is that being a male is a pre-condition for Prophethood.'"[284]

Al-Laqqānī mentions that there is disagreement with regards to the Prophethood of four women: Maryam, Āsiya, Sāra and Hājar. Al-Qurṭubī, as mentioned in his commentary upon Muslim, gave preference to considering Maryam a Prophetess. However, the more correct opinion is that none of these four women were Prophetesses.[285]

It has been said that the wisdom of sending only male Prophets and Messengers is because of men having greater aptitude and capability for the requirements of the role.[286]

Another reason given for not sending Messengers is to protect women as a Messenger is required to teach and instruct which necessitates interacting with all types of individuals of which many may be of foul character, and thus it is considered inappropriate to expose women to these types of individuals.[287]

---

[282] *Masāʾil al-Ikhtilāf Bayna al-Ashāʿira wal-Māturīdiyya* (Ibn Kamāl Pāshā), p. 68
[283] *Badʾ al-Amālī* (al-Ūshī), p. 96
[284] *Ḍawʾ al-Maʿālī* (al-Qārī), p. 96
[285] *ʿUmda al-Murīd* (al-Laqqānī), 2:798
[286] *Al-ʿAqīda al-Islāmiyya* (Ḥabannaka), p. 346
[287] *Al-Mukhtaṣar al-Mufīd* (al-Quḍāt), p. 127

Moreover, "the Messenger is the one who forbids and commands, he is the ruler and judge in his nation and he is the custodian of all of their affairs and thus if the Messenger was a woman then this may not be achieved in a complete manner."[288]

IV. *Being Devoid of any Repulsive Traits or Diseases*

Allah ﷻ has sent Prophets and Messengers to be followed and obeyed, and thus any trait or disease that is normally considered repulsive, such as leprosy and the like, is not appropriate for Messengers as it would drive people away. It is vital here to note that this does not mean that a Prophet cannot become afflicted by a disease or illness as not all diseases cause aversion or arouse distaste.[289]

V. *Revelation of Divine Teachings* [*Waḥiy*]

The revelation of Divine teachings is considered to be the most important decisive criterion to distinguish between a normal human being and a Prophet.

Linguistically, *waḥiy* can mean: a swift sign" [*al-ishāra al-sarīʿa*], writing [*kitāba*], a message [*risāla*], inspiration [*ilhām*] or concealed speech [*kalām khafī*], with its underlying principle being to make understand or instruct [*tafhīm*]. Therefore, any instruction given through a sign, inspiration, writing or speech is considered *waḥiy* in the linguistic sense.[290]

Technically, according to the Muslim theologians, it is the speech of Allah revealed to one of His Prophets ﷺ.[291]

Revelation and its Forms[292]

The speech of God that He ﷻ reveals to His Prophets can come in different forms. Below, I have tried to summarise these different forms:

[288] *Al-ʿAqīda al-Islāmiyya*, p. 346
[289] Ibid.; *Ḥāshiya al-Bājūrī ʿalā Umm al-Barāhīn*, p. 174
[290] *Al-Qawl al-Mufīd* (al-Muṭīʿī), p. 185; *Mufradāt*, p. 858
[291] *Al-Qawl al-Mufīd*, p. 185
[292] *Ḥāshiya al-ʿAqabāwī*, p. 10; *Al-Itqān* (al-Suyūṭī), p. 120; *Al-Qawl al-Mufīd*, p. 185-186

I. *Direct Divine Speech without an Intermediary*
This can happen in three ways, either through it being:

1. *Thrust directly into the heart* [*ilqā' fī al-qalb*]
It is said that Dāwūd ﷺ received the *Zabūr* in this manner.

2. *Or via a true dream*
An example of this is Ibrāhīm's ﷺ dream that instructed the sacrifice of his son.

3. *Or by hearing the perceptible speech of Allah* ﷻ *[kalām lafẓī] without seeing the Speaker*
An example of this is when Allah ﷻ spoke to Mūsā in the valley of Tuwā at the tree.

It is important to note here that nothing of the Qur'an has been revealed by the above forms of revelation.

II. *Through the Intermediary of an Angel*
This can also manifest in various ways:

1. *An angel can come to a Prophet whilst in a sleeping or unconscious state*
Some of the scholars considered the revelation of *Sūra al-Kawthar* to be from this category. On the authority of Anas ؓ, who said: "We were with the Messenger of Allah ﷺ one day, when he suddenly fell asleep. Afterwards, he ﷺ raised his head smiling so we asked: 'What is it that makes you smile, O Messenger of Allah?' He ﷺ said: 'A *Sūra* has just been revealed upon me.' He ﷺ then recited: ﴾*In the name of Allah, the Lord of mercy, the Giver of mercy. We have truly given abundance to you* [*O Prophet*]. *So pray to your Lord and make your sacrifice to Him alone. It is the one who hates you who has been cut off.*﴿ [108:1-3]"[293]

[293] *Ṣaḥīḥ Muslim*, 1:300:400

2. *Or the Message is thrust or inspired into the heart by an angel*

The Messenger of Allah ﷺ said: "Verily Jibrīl [*Rūḥ al-Qudus*] has thrust into my heart..."[294]

3. *Or, the angel takes the form of a man and speaks to the Prophet directly*

This was the case in the famous Hadith of Jibrīl ﷺ.

4. *Or the angel comes like the jingling of a bell*

On the authority of ʿĀʾisha ﷺ: "Ḥārith b. Hishām asked the Messenger of Allah ﷺ: 'How does revelation come to you?' He ﷺ said: 'Like the jingling of a bell—and that is the hardest upon me. Then, it passes at which point I have understood. Sometimes, an angel comes to me in the form of a man and so I understand what he says.'"[295]

5. *Or the angel appears in his original form*

On the authority of Jābir b. ʿAbdullah ﷺ, who said: "I heard the Messenger of Allah ﷺ say, whilst speaking about the pause in revelation, that: 'Once I was walking when I heard a sound from the heavens, and so I looked up to find the angel who came to me in *al-Ḥirāʾ*, sitting upon a chair between the heavens and earth. I became alarmed by it and returned [home] saying, "cover me, cover me" and so they wrapped me, after which Allah ﷻ revealed [the verses]: ﴾*You, wrapped in your cloak, arise and give warning*﴿ till [the verse]: ﴾*...keep away from all filth.*﴿ (71:1-5)[296]

THE NUMBER OF PROPHETS AND MESSENGERS

The belief of *Ahl al-Sunna* with regards to the number of Prophets sent by Allah is that no one is privy to this number except Allah. He ﷻ says: ﴾*We have sent other Messengers before you—some We have mentioned to you and some We have not...*﴿ [40:78]

---

[294] *Al-Muʿjam al-Kabīr* (al-Ṭabarānī), 8:166:7694

[295] *Musnad Aḥmad*, 42:146:25252; *Al-Muʿjam al-Kabīr* (al-Ṭabarānī), 3:259:3343; *Al-Mustadrak* (al-Ḥākim), 3:314:5213; *Ṣaḥīḥ Muslim*, 4:1816:2333

[296] *Ṣaḥīḥ al-Bukhārī*, 4:1895:4671

Hence, one should not believe in any specific number; rather, it is safer to say: "I believe in Allah ﷻ and everything that has come from Allah, and in every Prophet and Messenger sent," such that one does not believe someone who was not a Prophet to be a Prophet or someone who was not a Messenger to be a Messenger.[297]

There are, however, within the corpus of Hadith certain traditions that do make mention of their number. In a Hadith related by Ibn Ḥibbān in his *Ṣaḥīḥ*, the Messenger of Allah ﷺ mentions that there are a hundred and twenty-four thousand Prophets and three hundred and thirteen Messengers:

On the authority of Abū Dharr ؓ, who said: "I asked: 'O Messenger of Allah, how many Prophets are there?' He ﷺ replied: 'One hundred and twenty-four thousand.' I then asked: 'O Messenger of Allah, how many of them are Messengers [*Rusul*]?' He ﷺ said: 'three hundred and thirteen, a large number.'"[298]

However, due to the nature of this tradition, it cannot be used as evidence to assign a specific number. This is because the verse mentioned above is undeniable as has been mass-transmitted [*mutawātir*], whereas the tradition does not reach that level of certainty, since it is a single chain narration [*āḥād*] which cannot used to establish obligatory tenets of faith.[299]

PROPHETS MENTIONED IN THE QUR'AN

Twenty-five Prophets are mentioned by name in the Qur'an and it is necessary for every Muslim to believe in them by name. These twenty-five Prophets ؑ are:[300]

---

[297] *Baḥr al-Kalām* (Abū al-Mu'īn al-Nasafī), p. 239;
Al-Mukhtaṣar al-Mufīd (al-Quḍāt), p. 121, 124

[298] *Ṣaḥīḥ Ibn Ḥibbān*, 2:77:361. According to Shaykh Shu'ayb al-Arnā'ūṭ "its chain of transmission is extremely weak." [*Ṣaḥīḥ Ibn Ḥibbān*, 2:79]

[299] *'Umda al-Murīd* (al-Laqqānī), 2:776

[300] *Al-Mukhtaṣar al-Mufīd* (al-Quḍāt), p. 124;
Al-Jawāhir al-Kalāmiyya (al-Jazā'irī), p. 41

I.	Ādam ﷺ
II.	Nūḥ (Noah) ﷺ
III.	Idrīs (Enoch) ﷺ
IV.	Hūd ﷺ
V.	Ṣāliḥ ﷺ
VI.	Ibrāhīm (Abraham) ﷺ
VII.	Lūṭ (Lot) ﷺ
VIII.	Ismāʿīl (Ishmael) ﷺ
IX.	Al-Yasaʿ (Elisha) ﷺ
X.	Dhū al-Kifl (Ezekiel) ﷺ
XI.	Ilyās (Elijah) ﷺ
XII.	Yūnus (Jonah) ﷺ
XIII.	Isḥāq (Isaac) ﷺ
XIV.	Yaʿqūb (Jacob) ﷺ
XV.	Yūsuf (Joseph) ﷺ
XVI.	Shuʿayb (Jethro) ﷺ
XVII.	Mūsā (Moses) ﷺ
XVIII.	Hārūn (Aaron) ﷺ
XIX.	Dāwūd (David) ﷺ
XX.	Sulaymān (Solomon) ﷺ
XXI.	Ayyūb (Job) ﷺ
XXII.	Zakariyyā (Zechariah) ﷺ
XXIII.	Yaḥyā (John the Baptist) ﷺ
XXIV.	ʿĪsā (Jesus) ﷺ
XXV.	Muhammad ﷺ

The First Prophet

It is necessary to believe that the first Prophet sent by Allah to this earth was Ādam ﷺ, the father of all men.[301]

The Last Prophet and Revelation

With regards to the last Prophet, it is necessary to believe that the last Prophet sent by Allah ﷻ was our master Muhammad ﷺ. Last here means that there is no Prophet after him; believing in a Prophet after him is tantamount to disbelief. It is also important to know that the Sacred Law of our master Muhammad ﷺ has abrogated all other previous Sacred Laws, such that one cannot

[301] *Ḥāshiya al-ʿAqabāwī*, p. 22

take what has been given to previous Prophets as evidence, except in certain instances which have been clarified by the scholars of legal theory.[302]

The Greatest Prophet

It is obligatory to believe that the greatest of all the Prophets is our master Muhammad ﷺ: his noble virtues, qualities and character, both inner and outer, are like no other, surpassing all of creation in his magnificence and splendour. He ﷺ has been sent to all of creation, Arab and non-Arab, man and jinn.[303]

In conclusion, our master Muhammad ﷺ has three major traits[304] that distinguish him from all other Prophets:

I. He ﷺ is the greatest of all Prophets
II. He ﷺ is the last and final Prophet
III. He ﷺ has been sent to all of creation

The Necessary Attributes of Prophets and Messengers

The first necessary attribute of all Prophets is *ʿiṣma,* (infallibility). *ʿIṣma* is also sometimes expressed as *amāna* (fidelity). According to *Ahl al-Sunna* it is necessary to believe that all Prophets and Messengers are protected from sin and thus infallible [*maʿṣūm*]. Allah ﷻ protects both their outward and inward, in both their childhood and adulthood, before and after Prophecy, from committing any sinful act, regardless of whether that act was unlawful or offensive.[305]

Messengers are sent by Allah ﷻ to be followed, thus, if they were to engage in sinful behaviour it would mean by extension that Allah is asking for people to also engage in sinful behaviour—which would be absurd.[306]

---

[302] *Kubrā al-Yaqīniyāt al-Kawniyya* (al-Būṭī), p. 196 and p. 200
[303] *Ḥāshiya al-ʿAqabāwī*, p. 23
[304] That is, there are many other distinguishing traits; however, these are three that are normally mentioned in the science of theology due to their extreme importance with regards to belief.
[305] *Ḥāshiya al-ʿAqabāwī*, p. 20; *Al-Mukhtaṣar al-Mufīd* (al-Quḍāt), p. 124
[306] *Tuḥfa al-Murīd* (al-Bājūrī), p. 201

In addition to being infallible, it is also necessary to believe that the following are from the attributes of all Prophets and Messengers:[307]

II. *Veracity* [*Ṣidq*]

The opposite of veracity is lying, which is a sin. The Prophets as mentioned above are infallible, thus it is necessary that they be characterised with the attribute of veracity. Even though this attribute can be logically derived from *'iṣma*, the theologians single out this trait because of its great importance. Prophets convey on behalf of Allah and therefore it is necessary to believe that they are truthful in what they are conveying. Allah ﷻ says in the Qur'an: ﴾*...the promise of God and His Messenger is true.*﴿ [33:22]

III. *Sagacity* [*Faṭāna*]

This is unadulterated intelligence. With this attribute the Prophets have the capacity to establish the truthfulness of what they are calling to and refute any argument that contradicts the truth. Allah ﷻ says: ﴾*Argue with them in the most courteous way.*﴿ [16:125]

IV. *Conveying* [*Tablīgh*]

It is from the belief of *Ahl al-Sunna* that a Prophet who is also a Messenger conveys to his people everything that he has been ordered to convey by Allah. He ﷻ says: ﴾*O Messenger, proclaim everything that has been sent down to you from your Lord—if you do not, then you will not have communicated His Message, and God will protect you from people.*﴿ [5:67]

However, it is crucial to understand that there are matters a Messenger is not obliged to convey, and therefore may choose to withhold such information or only disclose it to particular individuals.

The Impossible with regards to the Prophets

The opposite of any of the aforementioned traits is impossible for Prophets, for example: sinning, lying, stupidity and concealing what they have been commanded to convey.

---

307 *Al-Jawāhir al-Kalāmiyya* (al-Jazā'irī), p. 46

Any trait that is considered shameful or lowly is also impossible for them, like a menial profession or an inferior lineage.[308]

The Possible with regards to the Prophets

Anything that is neither from the necessary nor impossible is considered from the realm of the possible for the Prophets, for example: eating, drinking, sleep, sexual intercourse and the like.[309]

Apparent Contraventions

The Messengers are infallible, as mentioned previously, and therefore it is inconceivable that they disobey Allah ﷻ in any way, shape or form. However, there are numerous instances where it appears that certain Messengers have engaged in sinful acts. For example, when Ādam ﵇ ate from the forbidden tree, or when Ibrāhīm ﵇ pointed towards and blamed the large idol for destructing the other idols when in reality it was he who had destroyed them, or when he said "I am ill" when he was not, or when he said regarding his wife Sāra, "this is my sister," and so on.[310]

The apparent deduction is that these are contraventions of Sacred Law; however, these events must be interpreted in a way that preserves the infallibility of the Prophets. Al-Taftazānī states:

> Whatever has been reported about the Prophets in which falsehood and disobedience is ascribed to them is to be rejected if it is recorded by way of individual narrations, and when it comes by way of *tawātur* it is to be interpreted beyond its literal meaning whenever possible; otherwise, it is possible to explain it as a case of doing the less preferable of two actions, or as something that happened before the Prophetic mission.[311]

---

[308] *Al-Jawāhir al-Kalāmiyya* (al-Jazā'irī), p. 48
[309] *Tuḥfa al-Murīd* (al-Bājūrī), p. 205
[310] *Ḥāshiya Al-ʿAqabāwī*, p. 20
[311] *Sharḥ al-ʿAqā'id al-Nasafiyya* (al-Taftazānī), p. 127-128

Therefore, it has been said that Ādam ﷺ ate the fruit from the tree forgetfully,[312] that Ibrāhīm ﷺ said "the large one" as a way of proving to them that the idol has no power, that he said "I am ill" to mean that his ultimate end is towards illness and death and he said "this is my sister" to mean "this is my sister in Islam."

وكذالكَ الملائِكةُ. ويجِبُ لِلرُّسُلِ عليهم الصلاةُ والسَّلامُ تَبليغُ ما أُمِرُوْا بِتَبْلِيغِهِ لِلْخَلْقِ من الأحكامِ وغَيْرِها.

> And likewise, the angels. It is necessary for Messengers—prayers and salutations be upon them—to convey [*tablīgh*] to creation that which they have been commanded to convey, from rulings and other matters...[313]

Just as we have affirmed the infallible nature of Prophets, it is also necessary to believe in the infallible nature of angels.[314] Allah ﷻ says in the Qur'an: ❮*Angels who never disobey God's commands to them, but do as they are ordered.*❯ [66:6]

In the following pages, we will take a more detailed look at angels, how they are defined and the different types of angels that one must believe in.

ANGELS: THE DEFINITION

An angel is defined as: a subtle spiritual and luminous entity that has the power to transform itself into different beautiful forms. Angels do not disobey Allah ﷻ, but do whatever they've been commanded. Some are constantly in prostration whilst others are constantly bowing; whatever role they have been given, they perform it continuously without break.[315]

[312] *Miftāḥ al-Janna* (al-Hāshimī), p. 315

[313] See: "The Necessary Attributes of Prophets and Messengers" on p. 115-116 for a discussion regarding the attribute of *tablīgh* (conveying).

[314] *Sharḥ ʿAqīda al-Dardīr*, p. 20

[315] *Sharḥ al-Kharīda al-Bahiyya* (al-Dardīr), p. 232; *Sharḥ ʿAqīda al-Dardīr*, p. 10-11

Angels are spirits that are created without the intermediary of a father, a mother or clay. In a tradition related by ʿĀʾisha ﵂, the Messenger of Allah ﷺ said: "Angels have been created from light, jinn have been created from smokeless fire, and Ādam has been created from that which your Lord has described[316] for you."[317]

Angels and their Different Types

Angels have been mentioned extensively in the Qurʾan in around seventy-five different verses, in over thirty-three different chapters, and thus their denial is tantamount to disbelief.[318] However, similarly to Prophets, it suffices to have a generic belief in the angels, although, there are some angels that one must believe in specifically, either by individual or by type. Below is a summary of the angels one must believe in:[319]

Generic Belief

This is to believe that Allah has angels that are characterised by traits appropriate for them, and that no one is privy to their exact number except Allah. He ﷻ says: ﴾*No one knows the soldiers of your Lord, except He...*﴿ [74:31][320]

Specific Belief

By Individual:

I. *Jibrīl* ﵇ *(Gabriel)* –

The Custodian of Revelation [*Amīn al-Waḥiy*][321]

The name of this mighty angel, according to al-ʿAqabāwī, is Aramaic in origin, consisting of two components: *jabr* and *ʾīl*. *Jabr* means "servant" and *ʾīl* means "God" or "the Merciful One."[322]

---

[316] This is referring to the verse in the Qurʾan: ﴾*He created mankind out of dried clay, like pottery.*﴿ [55:14]

[317] *Musnad Aḥmad*, 42:109:25194

[318] *Al-ʿAqīda al-Islāmiyya* (Ḥabannaka), p. 234

[319] *Sharḥ ʿAqīda al-Dardīr*, p. 21-22;
Sharḥ al-Kharīda al-Bahiyya (al-Dardīr), p. 232

[320] *Ḥāshiya al-ʿAqabāwī*, p. 21

[321] *Sharḥ ʿAqīda al-Dardīr*, p. 21

[322] A tradition in *Musnad Aḥmad* corroborates this. On the authority of Muḥammad b. ʿAmr b. ʿAṭāʾ, who said: "ʿAlī b. Ḥusayn said to me: 'The

There are phonetic variations with regards to his name: *Jabrīl*, *Jibrāʾīl* and *Jibrāl* have also been transmitted.[323]

Throughout the Qurʾan, Jibrīl ﷺ is described with multiple epithets and names. He has been called:

1. The Holy Spirit [*Rūḥ al-Qudus*] [2:87]
2. A Noble Messenger [*Rasūlun Karīm*] [81:19]
3. The one who possesses great strength [*Dhū al-Quwwa*] [81:20]
4. The one who is held in honour by Allah ﷻ [*Makīn*] [81:20]
5. Obeyed [*Muṭāʿ*] [81:21]
6. The Trustworthy Spirit [*al-Rūḥ al-Amīn*] [26:193]

Within the corpus of Hadith, certain narrations describe Jibrīl ﷺ with six-hundred wings. In one tradition, Ibn Masʿūd ؓ narrates: "Muhammad ﷺ saw Jibrīl: he had six-hundred wings."[324] And in another narration Ibn Masʿūd is reported to have said regarding the verse: ﴾*A second time he saw him*﴿ [53:13] that: "The Messenger of Allah ﷺ said: 'I saw Jibrīl at the Lote tree in his true form, he had six-hundred wings, each wing covering the horizon and hanging from his feathers were embellishments made from pearls and rubies.'"[325]

II. *Isrāfīl – The Custodian of the Trumpet* [*Amīn al-Ṣūr*]

The second angel one must believe in is the angel who has been given the responsibility of blowing the trumpet twice, with which everything in creation, except those that Allah chooses to spare, will perish and then be given life a second time after death. Allah ﷻ says: ﴾*The Trumpet will sound, and everyone in the heavens and earth will fall down senseless except those God spares. It will sound once again and they will be on their feet, looking on.*﴿ [39:68][326]

---

name of Jibrīl ﷺ is ʿAbdullah, and the name of Mikāʾīl is ʿUbaydullah.'" [*Musnad Aḥmad*, 33:345:20176]

[323] *Ḥāshiya al-ʿAqabāwī*, p. 21

[324] *Ṣaḥīḥ al-Bukhārī*, 4:1840:4575

[325] *Musnad Aḥmad*, 7:31:3915

[326] *Al-ʿAqīda al-Islāmiyya* (Ḥabannaka), p. 242

III. *Mikā'īl or Mīkāl (Michael) –*
   The Custodian of Rain and Provision [Amīn al-Arzāq]
The third angel that one must believe in is the angel Mikā'īl who is mentioned by Allah in the Qur'an. Allah ﷻ says in *Sūra al-Baqara:* ❲*If anyone is an enemy of God, His angels and His Messengers, of Jibrīl and* **Mikā'īl**, *then God is certainly the enemy of such disbelievers.*❳ [2:98]

Mikā'īl is considered the custodian of rain and provision. Ibn Kathīr states:

> Mikā'īl has been put in charge of rain and vegetation through which provision is created on this earth. And he has helpers that do what he commands them to do, with the command of Allah ﷻ: they divert the winds and clouds as the Lord, the most Exalted, wills.[327]

There are multiple narrations in which Mikā'īl is mentioned. In one Hadith, Anas b. Mālik ؓ narrates that: "The Messenger of Allah ﷺ asked Jibrīl: 'Why is it that I never see Mikā'īl smile?' He replied: 'Mikā'īl has not smiled since Hellfire was created.'"[328]

IV. *'Azrā'īl – The Custodian of Seizing Souls [Amīn Qabḍ al-Arwāḥ]*
The fourth angel is the angel of death or the one who has been charged with seizing souls. Allah ﷻ says: ❲*Say: "The angel of death put in charge of you will reclaim you, and then you will be brought back to your Lord."*❳ [32:11]

His name is said to be 'Azrā'īl, which according to al-Ṣāwī means 'Abd al-Jabbār, although it is important to note here that the name 'Azrā'īl has not been "explicitly mentioned in the Quran or in any sound Hadith."[329] Thus, to believe that the name of the angel of death is 'Azrā'īl is not a necessary tenet of faith. Al-Ṣāwī describes him as follows:

---

[327] *Al-Bidāya wal-Nihāya* (Ibn Kathīr), 1:49
[328] *Musnad Aḥmad*, 21:55:13343
[329] *Al-Bidāya wal-Nihāya*, 1:49. Al-Suyūṭī states: "His name 'Azrā'īl has not been related in any *marfū'* Hadith. It has been related from Wahb b. Munabbih that his name is 'Azrā'īl." [*Sharḥ al-Suyūṭī 'alā Sunan al-Nasā'ī*, 4:118]

> He is a mighty angel of colossal appearance—very terrifying. His head is in the highest sky, and his feet are on the edge of the lowest point of earth. Creation is between his eyes and he has helpers [*aʿwān*] who prepare the one dying: they draw out the soul until it reaches the throat, at which point he takes it with his own hands.[330]

Mujāhid states: "The ground has been rolled up for him, and so it is like a basin that he reaches from whenever he chooses."[331]

According to one opinion, he will take his own soul after taking the soul of everyone else, but when he experiences the pangs of death he will wish that he had not taken the soul of even a fly.[332]

V. *Munkar and Nakīr – The Interrogators*

The interrogators are two terrifying and frightening angels whose names, as mentioned in multiple traditions, are *Munkar* and *Nakīr*. They have been charged with the duty to question the deceased when he is placed in his grave with three vital questions:[333]

1. Who is your Lord?
2. What is your religion?
3. What do you say about this man?[334]

---

[330] *Sharḥ al-Ṣāwī ʿalā Jawhara al-Tawḥīd*, p. 357-358

[331] *Tafsīr Ibn Kathīr*, 6:61

[332] *Sharḥ al-Ṣāwī ʿalā Jawhara al-Tawḥīd*, p. 358

[333] *Muṣannaf ʿAbd al-Razzāq al-Ṣanʿānī*, 3:591:6760

[334] In some narrations, the wording is: who is your Prophet? It is crucial to mention here, that there is no evidence to indicate that the Messenger of Allah ﷺ will be represented pictorially in the grave. Al-Suyūṭī states in his *Urjūza al-Tathbīt fī Layla al-Tabyīṭ*: [*Ḥāshiya al-ʿAqabāwī*, p. 21]

Whoever claims that the Prophet is represented pictorially,
[Qāḍī] ʿIyāḍ said, that is not accepted,
And similarly, with regards to this Ibn Ḥajar has replied,
And said, no basis in the traditions is found regarding this.

There are many traditions that relate the questioning of the grave by these angels, indicating that it has reached the level of *tawātur* (mass-transmission); therefore there should be no doubt with regards to this matter.[335]

One such Hadith is narrated by Anas ﷺ, who said: "The Messenger of Allah ﷺ said: 'Verily the servant, when he is placed in his grave, his companions will leave and he will hear the patter of their shoes. Then at that point two angels will come to him, sit him up and ask: "What did you say about this man, Muhammad?" The believer will say: "I bear witness that he is the servant of God and His Messenger." It will then be said to him: "Look at your place in Hellfire, Allah ﷻ has replaced it for you with a place in Paradise."' The Messenger of Allah ﷺ said: 'The dead person will see both of his final destinations.'—Qatāda said: 'It was mentioned to us that the grave is made spacious for him.'—He ﷺ [then] said: 'But a disbeliever or a hypocrite will say to the angels: "I do not know, rather I used to say what the people used to say!" It will be said to him: "Neither did you know, nor did you heed the guidance." Then he will be hit with an iron hammer between his two ears and scream, and that scream will be heard by whatever is near to him, except human beings and jinn.'"[336]

In certain other traditions, there are details with regards to their appearance. They are described as "black [and] blue"[337] with "voices that resemble roaring thunder, vision that is lightening-like and hair that hangs down."[338] The colour of their eyes is said to be like the colour of "copper pots"[339] and their teeth are described as "fangs similar to the horns of a bull."[340]

[335] *Kubrā al-Yaqīniyāt al-Kawniyya* (al-Būṭī), p. 308
[336] *Musnad Aḥmad*, 19:289:12271
[337] *Sunan al-Tirmidhī*, 3:375:1071
[338] *Ithbāt ʿAdhāb al-Qabr* (al-Bayhaqī), 81:103
[339] *Al-Muʿjam al-Awsaṭ* (al-Ṭabarānī), 5:44:4629
[340] Ibid.

VI. *Riḍwān – The Guardian of Paradise* [*Khāzin al-Janna*]

The guardian of Paradise is mentioned in a Hadith in *Ṣaḥīḥ Muslim*, who when asked by the Messenger of Allah ﷺ to open the gate of Paradise, will say: "I have been ordered [to open it] only for you and not to open it for anyone before you."[341]

The name of the guardian of Paradise is said to be Riḍwān. Although, this name has not been mentioned in the Qur'an or in the corpus of sound traditions, it has been mentioned in some weaker traditions and it seems to have been widely accepted by the scholars as his name. Ibn Kathīr states: "The guardian of Paradise is an angel who is said to be called Riḍwān, which has been explicitly mentioned in several Hadith."[342]

VII. *Mālik* – The Guardian of Hellfire [*Khāzin al-Nār*]

The guardian of Hellfire is an angel called Mālik, as mentioned in a clear verse of the Qur'an. Allah ﷻ says: ❴*They will cry: "Mālik, if only your Lord would finish us off," but he will answer: "No! You are here to stay."*❵ [43:77] There is consensus between the scholars that the Mālik mentioned in this verse is "the guardian of Hellfire."[343]

This angel has also been mentioned in multiple traditions. In a long Hadith in *Ṣaḥīḥ al-Bukhārī*, the Messenger of Allah ﷺ whilst describing one of his dreams to his noble companions, said: "Two men came and took him to the Holy Land [*al-Arḍ al-Muqaddasa*]"[344] where he was made to see a variety of different events. From the things that he described was seeing "a hole similar to a clay oven, whose top was narrow and bottom was wide, and a fire was being kindled at the bottom of that hole. Whenever the fire-flame went up, the people were sent flying up to such an extent that they could just about fall out, but when the fire abated, they fell back down. Inside it were naked men and women." The Messenger of Allah ﷺ asked the two men: "Who is this?" to which he was later told in the Hadith by the two men that "the one kindling the fire was Mālik the guardian of Hellfire."[345]

---

[341] *Ṣaḥīḥ Muslim*, 1:188:197
[342] *Al-Bidāya wal-Nihāya* (Ibn Kathīr), 1:50
[343] *Al-Tafsīr al-Munīr* (al-Zuḥaylī), 25:189
[344] *Ṣaḥīḥ al-Bukhārī*, 1:465:1320
[345] Ibid.

With regards to his description, not much is known. However, there is a narration of Ibn Isḥāq, mentioned by Ibn Hishām whilst discussing the ascent of the Messenger of Allah to the Heavens, where he ﷺ is reported to have said: "Not an angel met me as I entered the heavens except that he was smiling and happy, speaking good and supplicating with it, until I met an angel from the angels. He said what they said and supplicated with what they supplicated, except that he did not smile, nor did I see him happy in the way I saw the others. And so, I asked Jibrīl: 'O Jibrīl, who is this angel who said what the others said but did not smile and whom I did not see happy the way I saw the others?' Jibrīl said to me: 'If he smiled to anyone before you, or if he was to smile to anyone after you, he would have smiled to you, but he does not smile—he is Mālik, the guardian of Hellfire.'"[346]

By Type:

I. *The Bearers of the Throne* [*Ḥamala al-ʿArsh*]

The angels who have been given the duty of bearing the throne of Allah are explicitly mentioned in the Qurʾan. Allah ﷻ says: ﴾*The angels will be on all sides of it and, on that Day, eight of them will bear the throne of your Lord above them.*﴿ [69:17] Currently, they are four in number, but there will be twice that many due to the enormity and immensity of that day as alluded to in the Qurʾan.

With regards to their description, the Messenger of Allah ﷺ said: "I was given permission to discuss an angel from the angels of Allah ﷻ, those that carry the throne of Allah: between the earlobe and the shoulder is the distance of seven hundred years."[347]

II. *The Helpers of ʿAzrāʾīl* [*Aʿwān ʿAzrāʾīl*]

These are angels that help the angel of death remove the soul from the body. Allah says: ﴾*When the angels take the souls of those who have wronged themselves.*﴿ [4:97]

[346] *Sīra Ibn Hishām*, 1:404
[347] *Sunan Abī Dāwūd*, 7:109:4727

III. *The Guardian Angels* [*Ḥafadha*]

Every person, regardless of age or creed, has guardian angels who watch over him. Allah ﷻ says: ﴾*...Every person has guardian angels in front of him and behind* [*him*], *watching over him by God's command.*﴿ [13:11]

Ibn Kathīr states in commentary of this verse:

> The servant has angels that follow one after the other, guarding by day and guarding by night, protecting him from evil and calamities [...] one behind him and one in front [of him]."[348]

He further states:

> Abū Mijlaz said: "A man from Murād[349] came to ʿAlī b. Abī Ṭālib whilst he was praying and said: 'Be on guard! There are people from Murād who want to kill you.' He [ʿAlī ؓ] replied: 'With every person there are two angels who protect him from that which has not been decreed. When the decree comes they withdraw, leaving him to his fate. Verily, one's appointed time is a strong protection [*ʿajal junna ḥaṣīna*].'"[350]

IV. *The Recording Angels* [*Kataba*]

Every person has two angels whose role is to record every single good or bad deed a person commits. Allah ﷻ says: ﴾*Over you stand watchers, noble recorders who know what you do.*﴿ [82:10-12]

These angels are also mentioned in a Hadith narrated by Abū Hurayra ؓ, who said: "The angels follow one after the other, angels by night and angels by morning. They gather at dawn and at *ʿaṣr* (afternoon), after which the ones that spent the night with you ascend to Him ﷻ, who asks them—and Allah is Omniscient—'How did you leave them?' They reply: 'We left them whilst they were praying, and we came to them whilst they were praying.'"[351]

---

[348] *Tafsīr Ibn Kathīr*, 4:437

[349] A name of a Yemeni tribe situated to the southwest of Maʿrib. [*Muʿjam Qabāʾil al-ʿArab al-Qadīma wal-Ḥadītha* (Kaḥḥāla), 3:1065]

[350] *Tafsīr Ibn Kathīr*, 4:439

[351] *Ṣaḥīḥ al-Bukhārī*, 1:203:530

With regards to their names, some of the scholars considered the words *raqīb* (vigilant) and *ʿatīd* (near or prepared) mentioned in verse eighteen in *Sūra al-Qāf* to be the names of these two angels. However, there is no consensus with regards to this, and thus, it is not a matter of essential creed.

Another Hadith describes the way in which the angel which records the bad deeds waits before writing it down. Abū Umāma said: "The Messenger of Allah ﷺ said: 'The one on the left lifts the pen for six hours on behalf of a Muslim servant who has sinned or done wrong; if he is overcome with remorse or repents then he leaves it, otherwise he writes down one [sin].'"[352]

With regards to their actual location [as they accompany mankind], then like their names, there is no consensus upon this matter and all the following varying opinions have been transmitted:[353]

1. The shoulders
2. The chin
3. The lips
4. The neck

The Muʿtazila and the Recording Angels

Not everyone accepted the existence of these angels. The *Muʿtazila* failed to reconcile their understanding of Divine knowledge which, according to them, renders the role and presence of recording angels as futile, leading them to deny their existence. Why would God, Who is Omniscient, need angels to record the deeds of His servants? The reply of *Ahl al-Sunna* was clear, in that, the presence of these angels in no way whatsoever negates the omniscience of Allah ﷻ or renders Him ignorant, rather the purpose is to establish proof against the servant on the Day of Judgement if the servant denies or claims to forget his actions.[354]

352 *Al-Muʿjam al-Kabīr* (al-Ṭabarānī), 8:185:7765
353 *Sharḥ al-Kharīda al-Bahiyya* (al-Dardīr), p. 233
354 *Baḥr al-Kalām* (Abū al-Muʿīn al-Nasafī), p. 197

V. *The Keepers of Hell* [*Zabāniyya*]

As mentioned in the Qur'an, the keepers of Hell are nineteen in number. Allah ﷻ says: ﴾*What will explain to you what the scorching Fire is? It spares nothing and leaves nothing: it scorches the flesh of humans. There are nineteen in charge of it—none other than angels appointed by Us to guard Hellfire—and We have made their number a test for the disbelievers.*﴿ [74:27-31]

The head of these angels is the angel Mālik mentioned previously.

VI. *The Keepers of Paradise* [*Khazana*]

The keepers of Paradise are mentioned in a clear verse of the Qur'an. Allah ﷻ says: ﴾*Those who were mindful of their Lord will be led in throngs to the Garden. When they arrive, they will find its gates wide open, and its* ***keepers*** *will say to them: "Peace be upon you. You have been good. Come in: you are here to stay."*﴿ [39:73]

The head of these keepers is said to be the angel Riḍwān mentioned previously.

بسم الله الرحمن الرحيم

PART III
MATTERS PERTAINING TO ESCHATOLOGY [*SAMʿIYYĀT*]

كالْيَومِ الأخِرِ وما فِيهِ: مِنَ الْحِسابِ، والعِقابِ، والصِّراطِ، والمِيزانِ، والجَنَّةِ، والنَّارِ، وبالْعَرْشِ، وبالكُرْسِيِّ، وبالكُتبِ السَّماوِيّةِ، والرُّسُلِ وما وَقَعَ لهم من أُمَمِهِم، وبالحُوْرِ العَيْنِ، والوِلْدانِ، والأولياءِ، وبإسرائِه صلى الله عليه وسلم، وبالمِعراجِ، وبأنَّ الشُّهَداءَ أحْياءٌ عند رَبِّهِم يُرْزَقُوْن، وبشفاعَةِ نبيِّنا محمَّدٍ صلى الله عليه وسلَّم، وبعلاماتِ السَّاعةِ، وتَجْدِيدِ التَّوبةِ من الذُّنُوبِ، والرِّضاءِ بالقَضاءِ والقَدَرِ.

Such as: the Last Day [*al-Yawm al-Ākhir*] and that which occurs in it from the reckoning [*ḥisāb*], punishment [*ʿiqāb*], the bridge [*ṣirāṭ*], the scales [*mīzān*], Paradise [*Janna*] and Hellfire [*Jahannam*]. And [it is necessary to believe in:] the throne [*ʿarsh*], the chair [*kursī*], the heavenly books, the Messengers—prayers and salutations be upon them—and what their nations did to them,[355] the maidens of Paradise, the everlasting youths, the saints, his ﷺ night journey, his ﷺ heavenly ascent, that martyrs are living, provided for by their Lord, the intercession of our Prophet Muhammad ﷺ, the signs of the Hour, the renewal of repentance from sins and contentment in *qaḍāʾ* and *qadar* (pre-destination).

[355] See: "Part II: Matters Pertaining to Prophethood [*Nubuwwāt*]" on p. 107-118 for a detailed discussion regarding the Messengers.

THE LAST DAY

Belief in the Last Day is a necessary component of Muslim creed. Multiple verses in the Qur'an mention this frightening event. Allah ﷻ says: ❮*On that Day, We shall roll up the skies as a writer rolls up [his] scrolls. We shall reproduce creation just as We produced it the first time. This is Our binding promise. We shall certainly do all these things.*❯ [21:104]

The magnitude and utmost importance of this issue is made apparent by its many names "as a multitude of names is an indication of the greatness of the named."[356] Some of the names mentioned in the Qur'an are:

I. *Yawm al-Qiyāma* (The Day of Resurrection)
II. *Al-Sā'a* (The Hour)
III. *Yawm al-Dīn* (The Day of Judgement)
IV. *Al-Ṭāmma* (The Great Calamity)
V. *Al-Ḥāqqa* (The Inevitable Hour)
VI. *Al-Ghāshiya* (The Overwhelming Event)
VII. *Al-Wāqi'a* (That which is Coming)
VIII. *Al-Qāri'a* (The Crashing Blow)
IX. *Al-Ṣākha* (The Deafening Blast)

There is no doubt that the Last Day is the greatest and most fateful of all the eschatological occurrences that we have been made privy to. Each person will stand in front of his Lord and be interrogated and held accountable for each and every thing he did, resulting in one entering either Paradise or Hellfire.[357]

After the sounding of the second horn by Isrāfīl, this day will begin, and it will end when everyone has entered their final abode, Paradise or Hell.[358] Below, I have tried to list a chronological timeline of events that will occur after the second sounding of the horn:

---

[356] *Al-Budūr al-Sāfira fī al-Aḥwāl al-Ākhira* (al-Suyūṭī), p. 143
[357] *Kubrā al-Yaqīniyāt al-Kawniyya* (al-Būṭī), p. 340
[358] *Ḥāshiya al-'Aqabāwī*, p. 23

I. The Resurrection [Nushūr or Baʿth]

Nushūr or baʿth is defined as: the resurrection of the dead from their graves by bringing together their original molecules from nothingness and returning the soul.[359]

In a one tradition narrated by Abū Hurayra 🙏, the Messenger of Allah explains the way creation will be resurrected. He 🙏 said: "Between the two soundings of the trumpet, there are forty." They asked: "O Abū Hurayra, do you mean forty days?" He replied: "I am not certain." They asked: "Forty months?" He replied: "I am not certain." They asked: "Forty years?" He replied: "I am not certain. Then Allah will make the skies rain,[360] causing them (the dead) to sprout the way vegetables sprout. Everything in man will decay, except one bone, and that is the coccyx bone; from it, creation will be reconstituted once again on the Day of Resurrection."[361]

In another, similar but longer tradition, ʿAbdullah b. Masʿūd 🙏, whilst describing the events towards the end of times, is reported to have said: "Then Allah 🙏 will send water[362] from beneath the throne like the fluid of man, their flesh and body will grow from that water the same way the earth brings forth vegetation from moist soil." And then ʿAbdullah b. Masʿūd recited: ❲It is God Who sends forth the winds, they raise up the clouds❳ [30:48] and: ❲We drive them to a dead land and with them revive the earth after its death; such will be the Resurrection.❳ [35:9][363]

---

[359] Lawāmiʿ al-Anwār al-Bahiyya (al-Saffārīnī), p. 2:157; Tuḥfa al-Murīd (al-Bājūrī), p. 279

[360] In another tradition related by al-Bayhaqī, Abū Hurayra 🙏 states: "The Messenger of Allah 🙏 said: 'Then Allah 🙏 will order the skies to rain for forty days, such that there will be twelve cubits [of rain] above them.'" [Al-Baʿth wal-Nushūr (al-Bayhaqī), 1:336]

[361] Ṣaḥīḥ Muslim, 4:2270:2955

[362] Based upon certain narrations this water is also known as the water of life [māʾ al-ḥayawān], as mentioned by al-Baghawī and others. [Maʿālim al-Tanzīl, 2:200]

[363] Al-Muʿjam al-Kabīr (al-Ṭabarānī), 9:354:9761

The Order of Resurrection

The first person for whom the earth will be cleaved open is the Messenger of Allah ﷺ, then his two companions, Abū Bakr al-Ṣiddīq and ʿUmar b. al-Khaṭṭāb, then the people of *al-Baqīʿ*, followed by the people of Mecca, the people of the Levant and then everyone else.[364]

On the authority of Abū Saʿīd, who said: "The Messenger of Allah ﷺ said: 'I am the liege lord of the sons of Ādam on the Day of Judgement, [and that is] no boast, and in my hand is the banner of praise, [and that is] no boast, and there will be no Prophet on that day—Ādam and other than him—except that they are under my banner, and I am the first for which the earth will be split asunder for.'"[365]

II. The Gathering [*Ḥashr*]

Linguistically, *ḥashr* means: to gather along whilst urging.[366] Technically, it means: the gathering of creation after having been resurrected on the plain of reckoning.[367]

This gathering is mentioned explicitly in *Sūra al-Kahf*. Allah says: ﴾*One day We shall make the mountains move, and you will see the earth as an open plain We shall gather all people together, leaving no one.*﴿ [18:47]

There are also various traditions that make mention of the gathering. On the authority of Sahl b. Saʿd, who said: "The Messenger of Allah ﷺ said: 'The people will be gathered on the Day of Judgement on a land that is white with a reddish tinge, like a white loaf of bread; there will be no sign of anyone[368] on it.'"[369]

In another Hadith, the Messenger of Allah ﷺ describes the manner in which people will be resurrected. On the authority of ʿĀʾisha, who said: "I heard the Messenger of Allah ﷺ say: 'People will be gathered on the Day of Judgement barefoot, naked

---

364 *Ḥāshiya al-Ṣāwī ʿalā al-Kharīda al-Bahiyya*, p. 26
365 *Sunan al-Tirmidhī*, 5:587:3615
366 *Muʿjam Maqāyīs al-Lugha* (Ibn Fāris), 2:66
367 *Tuḥfa al-Murīd* (al-Bājūrī), p. 278
368 That is, no houses, buildings or any type of human trace. [*Sharḥ al-Nawawī*, 17:134]
369 *Ṣaḥīḥ Muslim*, 4:2150:2790

and uncircumcised.' I said: 'Messenger of Allah, will all the women and men be looking at each other?' The Messenger of Allah replied: 'O 'Ā'isha, the affair is too dire for people to be looking at each other.'"[370]

Depending upon the rank of the person, people will be driven to the plain in different modes: the pious will be mounted and riding, the one with little works will be made to walk on his feet, whereas the disbeliever will be made to walk on his face.[371]

Terrors of the Plain [*Hawl al-Mawqif*]

After the people have been gathered on the plain they will be made to wait for the judgement to commence, which will be a severely agonising and torturous time as has been indicated in a Hadith narrated by al-Miqdād b. al-Aswad ﷺ, who said: "I heard the Messenger of Allah ﷺ say: 'The sun will come close to creation on the Day of Judgement until it will be a distance of a mile away from them [...] the people will be in proportion to their works in sweat, for some of them it will be to their ankles, others to their knees, others to their groins, whilst for others the sweat will bridle them.' And then the Messenger of Allah pointed with his hand to his mouth."[372]

There is a difference of opinion with regards to the period of waiting. According to some it is a thousand years, based on the verse: ﴾*On a Day that will measure a thousand years in your reckoning.*﴿ [32:5] Others thought it to be a period of fifty thousand years, based on the verse: ﴾*On a Day whose length is fifty thousand years.*﴿ [70:4][373]

III. Beginning of the Judgement [*Faṣl al-Qaḍā'*]

After the agonising and painful wait, the judgement will finally begin with the intercession of the Messenger of Allah ﷺ, relieving creation from the suffering and terrors of the plain of resurrection. This act of mediation by the Messenger is considered to be the supreme intercession [*al-shafā'a al-kubrā*].

---

[370] Ibid., 4:2194:2859

[371] *Tuḥfa al-Murīd* (al-Bājūrī), p. 278

[372] *Ṣaḥīḥ Muslim*, 4:2196:2864

[373] *Tuḥfa al-Murīd* (al-Bājūrī), p. 288

This event is mentioned in detail in a long Hadith related by al-Bukhārī and Muslim. It recounts how the pain and torment of waiting will become intolerable for creation to the point that they will beg and implore to be taken to any place other than the plain of resurrection, even if that would mean entering Hellfire! However, Allah ﷻ will inspire creation to ask the Prophets to intercede on their behalf. They will begin by going to Ādam ﷺ who will be too concerned with his own affair. Then they will go to Nūḥ, and then to Ibrāhīm, and then to Mūsā and then to ʿĪsā b. Maryam, all of whom, like Ādam ﷺ, will be too concerned about their own fate and refuse to intercede. It has been said that between each Prophet there will be a period of a thousand years. Finally, they will arrive at the feet of the best of creation, our master Muhammad ﷺ. The Messenger of Allah will accept the request, saying: "I am for it! I am for it!" He will intercede on behalf of all of creation, regardless of their faith. He then, as mentioned in the Hadith, will prostrate to Allah ﷻ and praise Him in a way inspired in him by Allah. He ﷺ will be addressed with the words: "O Muhammad, raise your head, speak and you will be heard, ask and you will be granted, and intercede for you will be granted intercession." The Messenger of Allah ﷺ will at that point say: "My nation, my nation."[374]

At this point, the lofty station of the Messenger of Allah ﷺ will be known to all, which is described in the Qur'an as the "station of praise" [*maqām al-maḥmūd*], called such due to the Abundance in praise he will be showered with at that moment.[375]

IV. Standing in front of Allah ﷻ [*ʿArḍ*]

Before the actual reckoning takes place, creation will be gathered before Allah as mentioned in *Sūra al-Kahf*. Allah ﷻ says: ﴾*They will be lined up before your Lord: "Now you have come to Us as We first created you, although you claimed We had not made any such appointment for you.*﴿ [18:48]

---

[374] *Ṣaḥīḥ al-Bukhārī*, 6:2727:7072; *Ṣaḥīḥ Muslim*, 1:182:193

[375] *Sharḥ al-Ṣāwī ʿalā al-Jawhara*, p. 401

V. The Reckoning [*Ḥisāb*]

The reckoning is when Allah ﷻ will hold His servants to account with regards to their actions, before they are taken away from the plain of resurrection.[376] This reckoning will be of two types:[377]

1. *Ḥisāb al-Munāqasha* (*Reckoning of Debate*)

This is the more severe of the two types of reckoning. If during the judgement process the servant is asked about the reason he performed a certain act, then, this is considered reckoning with debate. This type of reckoning has been mentioned in numerous traditions.

On the authority of ʿĀʾisha ﵂, who said: "The Messenger of Allah ﷺ said: 'Whoever's reckoning is debated, is punished.' I said: 'Does Allah not say: ﴿*Whoever is given his record in his right hand will have an easy reckoning.*﴾' [84:7-8] He ﷺ said: 'That is the exposition.'"[378]

2. *Ḥisāb al-ʿArḍ* (*Reckoning of Exposition*)

In this type of reckoning, the servant will be told about the acts that he performed but then be pardoned by Allah ﷻ.

This type of judgement is described in a Hadith related by both al-Bukhārī and Muslim, where the Messenger of Allah ﷺ is reported to have said: "Verily, Allah ﷻ will bring nigh the believer until He places over him His pardon and veil. He will say to him: 'Do you remember such and such sin? And, do you remember such and such sin?' To which he will reply: 'Yes, my Lord.' When He has made him admit his sins, the servant will feel certain that he has perished.

"Then, Allah will say to him: 'I veiled them for you in the world, and today I will forgive them for you.' After that he will be given his book of good deeds. As for the disbeliever and

---

[376] *Sharḥ al-Ṣāwī ʿalā al-Jawhara*, p. 376

[377] *Baḥr al-Kalām* (Abū al-Muʿīn al-Nasafī), p. 179

[378] *Ṣaḥīḥ al-Bukhārī*, 8:111:6536; *Ṣaḥīḥ Ibn Ḥibbān*, 16:370:7370; *Sunan al-Tirmidhī*, 4:617:2426

hypocrite, the witnesses will say: 'These are the ones that lied about their Lord. God's rejection is the due of those who do such wrong. [11:18]'"[379]

According to Abū al-Muʿīn al-Nasafī, everyone is judged with exposition [*ḥisāb al-ʿarḍ*].[380] However, there are some who are exempt from the reckoning of debate [*ḥisāb al-munāqasha*], they are:[381]

i. The Prophets
ii. The angels
iii. The ten guaranteed Paradise
iv. The seventy thousand from the nation of the Messenger of Allah ﷺ mentioned in certain traditions as those who will enter Paradise without any reckoning.[382]

---

[379] *Ṣaḥīḥ al-Bukhārī*, 2:862:2309; *Ṣaḥīḥ Muslim*, 4:2120:2768

[380] Abū al-Muʿīn al-Nasafī states: "As for the reckoning of exposition [*ḥisāb al-ʿarḍ*], it is [also] upon all the Prophets and companions. It will be said to them: "You did such and such and I have pardoned you." Whereas, in the reckoning of debate [*ḥisāb al-munāqasha*] it will be said: "Why did you do such and such?"" [*Baḥr al-Kalām*, p. 179]

Al-Rāzī in his *Tafsīr* is also of a similar opinion, he states whilst commenting upon the verse ﴾*We shall certainly question those to whom Messengers were sent, and We shall question the Messengers themselves,*﴿ [7:6] that: "This verse indicates that He, the Almighty, will reckon all of His servants, whether they are Messengers or those upon whom the Message has been sent, and it negates the opinion of those who claim that there is no reckoning upon the Prophets or disbelievers." [*Al-Tafsīr al-Kabīr*, 14:26]

Al-Saffārīnī, in a similar vein, states: "The previously mentioned Hadith indicates that anyone who will not enter Hellfire will not be questioned with debate, for anyone who is reckoned with debate is punished. However, as for the reckoning of exposition [*ḥisāb al-ʿarḍ*] then it is not withheld even from the Prophets and other than them." [*Al-Buḥūr al-Zākhira*, p. 678]

[381] *Baḥr al-Kalām* (Abū al-Muʿīn al-Nasafī), p. 179

[382] The Messenger of Allah ﷺ said: "Seventy thousand from my nation will enter Paradise without any judgement." They asked: "Who are they, O Messenger of Allah?" He ﷺ replied: "They are those that do not cauterise or perform *ruqya* and rely on Allah ﷻ." [*Ṣaḥīḥ Muslim*, 1:198:218]

It is also worth noting here that the nation of Muhammad ﷺ will be the first to be reckoned so that their standing is not prolonged, and they are the last of all the nations so that their stay in the graves is not prolonged.[383]

VI. The Book of Deeds

There are clear verses in the Qurʾan that describe the nature of this book and the moment it is given to the servant. Allah ﷻ says: ﴿*The record of their deeds will be placed open and you will see the guilty, dismayed at what they contain, saying: "Woe to us! What a record this is! It does not leave any deed, small or large, unaccounted for!" They will find everything they ever did placed in front of them; your Lord will not be unjust to anyone.*﴾ [18:49]

In another verse, Allah describes the way in which it will be received, those who receive it in the right hand will be felicitous, but those who receive it in the left hand will perish. He ﷻ says: ﴿*Anyone who is given his record in his right hand will say: "Here is my record, read it. I knew I would meet my Reckoning." And so, he will have a pleasant life in a lofty Garden, with clustered fruit within his reach. It will be said: "Eat and drink to your heart's content as a reward for what you have done in days gone by." But anyone who is given his record in his left hand will say: "If only I had never been given any record and knew nothing of my Reckoning. How I wish death had been the end of me. My wealth has been no use to me, and my power has vanished."*﴾ [69:19-30]

Every single person will be given their record of deeds in some type of book or scroll; ultimately, we have not been made privy to its real form. In one Hadith, the Messenger of Allah ﷺ describes how these books with fall by way of a wind sent by Allah ﷻ.

Abū Umāma said: "I heard the Messenger of Allah ﷺ say: 'My Lord has promised me to enter into Paradise seventy thousand from my nation without any judgement or punishment; with every thousand another seventy thousand and three handfuls from His handfuls.'" [*Sunan al-Tirmidhī*, 4:626:2437]

[383] *Ḥāshiya al-ʿAqabāwī*, p. 24

The Messenger of Allah ﷺ said: "The books, all of them are situated under the throne. When the moment to reckon arrives, Allah ﷻ will send a wind that will make them fly right and left. The first line written within it is: ﴾*Read your record. Today your own soul is enough to calculate your account.*﴿ [17:14]"[384]

This wind will cause these books to fall upon the necks of its owner with perfect precision. Following this, the angels will arrive and grab them from their necks and give it to them either in their right hand if he was a pious believer, or the left from behind his back if he was a disbeliever. The pious believer's book will be white with white writing; when he reads it, his face will lighten up. Whereas the disbeliever will receive a black book with black writing; when he reads it, his face will blacken.[385]

The first person to receive their book in the right hand will be 'Umar b. al-Khaṭṭāb ؓ, the second rightly guided caliph. The first person to receive it in their left hand will be al-Aswad b. 'Abd al-Asad, who was the first person to fight the Messenger of Allah ﷺ on the day of Badr. It has been mentioned that al-Aswad will extend his right hand to take his book at which point an angel will take his hand by force and dislocate it.[386]

VII. The Scales [*Mīzān*]

After the reckoning, but before traversing the bridge[387] and entering either Paradise or Hell, the deeds of each servant will be weighed upon a scale as mentioned in the Qur'an. Allah ﷻ says: ﴾*The one whose good deeds are heavy on the scales will have a pleasant life, but the one whose good deeds are light will have the Bottomless Pit for his home.*﴿ [101:6-9]

Just like the scales that we are familiar with in this world, the scales in the hereafter will also comprise of two pans or sides and a fulcrum; its true form, however, is only known to Allah.[388]

---

[384] *Al-Ḍu'afā' al-Kabīr* (al-'Uqaylī), 4:466

[385] *Tuḥfa al-Murīd* (al-Bājūrī), p. 290-291

[386] Ibid., p. 291

[387] *Sharḥ 'Aqīda al-Dardīr*, p. 26. There is also an opinion that the scales come after the bridge.

[388] Ibid.

The angel Jibrīl ﷺ, according to some, will be charged with the actual weighing, with Mikāʾīl by his side.[389]

The objective of the reckoning is to ascertain or calculate the amount of one's deeds; whereas the weighing is to check their worth. One's deeds can be compared to a bunch of things in a big sack. The reckoning is the same as sorting and separating the things in the bag, that is, separating the acceptable from the unacceptable, whereas "the weighing" is to take the accepted and unaccepted deeds and place them against each other to ascertain which type exceeds the other.

What is Weighed?

There are three main opinions with regards to what exactly will be weighed on the scales:[390]

1. *The Book of Deeds*

Most of the exegetes of the Qurʾan believed that it is the book of deeds that will be weighed on the scales.[391] Certain traditions seem to give strength to this opinion. For example, in a Hadith related by al-Tirmidhī, ʿAbdullah b. ʿAmr b. al-ʿĀṣ ﷺ said: "The Messenger of Allah ﷺ said: 'Verily, Allah ﷻ will bring forth a man from my nation, in front of all of creation, on the Day of Judgement. Ninety-nine scrolls will be spread out before him, each scroll as far as the eye can see. Then He will ask: "Do you deny anything from these? Have my recording angels wronged you?" He (the man) will reply: "No, my Lord." Allah will then ask: "Do you have an excuse?" He will [again] reply: "No, my Lord." Allah will say: "Certainly, you have with us a good deed and there is no oppression upon you today."

"'Then a card will pop out, inscribed upon it the words: "I bear witness that there is no god but Allah and I bear witness that Muhammad is the Messenger of Allah." Allah will then say: "Bring his scales." The man will then say [astonished]: "My Lord, what worth does this card have against all these scrolls?"

---

[389] *Ḥāshiya al-ʿAqabāwī*, p. 26
[390] *Sharḥ ʿAqīda al-Dardīr*, p. 26
[391] *Tuḥfa al-Murīd* (al-Bājūrī), p. 292

"'Allah will reply: "You will not be wronged." The scrolls will be placed on one side of the scales and the card on the other at which point the scrolls will be light and the card heavy, as nothing is of greater weight than the name of Allah ﷻ.'"[392]

2. *The Person*

Other traditions allude to the person himself being weighed. Imam Aḥmad relates: "Once, Ibn Masʿūd, whose shins were thin, was gathering *siwāk* from the *arāk*[393] [tree]. Suddenly, the wind exposed them, and people started to laugh. The Messenger of Allah ﷺ asked: 'What are you laughing about?' They replied: 'His thin shins, O Messenger of Allah.' He ﷺ said: 'Verily, by Whose hand my soul is in, they are **heavier on the scale** than [mount] Uḥud.'"[394]

3. *The Deeds*

The third opinion with regards to what will be weighed is the actual deeds of a person. Like the other two opinions, there are also traditions that support this view. For example, the Messenger of Allah ﷺ is reported to have said: "Purity is half of faith and *al-ḥamdulillah* fills the scales..."[395] and in another tradition, he ﷺ states: "Two words easy on the tongue, heavy on the scales and beloved to the All Merciful: *subḥān Allah wa-bi-ḥamdihi* (glory and praise be to Allah) and *subḥān Allah al-ʿAẓīm* (glory be to Allah, the Magnificent)."[396]

In summary, it is necessary to believe in the scales and that one's good deeds will be weighed against one's bad deeds, but the "how" should be relegated to Allah ﷻ.

VIII. The Bridge [*Ṣirāṭ*]

No one, including the Prophets, shall enter Paradise before traversing the bridge that is extended over Hellfire.

---

392 *Sunan al-Tirmidhī*, 5:24:2639

393 This is the Salvadora persica tree.

394 *Musnad Aḥmad*, 7:98:3990 and others

395 *Ṣaḥīḥ Muslim*, 1:203:223

396 *Ṣaḥīḥ al-Bukhārī*, 8:86:6406

Allah ﷻ says: ﴾*...but every single one of you will traverse it,*[397] *a decree from your Lord which must be fulfilled. We shall save the devout and leave the evildoers there on their knees.*﴿ [19:71-72]

The bridge has been described by the Messenger of Allah ﷺ in various traditions. In one long tradition related by both al-Bukhārī and Muslim, Abū Hurayra ؓ narrates that the Messenger of Allah ﷺ said: "...The bridge will be extended over the centre of Hell. I will be the first from the Messengers to pass over it with their nation. No one shall speak at that moment except the Messengers. The call of the Messengers on that day will be: 'O Lord, safety, safety!' On it are hooks like the thorns of *al-Saʿdān*,[398] have you seen the thorns of *al-Saʿdān*?" They replied: "Yes." He ﷺ said: "They are like the thorns of *al-Saʿdān* except that their hugeness is not known by anyone but Allah ﷻ. They will snatch people based upon their deeds: there will be those who will perish because of their [evil] deeds, and those who will be wounded and fall into Hell but will later be rescued."[399]

Other traditions describe the different speeds with which this terrifying bridge is traversed. It has been reported that the Messenger of Allah ﷺ said: "The believers will traverse upon it like the bat of an eyelid, like lightening, like wind, like a bird or like pedigree horses and camels. Some will escape and be safe, some will be lacerated and set free, whilst some will be pushed into the fire of Hell."[400]

In another Hadith, The Messenger of Allah ﷺ is reported to have said: "...And so they will come to Muhammad, who will stand and be given permission. Fidelity [*amāna*] and blood relations will be sent forth, situating themselves on the sides of the bridge, right and left. The first ones from you will pass over it like lightening [...] then, like the wind, then like a bird and fast

---

[397] The word in Arabic here is: *wāriduhā*. According to the exegetes of the Qurʾan, *wurūd* in this context can either mean: [1] to traverse over the bridge, [2] to approach Hell and surround it, or [3] to enter Hellfire. According to al-Zuḥaylī, the more correct opinion is: to traverse or pass. [*Al-Tafsīr al-Munīr*, 16:145]

[398] According to al-Mubarrid, *al-Saʿdān* is "a plant with many thorns." [*ʿUmda al-Qārī* (al-ʿAynī), 6:85]

[399] *Ṣaḥīḥ al-Bukhārī*, 1:277:773; *Ṣaḥīḥ Muslim*, 1:163:182

[400] *Ṣaḥīḥ al-Bukhārī*, 6:2706:7001; *Ṣaḥīḥ Muslim*, 1:167:183

men. Their actions will drive them whilst your Prophet will stand and say: 'My Lord, make safe, make safe,' until the servant's actions are depleted and a man will come who can no longer traverse except by crawling."[401]

With regards to the size of the bridge, in the same Hadith mentioned above, Muslim adds that Abū Saʿīd al-Khudrī said: "It has reached me that the bridge is thinner than a strand of hair and sharper than a sword."[402] This description of the bridge is well known between the general Muslim populace; however, according to Muṣṭafā al-ʿAqabāwī, the bridge is not static, that is, it will narrow and widen depending upon a person's actions.[403]

PARADISE [*JANNA*]

Paradise, which currently exists,[404] is the eternal[405] abode of reward and recompense, for the believers who will enter by the grace and mercy of Allah.[406] Allah ﷻ says: ﴾*God has promised the believers, both men and women, Gardens graced with flowing streams where they will remain. Good, peaceful homes in Gardens of lasting bliss; and—greatest of all—God's good pleasure. That is the supreme triumph.*﴿ [9:72]

There are also numerous traditions that describe the splendour and glory of Paradise. In one Hadith, Abū Hurayra ﷺ narrates that: "The Messenger of Allah ﷺ said: 'Allah ﷻ says: "I have prepared for my righteous servants that which no eye has seen, no ear has heard, and no heart has ever imagined, as is corroborated in the Qur'an." He ﷺ then recited: ﴾*No soul knows what joy is kept hidden in store for them as a reward for what they have done.*﴿ [32:17][407]

[401] *Ṣaḥīḥ Muslim*, 1:186:195
[402] Ibid.
[403] *Sharḥ ʿAqīda al-Dardīr*, p. 26
[404] The majority of the *Muʿtazila* believe that Paradise does not currently exist but will be created by Allah ﷻ on the Day of Judgement. [*Sharḥ al-ʿAqāʾid al-Nasafiyya* (al-Saʿdī), p. 160]
[405] The *Jahmiyya* denied the eternality of Paradise and Hell. [Ibid.]
[406] *Sharḥ ʿAqīda al-Dardīr*, p. 27
[407] *Ṣaḥīḥ Muslim*, 4:2174:2824

In another tradition, Abū Hurayra narrates that: "The Messenger of Allah said: 'Whoever enters Paradise will live in comfort and never be miserable, his clothes will never become shabby and his youth will never end.'"[408]

The Gates of Paradise

The Qur'an also makes mention of Paradise having *gates wide open* [39:73] but it does not make any reference to their quantity. However, certain traditions have made mention of their number, for example, Sahl b. Saʿd narrates that: "The Messenger of Allah said: 'Paradise has eight gates: it has a gate named *Rayyān*, no one except those who fasted shall enter it.'"[409]

Similarly, ʿUbāda b. Ṣāmit narrates that: "The Messenger of Allah said: 'Whoever says: "I bear witness that there is no god but Allah alone, without partner, and I bear witness that Muhammad is His servant and Messenger, and that ʿĪsā is the servant of Allah, the son of his mother and His word, bestowed upon Maryam and a spirit from Him, that Paradise is true, and that Hellfire is true," Allah will enter him into any one of the eight gates of Paradise he wishes.'"[410]

Various traditions and statements of the scholars have also alluded to the names of these gates, for example: *Ayman,*[411] *Ṣalāt, Jihād, Rayyān, Ṣadaqa,*[412] *al-Kāẓimīn al-ghayẓ wal-ʿāfīn ʿan al-nās, Tawba,* and *Rāḍḍīn.*[413]

The Degrees of Paradise [*Darajāt*]

The scholars have varied with regards to the degrees of Paradise. Three well known opinions exist with regards to this issue:[414]

---

408 Ibid., 4:2181:2836
409 *Ṣaḥīḥ al-Bukhārī*, 3:1188:3084
410 *Ṣaḥīḥ Muslim*, 1:57:28
411 Ibid., 1:184:194
412 Ibid., 2:711:1027
413 *Sharḥ Muslim lil-Nawawī*, 7:118
414 *Al-Qawl al-Mufīd* (al-Muṭīʿī), p. 151

I. *Seven*

This was the opinion of Ibn ʿAbbās ﷺ. The seven in descending order are:

1. *Al-Firdaws*
2. *Al-Maʾwā*
3. *Al-Khuld*
4. *Al-Naʿīm*
5. *ʿAden*
6. *Al-Salām*
7. *Al-Jalāl*

II. *Four*

This was the opinion of the majority, because of the two verses in *Sūra al-Raḥmān* which describe the cosmology of Paradise. Allah ﷻ says: ﴾*For those who fear [the time when they will be] standing before their Lord, there are* **two** *gardens.*﴿ [55:46] and then later in the same chapter He ﷻ says: ﴾*There are* **two other** *gardens below these two.*﴿ [55:62]

III. *One*

Some scholars were of the view there is only one Paradise and that the various names related with regards to it are simply attributes for one reality.

Paradise: Everlasting or Temporary?

The belief of *Ahl al-Sunna* is that the people of Paradise will not cease to exist, nor will Paradise cease to exist: ﴾*...those who believe and do good deeds will be the inhabitants of the Garden, there to remain forever.*﴿ [2:82]

The *Jahmiyya*, however, disagreed with *Ahl al-Sunna* and believed that Paradise is a temporary reality and at a certain point, depending upon the amount of a person's good deeds, will cease to exist.[415]

[415] *Sharḥ al-ʿAqāʾid al-Nasafiyya* (al-Saʿdī), p. 159

HELLFIRE [*JAHANNAM*]

Hellfire is the everlasting abode of retribution and punishment for the disbelievers. Allah ﷻ says: ﴿*Our Lord! You will truly humiliate those You commit to the Fire. The evildoers have no one to help them.*﴾ [3:192] Disobedient believers will also enter Hellfire; however, unlike disbelievers, their punishment will be temporary, depending on the extent of their sins.[416] The *Muʿtazila*, on the other hand, saw no difference between the disbeliever and the profligate believer who died without repenting; both, in their opinion, will be forever punished in Hellfire.[417]

The Degrees of Hell [*Darakāt*]

The Qurʾan, in *Sūra al-Nisāʾ*, refers to Hellfire having degrees. Allah ﷻ says: ﴿*The hypocrites will be in the lowest depths of Hell, and you will find no one to help them.*﴾ [4:145] We find that many of the scholars believe these degrees to be seven in number, like Paradise, although it is worth noting that no sound tradition has been related with regards to the number, names and people of each degree even though according to al-Qurṭubī "the like is not known by speculation; rather, it is known by way of revelation [*tawqīf*]."[418]

The seven degrees of Hell mentioned by the scholars are:[419]

I. *Jahannam* – for the sinful believers
II. *Laẓā* – for the Jews
III. *Al-Huṭama* – for the Christians
IV. *Al-Saʿīr* – for the Sabaeans
V. *Saqar* – for the Magians
VI. *Al-Jaḥīm* – for the idol worshippers
VII. *Al-Hāwiya* – for the hypocrites

Hellfire, like Paradise, currently exists and the disbelievers will reside in there forever.

---

[416] Ibid. p. 176
[417] Ibid. p. 177
[418] *Al-Tadhkira* (al-Qurṭubī), p. 840
[419] *Sharḥ al-Ṣāwī ʿalā Jawhara al-Tawḥīd*, p. 393

THE THRONE [ʿARSH]

The throne [ʿ*arsh*] is a mighty luminous creation that is situated above Paradise. Allah ﷻ says: ﴾*If they turn away, [O Muhammad,] say: "God is enough for me: there is no god but Him; I put my trust in Him; He is the Lord of the mighty* ***throne.***"﴿ [9:129]

There are very few details that have been transmitted with regards to the description of the throne; however, some scholars have mentioned that it is dome shaped, and that it is supported by four angels, and on the Day of Judgement it will be supported by eight.[420]

THE CHAIR [KURSĪ]

The chair [*kursī*] is a mighty luminous creation, underneath the throne but adjoined to it, and above the seven skies. It is said that there is a distance of five hundred years between it and the highest sky.[421]

Again, not much has been related with regards to the *kursī*; however, there is a tradition in which Abū Dharr al-Ghifārī ؓ states: "I asked the Messenger of Allah ﷺ: 'What is the greatest [verse] that has been revealed upon you?' He ﷺ said: 'The verse of the throne [*āya al-kursī*].' Then he ﷺ said: 'O Abū Dharr, what are the seven skies compared to the *kursī* except like a ring thrown into a vast desert. And the magnanimity of the ʿ*arsh* to the *kursī* is like the magnanimity of the desert to the ring.'"[422]

THE DIVINE BOOKS

Just as it is necessary to believe in the Prophets, those mentioned in the Qurʾan and those not mentioned, it is also necessary to believe in the Divine books, those mentioned specifically in the Qurʾan and those not mentioned.

---

420 *Tuḥfa al-Murīd* (al-Bājūrī), p. 296
421 *Ibid.*
422 *Ṣaḥīḥ Ibn Ḥibbān*, 2:77:361

Allah ﷻ says: ﴾*...but say: "I believe in whatever Scripture God has sent down..."*﴿ [42:15]

The following is a list of the Divine scriptures that have been mentioned in the Qurʾan that every Muslim must specifically believe in:

I. *The Four Books* (*in chronological order*)

1. *The Torah* [*Tawrāt*]

The Torah, which is a Hebrew word that means "education" or "law,"[423] is the book revealed to the Prophet Mūsā ﷺ.[424] Many also believe that the scrolls of Mūsā ﷺ mentioned in *Sūra al-Aʿlā* are part of the Torah.

2. *The Psalms* [*Zabūr*]

The *Zabūr*, which linguistically means "that which is written down," is the Divine book revealed to the Prophet Dāwūd ﷺ. Allah ﷻ says: ﴾*To Dāwūd We gave the book* [*of Psalms*].﴿ [4:164]

3. *The Gospel* [*Injīl*]

The *Injīl*, which is a Greek word that means "glad tidings," is the Divine book revealed to the Prophet ʿĪsā ﷺ. Allah ﷻ says: ﴾*He sent down the Torah and the Gospel.*﴿ [3:3]

It is crucial to note that current copies of the Torah, Psalms or the Gospel are not the books revealed by Allah ﷻ to Mūsā, Dāwūd or ʿĪsā ﷺ as they do not have a continuous chain of transmission to these Prophets and have over time been exposed to falsifications.

4. *The Qurʾan*

The word Qurʾan linguistically means "recitation." Technically, it means: "the word of God revealed upon the Prophet Muhammad ﷺ, written as a book, transmitted by way of *tawātur*, inimitable in all of its chapters and whose recital is an act of worship."[425]

---

[423] *Al-ʿAqīda al-Islāmiyya wa-Ususuhā* (Ḥabannaka), p. 473
[424] Ibid.
[425] *ʿUlūm al-Qurʾān al-Karīm* (ʿItr), p. 10

The Qur'an is the final revealed book and thus it has been protected and preserved by Allah 🕮 from any type of distortion or phonetic corruption. The words that are recited today are the same words revealed upon the Messenger of Allah 🕮 without an iota of doubt.

II.   *The Scriptures [Ṣuḥuf]*
      1. The Scriptures of Ibrāhīm 🕮
These have been explicitly mentioned in the Qur'an. Allah 🕮 says: ❴*All this is in the earlier scriptures, the scriptures of Ibrāhīm and Mūsā.*❵ [87:18-19]
These scriptures are lost, and no one is aware of their content. However, the tradition narrated below alludes to the fact that they were ten in number.

      2. The Scriptures of Mūsā 🕮
These are also explicitly mentioned in the Qur'an, as is evident in the verse cited above. However, as previously mentioned, many considered these to be included in the Torah itself. According to the Hadith below, they are ten in number.
      The above is what has been related in the Qur'an; however, the aforementioned tradition also refers to scriptures revealed to the Prophet Shīth, Idrīs and Ādam 🕮:
      On the authority of Abū Dharr al-Ghifārī 🕮, who said: "I said: 'O Messenger of Allah, how many books has Allah 🕮 revealed?' He 🕮 replied: 'A hundred scriptures and four books. Allah Almighty revealed to Shīth fifty scriptures, thirty scriptures to Idrīs, ten scriptures to Ibrāhīm and He revealed to Mūsā ten scriptures before [the revelation of] the Torah; and He revealed the Torah, *Injīl, Zabūr* and the Qur'an.'"[426]

---

[426] *Ṣaḥīḥ Ibn Ḥibbān*, 2:77:361. According to Shaykh Shuʿayb al-Arnāʾūṭ "the *sanad* of this Hadith is extremely weak."

THE MAIDENS OF PARADISE [*ḤŪR AL-ʿAYN*]

The maidens of Paradise are females with gazelle like eyes[427] created by Allah in Paradise; they are explicitly mentioned in numerous places in the Qur'an. Allah ﷻ says, describing them: ﴾*...and beautiful maidens like hidden pearls.*﴿ [56:22-23] And in another verse He ﷻ says: ﴾*We shall wed them to maidens with large, dark eyes.*﴿ [44:54]

Various traditions also make mention of these maidens of Paradise. One Hadith describes how a man who attained the lowest rank of Paradise "will enter his house and his two wives will enter after him. They will say: 'Praise be to Allah, Who has created you for us and us for you.'"[428] This man, who is at the lowest degree of Paradise, will say upon witnessing their immense beauty: 'No one has been given the likes of what I have been given.'"[429]

Al-Ālūsī also relates some traditions with regards to their creation. He states: "Abū Umāma narrates that: 'The Messenger of Allah ﷺ said: "The maidens of Paradise have been created from saffron." And Ibn al-Mubārak reports from Zayd b. Aslam, who said: "Allah ﷻ did not create the maidens of Paradise from clay; rather, He created them from musk, camphor and saffron.""'"[430]

THE EVERLASTING YOUTHS [*WILDĀN*]

The everlasting youths are a creation of Allah whose role is to serve the inhabitants of Paradise.[431] They will take the form "of the youths of the world, their beauty will be intense, and one will find pleasure and happiness when gazing at them."[432] Allah ﷻ says: ﴾*...everlasting youths will go round among them with glasses,*

[427] That is, having large dark eyes. Some said that the dark part of the eye is intensely black, and the white part is pure white, this giving the eye its beauty. [*Rūḥ al-Maʿānī* (al-Ālūsī), 25:135]
[428] *Ṣaḥīḥ Muslim*, 1:175:188
[429] Ibid., 1:175:188
[430] *Rūḥ al-Maʿānī* (al-Ālūsī), 25:136
[431] *Tafsīr Ibn Kathīr*, 8:292
[432] *Sharḥ ʿAqīda al-Dardīr*, p. 28

flagons, and cups of a pure drink that causes no headache or intoxication.》 [56:17-19] And in another verse He ﷻ says: 《*Everlasting youths will attend them—if you could see them, you would think they were scattered pearls.*》 [76:19]

THE SAINTS [*AWLIYĀʾ*]

It is necessary to believe in the existence of saints [*awliyāʾ*]. Allah ﷻ says: 《*But for the friends of God there is no fear, nor shall they grieve.*》 [10:62]

The word *walī* (pl. *awliyāʾ*) linguistically means "nearness."[433] Technically, it has two meanings:[434]

I. The person whose affairs have been protected by Allah, meaning that he is in the protectorate of Allah. Allah ﷻ says: 《*...and it is He Who protects the righteous.*》 [7:196]

II. The one who "protects" the worship and obedience of Allah ﷻ, such that his worship is continuous without being interrupted by sin.

Both these meanings must be present in a person for him to be considered a *walī*.[435] Hence, Imam Aḥmad al-Zarrūq defined a *walī* as someone who "protects [the rights of] Allah ﷻ in all his states, and the one who is protected by Allah in all his affairs. Thus, he does not turn to other than Him or supplicate to other than Him."[436]

It is important to note that the *awliyāʾ* have an esteemed rank with Allah and thus it is necessity to revere and honour them. In a famous Hadith related by al-Bukhārī, Abū Hurayra ؓ narrates that: "The Messenger of Allah ﷺ said: 'Verily, Allah ﷻ has said: "Whoever shows enmity to a friend of Mine, then I have declared war upon him."'"[437]

---

433 *Muʿjam Maqāyīs al-Lugha* (Ibn Fāris), 6:141
434 *Al-Risāla al-Qushayriyya*, p. 365
435 *ʿUmda al-Murīd* (al-Laqqānī), 3:1174
436 *Al-Taʿrīfāt al-Zarrūqiyya* (Ḥammādī), p. 77-78
437 *Ṣaḥīḥ al-Bukhārī*, 5:2384:6137

It is also crucial to understand that like the Prophets, the *awliyāʾ* are also protected [*maḥfūẓ*] from sin; however, the infallibility [*ʿisma*] of the Prophets is different to the protection of the *awliyāʾ*. The Prophets are protected completely from committing any sinful act whereas the *awliyāʾ* can sin or commit a wrong; however, they are protected from persisting in that sin and inspired with instant repentance, and it therefore does not affect their *wilāya* (sainthood).[438]

HIS ﷺ NIGHT JOURNEY [*ISRĀʾ*]

The *isrāʾ* is the night journey the Messenger of Allah ﷺ made from the scared precinct in Mecca to the Holy house in Jerusalem. He did so upon the equid *Burāq*, with Jibrīl ﷺ on his right and Mikāʾīl on his left.[439] This night journey has been explicitly mentioned in the Qurʾan. Allah ﷻ says: ﴾*Glory to Him Who made His servant travel by night from the sacred place of worship to the furthest place of worship.*﴿ [17:1] It has also been confirmed by various traditions and there is consensus [*ijmāʿ*] of the Muslims upon this event. Therefore, denial of this night journey is considered disbelief.[440]

HIS ﷺ HEAVENLY ASCENT [*MIʿRĀJ*]

The *miʿrāj* is the ascent of the Messenger of Allah ﷺ in body and spirit, whilst awake, from earth, past the seven skies to the furthest boundary to a point that only Allah knows. On this journey he saw his Lord and spoke to Him ﷻ.[441]

The *miʿrāj*, unlike the *isrāʾ*, has not been established by unequivocal proof and thus denying the *miʿrāj* does not result in disbelief but heresy.[442]

[438] *ʿUmda al-Murīd* (al-Laqqānī), 3:1175
[439] *Sharḥ al-Ṣāwī ʿalā Jawhara al-Tawḥīd*, p. 311
[440] *Baḥr al-Kalām* (Abū al-Muʿīn al-Nasafī), p. 192;
Tuḥfa al-Murīd (al-Bājūrī), p. 233
[441] *Sharḥ al-Ṣāwī ʿalā Jawhara al-Tawḥīd*, p. 311
[442] *Tuḥfa al-Murīd* (al-Bājūrī), p. 233

The Martyr [*Shahīd*]

In legal terms, a martyr is of two types:

I. *The Martyr of the World* [*Shahīd al-Dunyā*]

The martyr of the world, according to the school of Imam Abū Ḥanīfa, is a legally responsible believer who has been killed by a non-Muslim,[443] or by another Muslim unjustly and in a manner that does not necessitate[444] the *diya*.[445] According to the school of al-Shāfi'ī, however, it is anyone killed whilst fighting the disbelievers, and killed because of the fighting.[446] This type of martyr is not washed and is treated as a martyr in this world and the hereafter.

II. *The Martyr of the Hereafter* [*Shahīd al-Ākhira*]

The *murtath*[447] and the Muslim who died in a way that is deserving of the reward of a martyr, for example: by drowning, in a fire, by being crushed, by an internal disease, by the plague, during child birth, on a Friday night, whilst seeking knowledge or

---

[443] Regardless of whether that was whilst in battle or not.
['*Umda al-Ri'āya* (al-Laknawī), 2:376]

[444] That is, only the one killed intentionally [*al-qatl al-'amd*] is regarded a martyr, as the penalty for this type of crime does not include financial recompense [*diya*] but the death penalty [*qiṣāṣ*]. This definition includes those killed in battle, or by highway robbers, or whilst defending themselves, their family or their property.
[*Minḥat al-Sulūk* (al-'Aynī), p. 214]

[445] *Tuḥfa al-Mulūk* (al-Rāzī al-Ḥanafī), p. 128; '*Umda al-Ri'āya*, 2:373

[446] For example, regardless of whether he was killed by a disbeliever or not, was struck accidently by another Muslim or accidently struck himself with his own weapon. If he died because of an illness or without a reason or was intentionally struck by another Muslim, then he is not considered a martyr according to the original position of the school.
[*Mughnī al-Muḥtāj* (al-Shirbīnī), 2:34-35]

[447] This is a wounded Muslim soldier who ate, drank, slept, was healed, was brought under a roof, moved from the battlefield alive because of the fear of being trampled upon by horses, was alive and conscious for one entire period for prayer, or was bequeathed a worldly matter.
[*Tuḥfa al-Mulūk*, p. 129-130]

the like[448] are all considered martyrs of the hereafter. This means that they are washed and shrouded like a non-martyr but given the same promised reward of the martyr in the hereafter.

It is important to understand the above definitions of who is considered a martyr, as the necessity of believing that martyrs are alive, provided for by their Lord, in accordance with the verse of the Qur'an, ﴾*Do not think of those who have been killed in God's way as dead. They are alive with their Lord, well provided for*﴿ [3-169] is specifically for the first category, that is, the martyr of this world.

It must also be noted that even though we may fail to comprehend how the martyrs are kept alive, we must believe that this life is real and complete, and cease from delving into the unknown.[449]

THE INTERCESSION [*SHAFĀʿA*] OF OUR PROPHET MUHAMMAD ﷺ

Linguistically, the word *shafāʿa* means: a means [*wasīla*] or a request [*ṭalab*]. In customary usage, it is to ask for goodness from another for another.[450] Theologically, it means: to believe that the Messenger of Allah ﷺ will beseech Allah ﷻ to grace certain people with His mercy on the Day of Judgement,[451] and that his intercession will be accepted by Allah[452] and he will be the first to intercede before any other Prophet, angel or pious person.

There are numerous traditions which speak about the intercession of the Messenger of Allah ﷺ. In a Hadith related by Muslim, the Messenger of Allah ﷺ is reported to have said: "I am the first to intercede on the Day of Judgement and the first person whose intercession will be accepted."[453]

---

[448] There are many things that can make one attain the reward of being a martyr. Their number according to some, like al-Suyūṭī is around thirty, some said forty, whilst others said fifty.
[*Radd al-Muḥtār* (Ibn ʿĀbidīn), 3:153-154
[449] *Sharḥ al-Ṣāwī ʿalā Jawhara al-Tawḥīd*, p. 407
[450] *Ḥāshiya al-ʿAqabāwī*, p. 29; *Tuḥfa al-Murīd* (al-Bājūrī), p. 305
[451] That is, he ﷺ is *al-Shafīʿ*.
[452] That is, he ﷺ is *al-Mushaffaʿ*.
[453] *Ṣaḥīḥ Muslim*, 4:1782:2278

In another Hadith related by Tirmidhī, Abū Dāwūd and others he ﷺ said: "My intercession is for the people of my nation who have committed grave sins."[454] These Hadith are just a few from many traditions that have been narrated on this topic. In reality, these Hadith have reached the level of *tawātur* and thus it is impossible to deny the existence of the concept of the intercession. Imam al-Nawawī states:

> Qāḍī ʿIyāḍ said: "There are traditions that, as a whole, reach the level of *tawātur* with regards to the reality of the intercession for sinful Muslims; and both the early and later generations and those after them from *Ahl al-Sunna* have agreed upon it."[455]

The Types of Intercession

The intercession of the Messenger of Allah ﷺ is not of one type, but rather it has many forms. Many of the scholars have categorized his intercession into five different categories:[456]

I. *The Supreme Intercession* [*al-Shafāʿa al-Kubrā*]

This, as mentioned previously, is when the Messenger of Allah ﷺ will intercede on behalf of all of creation to end the torment of the plain of resurrection and begin the reckoning. This is specific for the Messenger of Allah ﷺ; that is, no one other than the Messenger of Allah will be given this privilege and honour.

II. *Entering Certain Believers into Paradise without any Reckoning*

After the Messenger of Allah ﷺ prostrates to Allah ﷻ and is granted intercession according to one narration, he will say: "My nation my Lord, my nation my Lord." It will be then said to him ﷺ: "O Muhammad, enter into paradise from your nation, for whom there is no reckoning, through the gate of *Ayman* from the gates of paradise."[457]

---

[454] *Sunan al-Tirmidhī*, 4:625:2435, *Sunan Abī Dāwūd*, 7:119:4739
[455] *Sharḥ Muslim lil-Nawawī*, 3:35
[456] Ibid.
[457] *Ṣaḥīḥ al-Bukhārī*, 4:1745:4435

The above two categories of intercession are specific for the Messenger of Allah ﷺ.[458]

III. *Preventing Believers deserving Hellfire from Entering into it*

On the authority of ʿAbdullah b. ʿAmr b. al-ʿĀṣ ﷺ, who said: "The Messenger of Allah ﷺ said: 'People of this *qibla* [i.e., Muslims], only Allah ﷻ knows their number, those who disobeyed Allah, had the audacity to sin and violated His commands, will enter the Hell-fire. And so, I will be given the permission to intercede [on their behalf].'"[459] Al-Subkī states:

> The sinful [*fāsiq*] Muslim who has died is under the will of Allah ﷻ; he is either punished and then entered into paradise, or he is forgiven by the pure grace of Allah or by way of intercession.[460]

Al-Maḥallī, commentating upon the word "intercession" then states: "by the Messenger ﷺ."[461] The *Muʿtazila* denied this type of intercession and believed that the sinful believer who died without repenting will remain forever in hell fire, and that to pardon or intercede on his behalf is impermissible.[462]

IV. *Removing believers from Hellfire*

According to another narration, after the Messenger of Allah ﷺ is granted intercession, he will say: "O my Lord, my nation, my nation." And so it will be said: "Go and take out from it whosoever has in his heart faith the weight of a barleycorn." And so he ﷺ will go and do [it] and then return and praise Him ﷻ with those [same] praises and fall down in prostration before Him. Then it will be said: "O Muhammad, raise your head and speak, you will be listened to, and ask, you will be granted [what you request and intercede, for your intercession will be accepted." He ﷺ will say: "O Lord, my nation! My nation!" It will

---

458 *ʿUmda al-Murīd* (al-Laqqānī), 4:1678;
Al-ʿAqīda al-Islāmiyya (al-Ḥabannaka), p. 570

459 *Al-Muʿjam al-Ṣaghīr* (al-Ṭabarānī), 1:80:103

460 *Jamʿ al-Jawāmiʿ* (al-Subkī), 4:397

461 *Sharḥ Jamʿ al-Jawāmiʿ* (al-Maḥallī), 4:397

462 Ibid.

be then said: "Go and take out from it whosoever has in his heart faith equal to the weight of a small ant or a mustard seed." He ﷺ will go and do so and return to praise Him ﷻ with the same praises, and fall down in prostration before Him. It will be said: "O Muhammad, raise your head and speak, you will be listened to, and ask, you will be granted [what you request and intercede, for your intercession will be accepted." He ﷺ will say: "O Lord, my nation! My nation!" It will be then said: "Go and take out all those in whose hearts there is faith equal to the lightest, lightest mustard seed and take them out of the Fire." He ﷺ will [then] go and do so.[463] Like the above category, the *Muʿtazila* rejected this type of intercession.

V. *Raising the people in Paradise within the degrees of Paradise*

In a Hadith Umm Salama ﷺ narrates that the Messenger of Allah ﷺ said on the death of Abū Salama ﷺ: "O Allah, forgive Abū Salama and raise his rank among those who are rightly-guided.'[464]

Other than the Messenger of Allah ﷺ, Allah ﷻ will allow some of His pious servants from amongst the Prophets, angels, companions, martyrs, scholars and saints, to intercede as well, each according to their rank with Allah ﷻ. This has been confirmed in the verse in the Qur'an: ﴿*On that Day, intercession will be useless except from those to whom the Lord of Mercy has granted permission and whose words He approves.*﴾ [20:109].

This has also been confirmed in various traditions, such as: On the authority of Abu Saʿīd al-Khudrī ﷺ, who said: "The Messenger of Allah ﷺ said: 'Verily, in my nation there are those who will intercede for large groups of people, those who will intercede for a tribe, those who will intercede for a band [of men], and those who will intercede for a man, until they are admitted into Paradise.'"[465]

And in another Hadith, also narrated by Abū Saʿīd al-Khudrī ﷺ, the Messenger of Allah is reported to have said whilst speaking about the events of the Day of Judgement that: "Allah

---

463 *Ṣaḥīḥ al-Bukhārī*, 6:2727:7072

464 *Ṣaḥīḥ Muslim*, 2:634:920

465 *Sunan al-Tirmidhī*, 4:627:2440

will say: 'The angels have interceded, the Prophets have interceded, the believers have interceded and nothing is left except the [intercession of the] most Merciful.'"[466]

The Signs of the Hour

The knowledge of when the Day Judgement will happen is unknown to all other than Allah. He ﷻ says: ﴾*They ask you about the Hour: "When will it happen?" Say: "My Lord alone has knowledge of it: He alone will reveal when its time will come, a time that is momentous in both the heavens and earth. All too suddenly it will come upon you."*﴿ [7:187] However, Allah has made us privy to the events that will occur before the hour, which are normally categorised as being either minor or major. Some of these events have come to us by way of *tawātur* and are thus necessary to believe in, and are considered part of a Muslim's creed. There are others that have come to us by way of solitary traditions and are thus not included in the necessary tenets of faith. The following are some of the major signs of the Hour that have been established with unequivocal proof and thus necessary to believe in:[467]

I. The Emergence of the Antichrist [*Dajjāl*]

The Antichrist is called *Dajjāl* in Arabic, which linguistically means "to cover." The Antichrist was thus given the nickname *Dajjāl* because of his covering of the truth with falsehood. His real name according to some is Ṣāf, his kunya is said to be Abū Yūsuf, and he will be of Jewish descent.[468]

He will first appear in the lands of Khorasan,[469] calling people towards obedience and virtue. But, this will be short-lived. His real motive will manifest when he will claim divinity, declaring himself God. He will roam the earth and enter every land, except

---

[466] *Ṣaḥīḥ Muslim*, 1:167:183

[467] *Sharḥ al-Kharīda al-Bahiyya* (al-Dardīr), p. 243; *Ḥāshiya al-ʿAqabāwī*, p. 30; *Kubrā al-Yaqīniyāt al-Kawniyya* (al-Būṭī), p. 318

[468] *Ḥāshiya al-ʿAqabāwī*, p. 29; *Kubrā Yaqīniyāt al-Kawniyya*, p. 318

[469] This is an area that covers northeast Iran, southern Turkmenistan and northern Afghanistan.

the blessed cities of Mecca and Medina; many, unfortunately, will be fooled by his miraculous displays and contraventions of the norm.

With regards to his appearance, it is said he has only one eye, whereas others are of the opinion that he will have two eyes, but in one of his eyes he will "be blind, with thick skin covering the eye,"[470] described in another Hadith as a "protruding grape."[471] The word *kāfir* (disbeliever) will be written between his eyes which will be read by every believer."[472]

Numerous traditions relate some of the details of what the *Dajjāl* will do and how he will be finally killed. What follows is a Hadith transmitted in the Musnad of Imam Aḥmad that describes events surrounding the *Dajjāl*:

On the authority of Jābir b. ʿAbdullah ﵁, who said: "The Messenger of Allah ﷺ said: 'The *Dajjāl* will emerge when religion is declining and knowledge is shunned. He will have forty nights in which he will traverse the earth. One day from it will be like a year, another day from it will be like a month, another day from it will be like a Friday. The rest of the days are like these days of yours. He will have a donkey that he will ride, which will have a width of forty cubits between its two ears. He will say to people: 'I am your Lord.' He is one-eyed and your Lord is not one-eyed. Between his eyes is written *kāfir*, spelled as: *kāf*, *fā* and *rā*, which every literate and illiterate believer will be able to read. He will travel to every water and spring, except Mecca and Medina, as Allah ﷻ has made them forbidden upon him and has placed angels at their entrance. He will have a mountain of bread and people will be in great difficulty, except those who follow him. He will have two rivers with him, of which I know of better than he. A river he will say is Paradise and a river he will call Hell. Whoever enters in the river he calls Paradise, is in Hell. And whoever enters that which he calls Hell, is in Paradise. Allah will send devils with him that will speak to people. He will come with a great trial. He will order the skies and the people will see it apparently rain. He will kill a person and then apparently

---

[470] *Ṣaḥīḥ Muslim*, 4:2259:2934
[471] Ibid., 1:154:169
[472] Ibid.

resurrect him. No one other than him will have power. He will say: 'Does anyone other than the Lord do something like this?' The Muslims will flee to a mountain called *Dukhān* in the Levant. He will go after them and surround them. The siege will intensify, and they will be in immense difficulty. Then ʿĪsā b. Maryam will descend at the [dawn] prayer and say: 'O people, what is preventing you from coming out to the liar and accursed one?' They will say, "this man must be a jinni" and so they will go to see who it is and it will be ʿĪsā b. Maryam. The prayer will commence, and it will be said to him: 'Lead us, Spirit of Allah.' He will say: 'Let your Imam go forward and lead you.' When they have prayed the dawn prayer they will come out to him. They then will see the liar dissolve just like salt dissolves in water. He [ʿĪsā ﷺ] will walk towards him [the *Dajjāl*] and kill him; even the trees and stones will say: 'O Spirit of Allah, this is a Jew [who followed the *Dajjāl*].' He will not leave anyone who followed him except that he will be killed."[473]

II. The Descent of ʿĪsā b. Maryam ﷺ, the Messiah

One of the most significant signs of the Hour is the descent of the Prophet ʿĪsā ﷺ. The belief of *Ahl al-Sunna* is that ʿĪsā ﷺ, who is currently alive, provided for by Allah ﷻ in the heavens, will physically descend onto this earth, not as a Messenger, but as a follower of the Sacred Law of the Messenger of Allah ﷺ.

The evidence for this event is unequivocal, clear and absolute. Verses in the Qur'an explicitly describe the ascent of ʿĪsā ﷺ, that he was not killed or crucified but rather raised to the heavens, that he will descend again, and that the people of the Book will believe in him as a Prophet.

Allah ﷻ says: ﴾*...and [they] said: "We have killed the Messiah, ʿĪsā, the son of Maryam, the Messenger of God." They did not kill him, nor did they crucify him, though it was made to appear like that to them; those that disagreed about him are full of doubt, with no knowledge to follow, only supposition: they certainly did not kill him—God raised him up to Himself. God is Almighty and Wise. There is not one of the people of the Book who will not believe in [ʿĪsā ﷺ] before his death, and on the Day of Resurrection he will be a witness against them.*﴿ [4:157-159]

---

[473] *Musnad Aḥmad*, 23:210:14954

In another verse Allah ﷻ says: ﴾*He* [*ʿĪsā* ﷺ] *is a sign of the Hour. Have no doubt about it.*﴿ [43:61] Both of these verses are explicit in showing that the Prophet ʿĪsā ﷺ has not died and that He will come again as a sign of the Hour and witness against the people of the Book.

In addition to these verses, numerous traditions have been related with regards to his descent leaving little room for doubt. Anwar Shāh al-Kashmīrī, the Indian Hadith scholar, has cited over a hundred Hadith and *āthār* (traditions) in his treatise *Al-Ṣarīḥ bi-mā Tawātara fī Nuzūl ʿĪsā* ﷺ, some of which are cited below:

On the authority of Ibn al-Musayyib, who heard Abū Hurayra ؓ say: "The Messenger of Allah ﷺ said: 'By Whose hand my soul is in, the time is surely near for the descent of ʿĪsā b. Maryam as a just leader: he will break the cross, kill the swine, establish the *jizya* and wealth will be so widespread such that no one will accept it.'"[474]

In another long tradition related by Muslim, al-Tirmidhī and others, al-Nawwās b. Samʿān ؓ is reported to have said that: "The Messenger of Allah ﷺ said: '...It will be at this time that Allah ﷻ will send the Messiah, the son of Maryam. He will descend at the white minaret on the eastern side of Damascus, wearing two beautiful garments lightly dyed with saffron and placing his hands on the wings of two angels. When he lowers his head, beads of perspiration will fall from his head; and when he raises it up, beads like pearls will slowly fall. Any disbeliever who smells his scent will perish. His breath will reach as far as he is able to see. He will then go after him [the *Dajjāl*] until he catches him at the gate of *Ludd* and kills him. Then, a people whom Allah had protected will come to ʿĪsā b. Maryam, and he will wipe their faces and inform them of their ranks in Paradise.'"[475]

On the authority of Abū Hurayra ؓ, who said: "The Messenger of Allah ﷺ said: 'How will you be when the son of Maryam descends upon you and is your Imam?'"[476]

---

[474] *Ṣaḥīḥ al-Bukhārī*, 2:774:2109
[475] *Ṣaḥīḥ Muslim*, 4:2250:2937; *Sunan al-Tirmidhī*, 4:510:2240
[476] *Ṣaḥīḥ Muslim*, 1:136:155

III. The Emergence of Gog and Magog [*Yaʾjūj wa-Maʾjūj*]

Gog and Magog, two tribes from the descendants of Yāfith the son of Nūḥ ﷺ,[477] are from the signs of the Hour that a Muslim must believe in. Allah, in the Qurʾan, describes the affair of these two tribes in detail. In *Sūra al-Anbiyāʾ*, He ﷻ says: ﴿*...and when the people of Gog and Magog are let loose and swarm swiftly from every highland.*﴾ [21:96]

And in *Sūra al-Kahf* He ﷻ says, describing how they were trapped between two mountain sides by *Dhū al-Qarnayn*: ﴿*He travelled on. Then, when he reached a place between two mountain barriers, he found beside them a people who could barely understand him. They said: "Dhū al-Qarnayn, Gog and Magog are ruining this land. Will you build a barrier between them and us if we pay you a tribute?" He answered: "The power my Lord has given me is better than any tribute, but if you lend me your strength, I will put up a fortification between you and them. Bring me lumps of iron!" Then, when he had filled the gap between the two mountainsides [he said:] "Work your bellows!" Then, when he had made it glow like fire, he said: "Bring me molten metal to pour over it!" Their enemies could not scale the barrier, nor could they pierce it, and he said: "This is a mercy from my Lord. But when my Lord's promise is fulfilled, He will raze this barrier to the ground; my Lord's promise always comes true."*﴾ [18:92-98]

Like the previous signs, there are many Hadith with regards to the coming of Gog and Magog. Below, are two traditions: the first is a very long tradition found in the Ṣaḥīḥ of Imam Muslim and the second is from the Musnad of Imam Aḥmad.

On the authority of al-Nawwās b. Samʿān ؓ, who said: "The Messenger of Allah ﷺ said: 'Allah ﷻ will reveal to ʿĪsā after having killed the Antichrist: "I have brought forth from amongst My servants such people against whom none has strength over, so take My servants to Mount Sinai." Allah will release Gog and Magog and they will swarm swiftly from every highland. The first of them will pass the lake of Tiberias (Sea of Galilee) and drink from it; when the last of them pass by it they will say: "There was once water here."

[477] *Sharḥ al-Kharīda al-Bahiyya* (al-Dardīr), p. 246

"'...'Īsā and his companions will then be besieged till the head of an ox will be more valuable to them than one hundred dinars is for you today. 'Īsā and his companions will supplicate, and so Allah ﷻ will send worms that will attack their necks, they will wake up in the morning dead like the death of one single person. Then, 'Īsā and his companions will come back down but they will not find even a single span except that it will be filled with their putrid and offensive smell. 'Īsā and his companions will supplicate to Allah Who will send birds with Bactrian camel-like necks that will carry them and throw them where Allah wills.

"'...Then, Allah ﷻ will send rain which no house, whether made of mud-bricks or camel-hair, will keep out: it will wash the Earth till it leaves it looking like a mirror. Then, it will be said to the earth: 'Bring forth your fruit and restore your blessing.' Therefore, on that day pomegranate will grow that will be enough for a group of people to eat and seek shelter using its shell. Milk will be made plentiful, such that a milch cow will give so much milk that will be enough for a large group of people to drink, the milch camel will give so much milk that a whole tribe will be able to drink from it and milch goats enough to suffice a small group of people.

"'...At that time, Allah ﷻ will send a pleasant wind which will take them from under their armpits. He will take the life of every Muslim and only the wicked will survive who will commit adultery shamelessly like donkeys—upon them, the Hour will fall.'"[478]

The second Hadith is narrated by Abū Hurayra ؓ, who said: "The Messenger of Allah ﷺ said: 'Gog and Magog dig into the barrier every day, until they can nearly see the rays of the sun. The one in charge says: "Return, you will dig again tomorrow." They return only for it to be thicker than before. Then, when their time arrives, and Allah, Mighty and Sublime, wishes to release them upon the people, they will dig until they can nearly see the rays of the sun. The one in charge will say: "Return, you will dig again tomorrow, God willing," [ending his speech by] making a clause. Then, they will come back to it and find it as they had left it.

[478] *Ṣaḥīḥ Muslim*, 4:2250:2937

"'So, they will dig through it, and come out upon the people. They will drink all the water, and the people will seek protection from them in their fortresses. They will shoot their arrows into the sky, and they will come seemingly bloodstained. They will say: "We have overcome the inhabitants of the earth, and conquered the inhabitants of the heaven." Then, Allah ﷻ will send down upon them worms [*naghaf*] upon their necks that will kill them.' Then, the Messenger of Allah ﷺ said: 'By He in Whose hand is my soul, the beasts of the earth will fatten and gain weight from their flesh and blood.'"[479]

IV. Emergence of the Creature [*Dābba*]

The concept of the creature [*dābba*] which is explicitly mentioned in the Qurʾan, is another sign of the Hour that is a necessary component of faith. Allah ﷻ says: ﴾*When the verdict is given against them, We shall bring a creature out of the earth, which will tell them that people had no faith in Our revelations.*﴿[480] [27:82]

On the authority of ʿAbdullah b. ʿUmar ﷺ, who said: "I memorised a Hadith from the Messenger of Allah ﷺ which I have not yet forgotten. I heard the Messenger of Allah say: 'The first of the signs that will appear is the rising of the sun from the place it sets and the emergence of the creature in the afternoon. Whichever of these two occurs before the other, and then the other is right behind it.'"[481]

On the authority of Abū Hurayra ﷺ, who said: "The Messenger of Allah ﷺ said: 'The Beast will emerge carrying the ring of Sulaymān b. Dāwūd, and the staff of Mūsā b. ʿImrān ﷺ. He will illuminate the face of the believer with the staff and stamp the nose of the disbeliever with the ring, until the people gather and begin to address one another with the words 'O believer!' or 'O disbeliever!'"[482]

---

[479] *Musnad Aḥmad*, 16:369:10632

[480] Other valid interpretations of this verse are that the creature will tell who is from the people of Paradise, and who is from the people of Hell, or tell them about the falsity of other faiths and the truth of Islam. [*Sharḥ al-Kharīda al-Bahiyya* (al-Dardīr), p. 248]

[481] *Ṣaḥīḥ Muslim*, 4:2260:2941

[482] *Sunan Ibn Mājah*, 5:522:4066

Certain Hadith also speak about how and where the creature will emerge. In a Hadith related by al-Ḥākim, the Messenger of Allah ﷺ states that the creature will appear three times:[483]

I. Firstly, it will appear in the furthest Yemen giving it reputation in the desert. It will be unknown in the city, that is Mecca, at this time.
II. Its second appearance after staying low for a long period will be somewhere near Mecca. The news of its arrival will spread to both the people of the desert and Mecca.
III. Then, after another long period of hiding, it will appear in *al-Masjid al-Ḥarām* (the Sacred Mosque in Mecca).

Imam al-Dardīr states:

> It will emerge whilst ʿĪsā ﷺ is circumambulating the House [*Kaʿba*] with the Muslims. The earth will shake beneath them and *al-Ṣafā*, that which is near *al-Mashʿar*, will be cleft open. The head of the creature will come out from *al-Ṣafā*: a horse will gallop for three days and a third of it (that is, the head) will still not have emerged. After it comes out its head will touch the clouds.[484]

V. The Rising of the Sun from the West

The fifth major sign of the Hour, and a necessary component of Islamic creed, is the rising of the sun from the west, at which point the door of repentance will be forever closed. The Qurʾan alludes to this event in *Sūra al-Anʿām* where Allah ﷻ says: ❮*But on the Day some of your Lord's signs come, no soul will profit from faith if it had none before or has not already earned some good through its faith.*❯ [6:158] According to multiple traditions, this verse is referring to the sign of the sun rising from the west. Abū Saʿīd al-Khudrī states ﷺ that the Messenger of Allah ﷺ, when asked about this verse, said: "The sun rising from the west."[485]

Numerous Hadith have also confirmed this event, like the one mentioned above and the tradition in *Ṣaḥīḥ Muslim* related

---

[483] *Al-Mustadrak* (al-Ḥākim), 4:530:8490
[484] *Sharḥ al-Kharīda al-Bahiyya* (al-Dardīr), p. 249
[485] *Musnad Aḥmad*, 17:368:11266

previously in the chapter of the emergence of the creature. They all affirm that "the Day of Judgement will not come to pass until the sun rises from west."[486]

THE RENEWAL OF REPENTANCE FROM SINS

Repentance [*tawba*] linguistically means "to return."[487] Technically, it is to:[488]

I. Abandon the sin
II. Have remorse, for the sake of Allah ﷻ, for committing the sin
III. Have firm resolve never to commit the sin again

These are the three pillars of repentance for a sin that transgressed the rights of Allah ﷻ. If, however, one transgressed against another person, then one must, in addition to these three pre-conditions, return the right of that person and seek his pardon.[489]

The creed of *Ahl al-Sunna* with regards to sin and repentance is that Allah accepts the repentance of the one who sincerely repents. He ﷻ says: ﴾*Believers, turn to God in sincere repentance. Your Lord may well cancel your bad deeds for you and admit you into Gardens graced with flowing streams...*﴿ [66:8] and in another verse, He ﷻ says: ﴾*Believers, all of you, turn to God in repentance so that you may prosper.*﴿ [24:31] These verses are clear in affirming the concept of repentance.

In addition to repentance, it is also necessary to believe that repentance can also be renewed. That is, if one sinned after having repented, repentance can be made again, and Allah will accept that repentance if sincere. There is no limit to repentance as the mercy of Allah is vast: He ﷻ is the oft forgiving and the One Who ﴾*loves those who turn to Him.*﴿ [2:222]

---

486 *Ṣaḥīḥ al-Bukhārī*, 4:1697:4359
487 *Muʿjam Maqāyīs al-Lugha* (Ibn Fāris), 1:357
488 *Riyāḍ al-Ṣāliḥīn* (al-Nawawī), p. 33
489 *Tuḥfa al-Murīd* (al-Bājūrī), p. 319

One can find a plethora of traditions that speak about forgiveness and its virtue in the corpus of Hadith literature. Below, are a few of these well-known Hadith:

The Messenger of Allah said ﷺ: "O people, repent to Allah ﷻ, for verily I repent to Allah a hundred times each day."[490] And in another narration he ﷺ said: "seventy times each day."[491]

The Messenger of Allah ﷺ said: "The one who has repented from sins is like the one with no sin."[492]

The Messenger of Allah ﷺ said: "By Him in Whose hand is my soul, if you did not sin Allah would get rid of you and create a people who did sin and then sought forgiveness, and He ﷻ would forgive them."[493]

The Messenger of Allah ﷺ said: "Verily Allah, Mighty and Sublime, accepts the repentance of a servant as long as the soul has not reached the gullet [*gharghara*]."[494]

QAḌĀʾ AND *QADAR* (PRE-DESTINATION)

Belief in *qaḍāʾ* and *qadar*, the good from it and the bad, is a necessary pillar of faith. In the Hadith of Jibrīl ﷺ, narrated by ʿUmar b. al-Khaṭṭāb ؓ, the Messenger of Allah ﷺ, when asked about faith [*īmān*], says it is: "To believe in Allah ﷻ, His angels, His books, His Messengers, the Day of Judgement and *qadar*, the good from it and the bad..."[495]

Qaḍāʾ

Qaḍāʾ linguistically means: the completion of something and its execution precisely and thoroughly whether that be a word, act or intention.[496] Allah ﷻ says: ﴾*...and in two Days He formed [qaḍāʾhunna] seven heavens.*﴿ [41:12]

490 *Ṣaḥīḥ Muslim*, 4:2075:2702
491 *Ṣaḥīḥ al-Bukhārī*, 5:2324:5948
492 *Sunan Ibn Mājah*, 2:1419:4250
493 *Ṣaḥīḥ Muslim*, 4:2106:2749
494 *Sunan al-Tirmidhī*, 5:547:3537
495 *Ṣaḥīḥ Muslim*, 1:38:8 and others
496 *Muʿjam Maqāyīs al-Lugha* (Ibn Fāris), p. 5:99;
Al-ʿAqīda al-Islāmiyya wa-Ususuhā (Ḥabannaka), p. 626

In Islamic theology, however, it carries a different signification. Imam al-Ashʿarī defined it as the pre-eternal will of Allah ﷻ that is connected to creation, meaning that it relates to the way they will be brought into existence.[497] This can also be explained as the pre-eternal knowledge of Allah of how everything will be created in the future.[498] For example, He ﷻ knows and wills in pre-eternity the creation of so and so in a certain country at a certain time, and He knows in pre-eternity that that person would perform such and such an act.

Al-Māturīdī differed with al-Ashʿarī and considered *qaḍāʾ* as the bringing of these things into existence by Allah ﷻ with extra precision and perfection, in accordance with His pre-eternal knowledge and will.[499]

Qadar

Qadar linguistically means "determining the quantity of something."[500] With regards to its technical usage, the *Ashʿarīs* consider the *Māturīdī* definition of *qaḍāʾ* to be *qadar*, and the *Māturīdīs* vice versa. The difference between the schools with regards to these two terms, as is evident, returns to the use of language.

However, what both schools do agree upon is that every Muslim must believe that:

I. Allah ﷻ knows of everything in pre-eternity, and this has been recorded in the preserved tablet.
II. Allah ﷻ specified the attributes of everything in pre-eternity, as has been outlined in the chapter of the will of Allah, and then brought these things into existence at their specific time in accordance with His pre-eternal knowledge.

---

497 *Al-ʿAqīda al-Islāmiyya wa-Ususuhā*, p. 626; *Tuḥfa al-Murīd* (al-Bājūrī), p. 189

498 *Kubrā al-Yaqīniyāt al-Kawniyya* (al-Būṭī), p. 160

499 Ibid.

500 *Al-ʿAqīda al-Islāmiyya wa-Ususuhā* (Ḥabannaka), p. 626

III. *Qaḍā'* and *qadar* do not infer that man is compelled, as many wrongly believe. According to al-Khaṭṭābī, they merely signify "the informing of the pre-eternal knowledge of Allah ﷻ with regards to what the servant will acquire, and bringing them into existence by the omnipotence of Allah."[501]

Hopefully, this is a sufficient summary of the concepts of *qaḍā'* and *qadar*. I would like to conclude by reminding ourselves of the Hadith of the Messenger of Allah ﷺ who has directed us towards not delving into the intricacies of these two matters:

On the authority of ʿAbdullah b. Masʿūd ؓ, who said: "The Messenger of Allah ﷺ said: 'If my companions are mentioned, restrain yourselves; if the stars are mentioned, restrain yourselves; and if the decree is mentioned, restrain yourselves.'"[502]

This is the end of the commentary of the Creed of Imam al-Dardīr. I sincerely hope that it will be a means of benefit to those who desire to learn about their faith and Creator, the Messengers, angels and the life to come. It is evident that Islam has left a rich corpus of knowledge surrounding topics pertaining to belief, and the scholars of previous generations strove tirelessly to elucidate, exposit and protect these beliefs from corruption and unorthodoxy. I ask Allah that He ﷻ accepts this work and allows it to be a source of clarity for Muslims for generations to come.

---

[501] *Sharḥ al-Nawawī ʿalā al-Muslim*, 1:155

[502] *Al-Muʿjam al-Kabīr* (al-Ṭabarānī), 10:198:10448

BIBLIOGRAPHY

1. ʿĀbidīn, Muḥammad Amīn b. ʿUmar b., *Radd al-Muḥtār ʿalā al-Durr al-Mukhtār*, 12 vols., ed. Muḥammad Ṣubḥī Ḥasan Ḥallāq & ʿĀmir Ḥusayn. Beirut, Lebanon: Dār Iḥyāʾ al-Turāth al-ʿArabī, 1418/1998.
2. Ālūsī, Shihāb al-Dīn Maḥmūd b. ʿAbdullah al-, *Rūḥ al-Maʿānī fī Tafsīr al-Qurʾān al-ʿAẓīm wal-Sabʿ al-Mathānī*, 30 vols. Beirut, Lebanon: Dār Iḥyāʾ al-Turāth al-ʿArabī (Idāra al-Ṭibāʿa al-Mūnīriyya), n.d.
3. Āmidī, Sayf al-Dīn al-, *Ghāya al-Marām fī ʿIlm al-Kalām*, ed. Ḥasan Maḥmūd ʿAbd al-Laṭīf. Cairo, Egypt: al-Majlis al-Aʿlā lil-Shuʾūn al-Islāmiyya, 1391/1971.
4. Amīr Ḥāj al-Ḥanafī, Abū ʿAbdullah Shams al-Dīn Muḥammad b. Muḥammad b., *Al-Taqrīr wal-Taḥbīr*, 3 vols., ed. ʿAbdullah Maḥmūd Muḥammad ʿUmar. Beirut, Lebanon: Dār al-Kutub al-ʿIlmiyya, 1419/1999.
5. Andalusī, Abū Ḥayyān Muḥammad b. Yūsuf al-, *Al-Baḥr al-Muḥīṭ fī al-Tafsīr*, 10 vols., ed. Sidqī Muḥammad Jamīl. Beirut, Lebanon: 1420/2000.
6. ʿAqabāwī, Muṣṭafā b. Aḥmad al-, *Sharḥ ʿAqīda al-Dardīr & Ḥāshiya ʿalā Sharḥ ʿAqīda al-Dardīr*. Cairo, Egypt: Muṣṭafā al-Bābī al-Ḥalabī, 1368/1949.
7. Archie, Lee C, "William Paley, 'The Teleological Argument,'" *Philosophy of Religion* (June 26, 2006) http://philosophy.lander.edu/intro/paley.shtml. Accessed, 14, Aug, 2018.
8. ʿAsākir, ʿAlī b. al-Ḥasan b., *Tabyīn Kadhib al-Muftarī fī mā Nusiba ilā al-Imām Abū al-Ḥasan al-Ashʿarī*. Beirut, Lebanon: Dar al-Kutub al-ʿArabī, 1404/1984.
9. ʿAsākir, ʿAlī b. al-Ḥasan b., *Tārīkh Dimashq*, 80 vols., ed. ʿAmr b. Gharāma al-ʿUmrawī. Damascus, Syria: Dār al-Fikr, 1415/1995.
10. Aṣfahānī, al-Rāghib al-, *Mufradāt Alfāẓ al-Qurʾān*, ed. Ṣafwān ʿAdnān al-Dāwūdī. Damascus, Syria: Dār al-Qalam, 1432/2011.

11. ʿAṭāʾillah al-Iskandarī, Aḥmad b. Muḥammad b., *Al-Ḥikam* (published with the commentary of the *Ḥikam* by Ibn ʿAjība), ed. ʿĀṣim Ibrāhīm al-Kayyālī. Beirut, Lebanon: Dār al-Kutub al-ʿIlmiyya, n.d.

12. ʿAynī, Maḥmūd b. Aḥmad Badr al-Dīn al-, *Minḥat al-Sulūk fī Sharḥ Tuḥfa al-Mulūk*, ed. Aḥmad al-Kubaysī. Syria, Lebanon, Kuwait: Dār al-Nawādir, 1432/2011.

13. ʿAynī, Maḥmūd b. Aḥmad Badr al-Dīn al-, *ʿUmda al-Qārī Sharḥ Ṣaḥīḥ al-Bukhārī*, 25 vols. in 12. Beirut, Lebanon: Dār Iḥyāʾ al-Turāth al-ʿArabī, 1431/2010.

14. Baghawī, al-Ḥusayn b. Masʿūd al-, *Maʿālim al-Tanzīl fī Tafsīr al-Qurʾān*, 5 vols., ed. ʿAbd al-Razzāq al-Mahdī. Beirut, Lebanon: Dār Iḥyāʾ al-Turāth al-ʿArabī, 1420/1999.

15. Baghdādī, Aḥmad b. ʿAlī al-Khaṭīb al-, 2 vols., ed. Muḥammad al-ʿAjjāj al-Khaṭīb. Beirut, Lebanon: Muʾassasa al-Risāla.

16. Baghdādī, Aḥmad b. ʿAlī al-Khaṭīb al-, *Al-Jāmiʿ li-Akhlāq al-Rāwī wa-Ādāb al-Sāmiʿ*, 2 vols., ed. Maḥmūd Ṭaḥḥān. Riyadh, Saudi Arabia: Maktaba al-Maʿarif, 1403/1989.

17. Bājūrī, Ibrāhīm al-, *Tuḥfa al-Murīd ʿalā Jawhara al-Tawḥīd*, ed. ʿAlī Jumuʿa. Cairo, Egypt: Dār al-Salām, 1433/2012.

18. Bayāḍī al-Ḥanafī, Kamāl al-Dīn Aḥmad al-, *Ishārāt al-Marām min ʿIbārāt al-Imām* (A commentary on *al-Fiqh al-Akbar*), ed. Yūsuf ʿAbd al-Razzāq. Karachi, Pakistan: Zam Zam Publishers, 1425/2004

19. Bayḍāwī, ʿAbdullah b. ʿUmar al-, *Anwār al-Tanzīl wa-Asrār al-Tāʾwīl* (*al-Tafsīr al-Bayḍāwī*), 5 vols., ed. Muḥammad ʿAbd al-Raḥmān al-Marʿashlī. Beirut, Lebanon: Dār Iḥyāʾ al-Turāth al-ʿArabī, 1418/1998.

20. Bayḍāwī, ʿAbdullah b. ʿUmar al-, *Sharḥ Asmāʾ Allah al-Ḥusnā*, ed. Khālid al-Jundī. Beirut, Lebanon: Dār al-Maʿrifa, 1430/2009.

21. Bayhaqī, Aḥmad b. al-Ḥusayn Abū Bakr al-, *Al-Asmāʾ wal-Ṣifāt*, ʿAbdullah b. Muḥammad al-Ḥāshidī. Jeddah, Saudi Arabia: Maktaba al-Sawādī, 1413/1993

22. Bayhaqī, Aḥmad b. al-Ḥusayn Abū Bakr al-, *Al-Baʿth wal-Nushūr*, ed. ʿĀmir Aḥmad Ḥaydar. Beirut, Lebanon: Markaz al-Khadamāt wal-Abḥāth al-Thaqāfiyya, 1406/1986

23. Bayhaqī, Aḥmad b. al-Ḥusayn Abū Bakr al-, *Ithbāt ʿAdhāb al-Qabr wa-Suʾāl al-Malakayn*, ed. Sharaf al-Quḍāt. Amman, Jordan: Dar al-Furqān, 1405/1985.

24. Bukhārī, Muḥammad b. Ismāʿīl al-, *Ṣaḥīḥ al-Bukhārī*, 7 vols. in 1, ed. Muṣṭafā Dīb al-Bughā. Damascus, Syria and Beirut, Lebanon: Dār Ibn Kathīr and Yamāma, 1414/1993

25. Būṭī, Muḥammad Saʿīd Ramaḍān al-, *Kubrā al-Yaqīniyyāt al-Kawniyya*. Damascus, Syria: Dār al-Fikr, 1417/1997.

26. Dardīr, Abū al-Barakāt Aḥmad b. Muḥammad al-, *Al-Kharīda al-Bahiyya & Sharḥ al-Kharīda al-Bahiyya*, ed. Muṣṭafā Maḥmūd Rasūl. Cairo, Egypt: Dār al-Baṣāʾir, 2010.

27. Dāwūd al-Sijistānī, Sulaymān b. al-Ashʿath Abū, *Sunan Abī Dāwūd*, 7 vols., ed. Shuʿayb al-Arnāʾūṭ & Muḥammad Kāmil Balalī. Beirut, Lebanon: Dār al-Risāla al-ʿĀlamiyya, 1430/2009.

28. Dhahabī, Shams al-Dīn al-, *Siyar al-Aʿlām al-Nubalāʾ*, 25 vols., ed. Shuʿayb al-Arnāʾūṭ. Beirut, Lebanon: Muʾassasa al-Risāla, 1405/1985.

29. Dughaym, Samīḥ, *Mawsūʿa Muṣṭalaḥāt ʿIlm al-Kalām al-Islāmī*, 2 vols. Beirut, Lebanon: Maktaba Lubnān Nāshirūn, 1418/1998.

30. Dūrī, Qaḥṭān al-, *ʿAqīda al-Islāmiyya wa-Madhāhibuhā*. Beirut, Lebanon: Books-Publisher, 1437/2016.

31. Effendī, Ramaḍān b. Muḥammad, *Sharḥ al-ʿAqāʾid al-Nasafiyya*, ed. Morʾī Ḥasan al-Rashīd. Beirut, Lebanon: Dar Nūr al-Ṣabāḥ, 1433/2012.

32. Encyclopaedia of Islam, second edition, Edited by: P. Bearman, Th. Bianquis, C.E. Bosworth, E. van Donzel, W.P. Heinrichs. Consulted online on 30 April 2018 http://dx.doi.org/10.1163/1573-3912_islam_SIM_0699.

33. Fāris, Abū al-Ḥusayn Aḥmad b., *Muʿjam Maqāyīs al-Lugha*, 6 vols., ed. ʿAbd al-Salām Muḥammad Hārūn. Beirut, Lebanon: Dār al-Jīl, 1419/1999 (reprinted by: Dār ʿĀlam al-Kutub)

34. Foudah, Saʿīd ʿAbd al-Laṭīf, *Al-Shiʿār fī al-ʿAqāʾid* (An abridgement of Imam al-Bayhaqī's *al-Iʿtiqād wal-Hidāya*). Beirut, Lebanon: Dār al-Dhakhāʾir.

35. Fayrūzābādī, Muḥammad b. Yaʿqūb al-, *Qāmūs al-Muḥīṭ*, ed. Muḥammad Naʿīm al-ʿArqasūsī. Beirut, Lebanon: Muʾassasa al-Risāla, 1426/2005.

36. Ghazālī, Abū Ḥāmid Muḥammad b. Muḥammad al-, *Al-Iqtiṣād fī al-Iʿtiqād*, ed. Anas al-Sharfāwī. Jeddah, Saudi Arabia: Dār al-Minhāj, 1437/2016.

37. Ghazālī, Abū Ḥāmid Muḥammad b. Muḥammad al-, *Al-Maqṣad al-Asnā fī Sharḥ Maʿānī al-Asmāʾ al-Ḥusnā*, ed. Bassām al-Jābī. Beirut, Lebanon: Dār Ibn Ḥazm, 1424/2003

38. Ghaznawī, Jamāl al-Dīn Aḥmad b. Muḥammad al-, *Kitāb Uṣūl al-Dīn*, ed. ʿUmar al-Dāʿūq. Beirut, Lebanon: Dar al-Bashāʾir al-Islāmiyya, 1418/1998.

39. Ḥākim al-Naysāpūrī, Muḥammad b. ʿAbdullah al-, *Al-Mustadrak ʿalā al-Ṣaḥīḥayn*, 4 vols., ed. Muṣṭafā ʿAbd al-Qādir ʿAṭā. Beirut, Lebanon: Dār al-Kutub al-ʿIlmiyya, 1411/1990.

40. Haleem, M.A.S. Abdel, *The Qurʾan: A New Translation*. Oxford: Oxford University Press, 2004

41. Hamadhānī, ʿAbd al-Jabbār b. Aḥmad, *Sharḥ al-Uṣūl al-Khamsa*, ed. ʿAbd al-Karīm ʿUthmān. Cairo, Egypt: Maktaba Wahba, 1416/1996.

42. Ḥamawī, Aḥmad b. Muḥammad Makkī al-, *Taqlīd al-Qalāʾid ʿalā Manẓūma al-ʿAqāʾid*, ed. Muḥammad Ṣalāḥ Taqwā. Amman, Jordan: Dār al-Fatḥ, 2018/1439.

43. Ḥammādī, Nizār, *Al-Taʿrīfāt al-Zarrūqiyya lil-Ḥaqāʾiq al-Ṣūfiyya*. Tunis, Tunisia: Dār Ibn al-Imām b. ʿArafa, n.d.

44. Ḥanbal, Aḥmad b Muḥammad b., *Musnad Aḥmad b. Ḥanbal*, ed. Shuʿayb al-Arnāʾūṭ, ʿĀdil Murshid, et al. Beirut, Lebanon: Muʾassasa al-Risāla, 1421/2001.

45. Ḥanīfa, Nuʿmān b. Thābit Abū, *Waṣiyya al-Imam Abū Ḥanīfa*, ed. Muḥammad al-Ṣubḥī al-ʿĀyidī and Ḥamza al-Bakrī. Amman, Jordan: Dār al-Fatḥ, 1430/2009.

46. Hāshimī, Muḥammad b. Aḥmad b. al-, *Miftāḥ al-Janna Sharḥ ʿAqīda Ahl al-Sunna*. N.p, 1413/1993

47. Hāshimī, Muḥammad b. Aḥmad b. al-, *Sharḥ Naẓm ʿAqīda Ahl al-Sunna*, ed. ʿAbd al-Raḥmān al-Shaʿʿār. Beirut, Lebanon: Dār al-Imām Yūsuf al-Nabhānī, 1437/2016

48. Hasker, William, Occasionalism, Muslim Philosophy, 1998, [website], accessed 10 June, 2018 www.muslimphilosophy.com/ip/rep/K057.htm#K057SECT3.

49. Haytamī, Shihāb al-Dīn b. Ḥajar al-, *Al-Fatāwā al-Ḥadīthiyya*. Beirut, Lebanon: Dār al-Maʿrifa, n.d.

50. Humām, Kamāl al-Dīn Muḥammad b. ʿAbd al-Wāḥid b. al-, *Al-Musāyara*, ed. Maḥmūd ʿUmar al-Dimyāṭī. Beirut, Lebanon: Dār al-Kutub al-ʿIlmiyya, 1422/2002.

51. Huṣnī, Taqī al-Dīn al-, *Dafʿu Shubah man Shabbaha wa-Tamarrada wa-Nasaba dhālika ilā al-Sayyid al-Jalīl al-Imam Aḥmad*, ed. Muḥammad Zāhid al-Kawtharī. Beirut, Lebanon: Dār al-Kutub al-ʿIlmiyya, 1430/2009.

52. Ḥibbān, Muḥammad Ṣaḥīḥ b., 18 vols., ed. Shuʿayb al-Arnāʾūṭ. Beirut, Lebanon: Muʾassasa al-Risāla, 1408/1988.

53. Hishām, ʿAbd al-Mālik b., *Al-Sīra al-Nabawiyya*, 2 vols., ed. Muṣṭafā al-Saqqā, Ibrāhīm al-ʿAbyārī & ʿAbd al-Ḥāfiẓ al-Shalabī. Cairo, Egypt: 1374/1955.

54. Kamāl Pāshā, Shams al-Dīn Aḥmad b. Sulaymān b., *Masāʾil al-Ikhtilāf Bayna al-Ashāʿira wal-Māturīdiyya*, ed. Saʿīd ʿAbd al-Laṭīf Foudah. Beirut, Lebanon: Dār al-Dhakhāʾir, 1436/2015. English translation: *The Differences between the Ashʿaris & Maturidis*. Rotterdam, Netherlands: Sunni Publications, 2018.

55. Kathīr, Abū al-Fidāʾ Ismāʿīl b. ʿUmar b., *Al-Bidāya wal-Nihāya*, 14 vols., ed. ʿAlī Shīrī. Beirut, Lebanon: Dār Iḥyāʾ Turāth al-ʿArabī, 1408/1988.

56. Kathīr, Abū al-Fidāʾ Ismāʿīl b. ʿUmar b., *Tafsīr al-Qurʾān al-ʿAdhīm*, 8 vols., ed. Sāmī b. Muḥammad Salāma. Riyadh, Saudi Arabia: Dār Ṭayba lil-Nashr wal-Tawzīʿ, 1420/1999.

57. Khallikān, Aḥmad b. Muḥammad b., *Wafayāt al-Aʿyān wa-Anbāʾ Abnāʾ al-Zamān*, 8 vols., ed. Iḥsān ʿAbbās. Beirut, Lebanon: Dār Ṣādir, 1398/1978.

58. Mājah, Muḥammad b. Yazīd al-Qazwīnī b., *Sunan Ibn Maja*, 6 vols., ed. Bashār ʿAwwād Maʿrūf. Beirut, Lebanon: Dār al-Jīl, 1419/1998.

59. ʿĪsā, ʿAbd al-Qādir, *Ḥaqāʾiq ʿan al-Taṣawwuf*. Aleppo, Syria: Dar al-ʿIrfān, 2007/1428. English translation: *Realities of Sufism*. Rotterdam, the Netherlands: Sunni Publications, 2013.

60. ʿItr, Nūr al-Dīn, *ʿUlūm al-Qurʾān al-Karīm*. Damascus, Syria: Maṭbaʿa al-Ṣabāḥ, 1417/1996.

61. Jawzī, ʿAbd al-Raḥmān b. ʿAlī al-, *Dafʿ Shubha al-Tashbīh*, ed. Muḥammad Zāhid al-Kawtharī. Beirut, Lebanon: Dār al-Kutub al-ʿIlmiyya, 1430/2009.

62. Jazāʾirī, Ṭāhir al-, *Al-Jawāhir al-Kalāmiyya fī ʿĪḍāḥ al-ʿAqīda al-Islāmiyya*. Beirut, Lebanon: Dār Ibn Ḥazm, 1406

63. Jurjānī, al-Sayyid al-Sharīf ʿAlī b. Muḥammad al-, *Sharḥ al-Mawāqif*, ed. Maḥmūd ʿUmar al-Dimyāṭī. Beirut, Lebanon: Dār al-Kutub al-ʿIlmiyya, 1419/1998.

64. Jazūlī, Muḥammad b. Sulaymān al-, *ʿAqīda al-Jazūlī*, ed. Khalid Zuhrī. Kuwait: Dār al-Ḍiyāʾ lil-Nashr wal-Tawzīʿ, 1435/2014.

65. Kaḥḥāla, ʿUmar b. Riḍā, *Muʿjam al-Muʾallafīn*, 15 vols. Beirut, Lebanon: Dār Iḥyāʾ al-Turāth al-ʿArabī & Maktaba al-Muthannā, 1376/1957

66. Kaḥḥāla, ʿUmar b. Riḍā, *Muʿjam Qabāʾil al-ʿArab al-Qadīma wal-Ḥadītha*, 5 vols. Beirut, Lebanon: Muʾassasa al-Risāla, 1994/1414.

67. Kāsānī al-Ḥanafī, ʿAlā al-Dīn Abū Bakr b. Masʿūd al-, *Badāʾī al-Ṣanāʾī fī Tartīb al-Sharāʾī*, 7 vols. Beirut, Lebanon: Dār al-Kutub al-ʿIlmiyya, 1406/1986.

68. Kawtharī, Muḥammad Zāhid al-, *Ḥāshiya ʿalā al-Sayf al-Ṣaqīl fī al-Radd ʿalā Ibn Zafīl* (*li-Taqī al-Dīn al-Subkī*). *Takmila al-Radd ʿalā Nūniyya Ibn al-Qayyim*. Egypt, Cairo: Dar al-Salam, 1433/2012.

69. Kawtharī, Muḥammad Zāhid al-, *Muqaddimāt al-Imām al-Kawtharī*. Egypt, Cairo: Al-Maktaba al-Azhariyya li l-Turāth, n.d.

70. Kayyālī, Muḥammad ʿĀdil al-, *ʿAqīda al-Salaf al-Ṣāliḥ Ahl al-Sunna wal-Jamāʿa fī Āyāt wa-Aḥādīth al-Ṣifāt*. Tarīm, Yemen: Dār al-Faqīh lil-Nashr wal-Tawzīʿ, 1420/1999.

71. Keller, Nūḥ Hā Mīm, *Kalam and Islam* (text of a talk given to the Aal al-Bayt Institute of Islamic Thought on 4 January 2005 in Amman, Jordan)

72. Khalīfa, Kaylānī Muḥammad, *Manhaj al-Ḥanafiyya fī Naqd al-Ḥadīth*. Cairo-Alexandria, Egypt: Dār al-Salām, 1431/2010.

73. Laknawī, ʿAbd al-Ḥayy al-, *Al-Fawāʾid al-Bahiyya fī Tarājim al-Ḥanafiyya*, ed. Aḥmad al-Zuʿbī. Beirut, Lebanon: Dār al-Arqam, 1419/1998.

74. Laknawī, ʿAbd al-Ḥayy al-, *ʿUmda al-Riʿāya ʿalā Sharḥ al-Wiqāya*, 7 vols., ed. Ṣalāḥ Abū al-Ḥāj. Beirut, Lebanon: Dār al-Kutub al-ʿIlmiyya, 1430/2009.

75. Laqqānī, Ibrāhīm al-, *Jawhara al-Tawḥīd* (printed with al-Bājūrī's commentary *Tuḥfa al-Murīd*), ed. ʿAlī Jumuʿa. Cairo, Egypt: Dār al-Salām, 1433/2012.

76. Laqqānī, Ibrāhīm al-, *'Umda al-Murīd Sharḥ Jawhara al-Tawḥīd*, 4 vols., ed. 'Abd al-Mannān and Jādullah Bassām. Amman, Jordan: Dār al-Nūr, 1437/2016.

77. Maḥallī, Jalāl al-Dīn al-, *Sharḥ Jam' al-Jawāmi'*, (printed with *al-Āyāt al-Bayyināt* of Ibn Qāsim al-'Abbādī), 4 vols., ed. Zakariyyā 'Umayrāt. Beirut, Lebanon: Dār al-Kutub al-'Ilmiyya, 1433/2012

78. Makhlūf, Muḥammad b. Muḥammad, *Shajarāt al-Nūr al-Zakiyya fī Ṭabaqāt al-Mālikiyya*, 2 vols. Beirut, Lebanon, Dar al-Kutub al-'Ilmiyya, 1424/2003.

79. Maqrīzī, Aḥmad b. 'Alī al-, *Al-Mawā'iẓ wal-I'tibār bi-dhikr al-Khiṭaṭ wal-Āthār*, 4 vols. Beirut, Lebanon: Dār al-Kutub al-'Ilmiyya, 1997/1418.

80. Mārighnī al-Mālikī, Ibrāhīm b. Aḥmad al-, *Ṭāli' al-Bushrā 'alā al-'Aqīda al-Ṣughrā*, ed. Nizār Ḥammādī. Tunis, Tunisia, 1432/2012.

81. Mawṣilī, 'Abdullah b. Maḥmūd al-, *Al-Ikhtiyār li-Ta'līl al-Mukhtār*, 4 vols., ed. Shu'ayb al-Arnā'ūṭ. Beirut, Lebanon: al-Risāla al-'Ālamiyya, 1431/2010.

82. Ḥabannaka al-Maydānī, 'Abd al-Raḥmān Ḥasan, *Al-'Aqīda al-Islāmiyya wa-Ususuhā*. Damascus, Syria: Dār al-Qalam, 1433/2012.

83. Muḥāsibī, al-Ḥārith al-, *Risāla al-Mustarshidīn*, ed. (with extensive footnotes) Shaykh 'Abd al-Fattāḥ Abū Ghudda. Cairo, Egypt: Dār al-Salām, 1435/2014.

84. Mullā, Abū Bakr al-, *Maslak al-Thiqāt fī Nuṣūṣ al-Ṣifāt*, ed. 'Umar b. Muḥammad al-Shaykhalī. Damascus, Syria: Dār al-Hudā wal-Rashād, 1431/2010.

85. Murādī, Abū al-Faḍl Muḥammad Khalīl b. 'Alī al-, *Silk al-Durar fī A'yān al-Qarn al-Thānī 'Ashar*. Beirut, Lebanon: Dār Ibn Ḥazm & Dar al-Bashā'ir al-Islāmiyya, 1408/1988.

86. Muslim b. Al-Ḥajjāj, *Ṣaḥīḥ Muslim*, 5 vols., ed. Muḥammad Fu'ād 'Abd al-Bāqī. Beirut, Lebanon: Dār Iḥyā' al-Kutub al-'Arabiyya, 1412/1991.

87. Muṭī'ī, Muḥammad al-Bakhīṭ al-, *Al-Qawl Mufīd fī 'Ilm al-Tawḥīd*, (commentary of *Wasīla al-'Abīd* by Muḥammad al-Ṭāḥirī). Cairo, Egypt: Dār al-Baṣā'ir, 1432/2011.

88. Nadīm, Ibn al-, *Al-Fihrist*, ed. Ibrāhīm Ramaḍān. Beirut, Lebanon: Dār al-Ma'rifa, 1417/1997.

89. Nasafī, Abū al-Muʿīn Maymūn b. Muḥammad al-, *Baḥr al-Kalām*, ed. Muḥammad al-Barsījī. Amman, Jordan: Dār al-Fatḥ, 1435/2014.

90. Nasafī, Abū al-Muʿīn Maymūn b. Muḥammad al-, *Tabṣira al-Adilla fī Uṣūl al-Dīn*, ed. Ḥusayn Atay. Ankara, Turkey: Riʾāsa al-Shuʾūn al-Dīniyya li-Jumhūriyya al-Turkiyya, 1414/1993.

91. Nasafī, Najm al-Dīn al-, *Al-ʿAqāʾid al-Nasafiyya*, ed. Morʾī Ḥasan al-Rashīd. Beirut, Lebanon: Dar Nūr al-Ṣabāḥ, 1433/2012.

92. Nawawī, Yaḥyā b. Sharaf al, *Al-Minhāj bi-Sharḥ Ṣaḥīḥ Muslim b. al-Ḥajjāj*, 18 vols. in 9, ed. Cairo, Egypt: al-Maṭbaʿa al-Miṣriyya, 1348/1929.

93. Nawawī, Yaḥyā b. Sharaf al-, *Riyāḍ al-Ṣāliḥīn*, ed. Shuʿayb al-Arnāʾūṭ. Beirut, Lebanon: Muʾassasa al-Risāla, 1430/2009.

94. Patton, Walter M., Aḥmad b. Ḥanbal and the *Miḥna*. Leiden, Netherlands: E.J. Brill, 1897

95. Qārī, Mullā ʿAlī al-, *Ḍawʾ al-Maʿālī Sharḥ Badʾ al-Amālī*, ed. ʿAbd al-Ḥamīd al-Turkmānī. Amman, Jordan: Dār al-Fatḥ, 1436/2015.

96. Qārī, Mullā ʿAlī al-, *Minaḥ al-Rawḍ al-Azhar fī Sharḥ al-Fiqh al-Akbar*, ed. Wahbī Sulaymān Ghawjī. Beirut, Lebanon: Dār al-Bashāʾir al-Islāmiyya, 1419/1998.

97. Qārī, Mullā ʿAlī al-, *Mirqāt al-Mafātīḥ Sharḥ Mishkāt al-Maṣābīḥ*. Beirut, Lebanon: Dār al-Fikr, 1423/2002.

98. Qayyim al-Jawziyya, Abū ʿAbdullah Muḥammad b. al-, *Madārij al-Sālikīn Bayna Manāzil Iyyāka Naʿbudu wa-Iyyāka Nastaʿīn*, 2 vols., ed. Muḥammad Muʿtaṣim Billah. Beirut, Lebanon: Dār al-Kitāb al-ʿArabī, 1417/1996.

99. Quḍat, Nūḥ ʿAlī Salmān al-, *Al-Mukhtaṣar al-Mufīd fī Sharḥ Jawhara al-Tawḥīd*. Amman, Jordan: Dār al-Rāzī, 1420/1999.

100. Qurṭubī, Muḥammad b. Aḥmad al-, *Al-Tadhkira bi-Aḥwāl al-Mawtā wa-Umūr al-Ākhira*, ed. Ṣādiq b. Muḥammad. Riyadh, Saudi Arabia: Maktaba Dār al-Minhāj, 1425/2005.

101. Qushayrī, Abū al-Qāsim ʿAbd al-Karīm b. Ḥawāzin al-, *Al-Risāla al-Qushayriyya fī ʿIlm al-Taṣawwuf*, ed. Hānī al-Ḥāj. Cairo, Egypt: al-Maktaba al-Tawfīqiyya, n.d.

102. Quṭlubghā al-Sūdūnī, Qāsim b., *Ḥāshiya ʿAlā al-Musāyara*, ed. Maḥmūd ʿUmar al-Dimyāṭī. Beirut, Lebanon: Dār al-Kutub al-ʿIlmiyya, 1423/2002.

103. Quṭlubghā al-Sūdūnī, Qāsim b., *Tāj al-Tarājim*, ed. Muḥammad Khayr Ramaḍān Yūsuf. Damascus, Syria: Dār al-Qalam, 1413/1992.

104. Rāzī al-Ḥanafī, Zayn al-Dīn Muḥammad b. Abī Bakr al-, *Tuḥfa al-Mulūk*, ed. Ṣalāḥ Abū al-Ḥāj. Amman, Jordan: Dār al-Fārūq, 1427/2006.

105. Rāzī, Fakhr al-Dīn Muḥammad b. ʿUmar al-, *Muḥassil Afkār al-Mutaqaddimīn wal-Mutʾakhirīn min al-ʿUlamāʾ wal-Ḥukamāʾ wal-Mutakallimīn*. Cairo, Egypt: Maṭbaʿa al-Ḥusayniyya al-Miṣriyya, n.d.

106. Rāzī, Fakhr al-Dīn Muḥammad b. ʿUmar al-, *Al-Tafsīr al-Kabīr*, 32 vols. Damascus, Syria: Dār al-Fikr, 1401/1981.

107. Renard, John, *Islamic Theological Themes A Primary Source Reader*. Oakland, California, University of California Press, 2014.

108. Richardson, Kara, "*Causation in Arabic and Islamic Thought*," *The Stanford Encyclopaedia of Philosophy* (Winter 2015 edition), Edward N. Zalta (ed.), https://plato.stanford.edu/archives/win2015/entries/arabic-islamic-causation.

109. Rudolph, Ulrich, *Al-Māturīdī and the Development of Sunni Theology in Samarqand*, tr. Rodrigo Adem. Leiden, Brill: 2015.

110. Saʿdī, ʿAbd al-Malik al-, *Sharḥ al-ʿAqāʾid al-Nasafiyya*. Amman, Jordan: Dar al-Nūr al-Mubīn, 1435/2014.

111. Ṣaffār al-Bukhārī, Ibrāhīm b. Ismāʿīl al-, *Talkhīṣ al-Adilla li-Qawāʾid al-Tawḥīd*, 2 vols., ed. Anjalīka Burudarshan. Beirut, Lebanon: Muʾassasa al-Rayyān, 1432/2011.

112. Saffārīnī al-Ḥanbalī, Muḥammad b. Aḥmad al-, *Lawāmiʿ al-Anwār al-Bahiyya wa-Sawāṭiʿ al-Asrār al-Athariyya*. Damascus, Syria: Muʾassasa al-Khāfiqayn wa-Maktabatihā, 1402/1982.

113. Saffārīnī al-Ḥanbalī, Muḥammad b. Aḥmad al-, *Al-Buḥūr al-Zākhira fī ʿUlūm al-Ākhira*, 2 vols., ed. Muḥammad Ibrāhīm Shomān. Kuwait: Sharika Ghirās lil-Nashr wal-Tawzīʿ, 1428/2007.

114. Ṣanʿānī, ʿAbd al-Razzāq al-, *Al-Muṣannaf*, 12 vols., ed. Ḥabīb al-Raḥmān al-Aʿẓamī. India: al-Majlis al-ʿIlmī, 1403/1983.

115. Sanūsī, Muḥammad b. Yūsuf al-, *Sharḥ al-ʿAqīda al-Kubrā*, ed. al-Sayyid Yūsuf Aḥmad. Beirut, Lebanon: Dār al-Kutub al-ʿIlmiyya, 1427/2006. Istanbul, Turkey: al-Maktaba al-Hāshimiyya, 1436/2015.

116. Sanūsī, Muḥammad b. Yūsuf al-, *Sharḥ Umm al-Barāhīn*. Istanbul, Turkey: al-Maktaba al-Hāshimiyya, 1436/2015.

117. Sarakhsī, Shams al-Aʾimma Muḥammad b. Aḥmad al-, *Al-Mabsūṭ*, 30 vols. in 12, ed. Samīr Muṣṭafā Dabab. Beirut, Lebanon: Dār Iḥyāʾ al-Turāth al-ʿArabī, n.d.

118. Ṣāwī, Aḥmad b. Muḥammad al-, *Sharḥ al-Ṣāwī ʿalā Jawhara al-Tawḥīd*, ed. ʿAbd al-Fattāḥ al-Bizm. Damascus, Syria: Dār Ibn Kathīr, 1431/2010.

119. Shahrastānī, Muḥammad b. ʿAbd al-Karīm al-, *Al-Milal wal-Niḥal*, ed. ʿAmīd ʿAlī Mahna & ʿAlī Ḥasan Fāʿūr. Beirut, Lebanon: Dār al-Maʿrifa, 1414/1993.

120. Sharīf, Kamāl b. Abī, *Al-Musāmara Sharḥ al-Musāyara*, ed. Maḥmūd ʿUmar al-Dimyāṭī. Beirut, Lebanon: Dar al-Kutub al-ʿIlmiyya, 1423/2002.

121. Shalabī, Shihāb al-Dīn Aḥmad b. Muḥammad al-, *Ḥāshiya al-Shalabī ʿalā Tabyīn al-Ḥaqāʾiq*, 7 vols., ed. Aḥmad ʿIzzū ʿInāya. Beirut, Lebanon: Dār al-Kutub al-ʿIlmiyya, 1431/2010.

122. Shirbīnī, Muḥammad b. Aḥmad al-Khaṭīb al-, *Mughnī al-Muḥtāj ilā Maʿrifa Maʿānī Alfāẓ al-Minhāj*, 6 vols. Beirut, Lebanon: Dār al-Kutub al-ʿIlmiyya, 1415/1994.

123. Sinān, Ḥamad al-, and ʿAnjarī, Fawzī al-, *Ahl al-Sunna al-Ashāʿira. Shahāda ʿUlamāʾ al-Umma wa-Adillatuhum*. Kuwait: Dār al-Ḍiyāʾ lil-Nashr wal-Tawzīʿ, 1427/2006. English translation: *Ahl al-Sunna the Ashʿaris. The Testimony and Proofs of the Scholars*. Rotterdam, the Netherlands: Sunni Publications, 2016.

124. Suʿūd al-ʿImādī, Muḥammad b. Muḥammad Abū, *Irshād al-ʿAql al-Salīm ilā Mazāyā al-Qurʾān al-Karīm*, 9 vols. Beirut, Lebanon: Dār Iḥyāʾ al-Turāth al-ʿArabī, n.d.

125. Subkī, Tāj al-Dīn al-, *Jamʿ al-Jawāmiʿ* (printed with *al-Āyāt al-Bayyināt* of Ibn Qāsim al-ʿAbbādī), 4 vols., ed. Zakariyyā ʿUmayrāt. Beirut, Lebanon: Dār al-Kutub al-ʿIlmiyya, 1433/2012

126. Subkī, Tāj al-Dīn al-, *Ṭabaqāt al-Shāfiʿiyya al-Kubrā*, 10 vols., ed. Maḥmūd Muḥammad al-Ṭanājī & ʿAbd al-Fattāḥ al-Ḥalū. Cairo, Egypt: Hijr lil-Ṭibaʿa wal-Nashr wal-Tawzīʿ, 1413/1993.

127. Sūdānī, Wuld ʿAdlān al-, *Jāmiʿ Zubad al-ʿAqāʾid al-Tawḥīdiyya fī Maʿrifa al-Dhāt al-Mawṣūf bil-Ṣifāt al-ʿĀliya*. Cairo, Egypt: Muṣṭafā al-Bābī al-Ḥalabī, 2nd ed., 1367/1948.

128. Suyūṭī, Jalāl al-Dīn b. Abī Bakr al-, *Al-Itqān fī ʿUlūm al-Qurʾān*, ed. Fawwāz Aḥmad Zamarlī. Beirut, Lebanon: Dār al-Kitāb al-ʿArabī, 1433/2012.

129. Suyūṭī, Jalāl al-Dīn b. Abī Bakr al-, *Al-Budūr al-Sāfira fī al-Aḥwāl al-Ākhira*, ed. Muḥammad Ḥasan. Beirut, Lebanon: Dār al-Kutub al-ʿIlmiyya, 1417/1996.

130. Suyūṭī, Jalāl al-Dīn b. Abī Bakr al-, *Al-Jāmiʿ al-Ṣaghīr fī al-Aḥādīth al-Bashīr al-Nadhīr*, 2 vols. Beirut, Lebanon: Dar al-Kutub al-ʿIlmiyya, 1425/2004.

131. Suyūṭī, Jalāl al-Dīn b. Abī Bakr al-, *Sharḥ al-Suyūṭī ʿalā Sunan al-Nasāʾī*, 8 vols., ed. ʿAbd al-Fattāḥ Abū Ghudda. Aleppo, Syria: Maktaba al-Maṭbūʿāt al-Islāmiyya, 1406/1986.

132. Ṭabarānī, Sulaymān b. Aḥmad al-, *Al-Muʿjam al-Ṣaghīr*, 2 vols., ed. Muḥammad Shakūr. Beirut, Lebanon & Amman, Jordan: Dār ʿAmmār, 1405/1985

133. Ṭabarānī, Sulaymān b. Aḥmad al-, *Al-Muʿjam al-Awsaṭ*, ed. Shuʿayb al-Arnāʾūṭ. Beirut, Lebanon: Dār al-Risāla al-ʿĀlamiyya, 1431/2010.

134. Ṭabarānī, Sulaymān b. Aḥmad al-, *Al-Muʿjam al-Kabīr*, ed. Ḥamdī b. ʿAbd al-Majīd al-Silafī. Cairo, Egypt: Maktaba Ibn Taymiyya, n.d.

135. Ṭāḥirī, Muḥammad al-, *Wasīla al-ʿAbīd* (printed with Muḥammad al-Bakhīṭ al- Muṭīʿī's commentary: *Al-Qawl Mufīd fī ʿIlm al-Tawḥīd*). Cairo, Egypt: Dār al-Baṣāʾir, 1432/2011.

136. Taftazānī, Saʿd al-Dīn al-, *A commentary on the Creed of Islam*, ed. Austin P. Evans, tr. Earl Edgar Elder. New York: Columbia University Press, 1950.

137. Taftazānī, Saʿd al-Dīn al-, *Sharḥ al-ʿAqāʾid al-Nasafiyya*, ed. Ṭāhā ʿAbd al-Raʾūf Saʿd. Cairo, Egypt: Al-Maktaba al-Azhariyya lil-Turāth, 1433/2012.

138. Taftazānī, Saʿd al-Dīn al-, *Sharḥ al-Maqāṣid*, 5 vols., ed. ʿAbd al-Raḥmān ʿUmayra. Beirut, Lebanon: ʿĀlam al-Kutub, 1419/1998.

139. Thānwī, Muḥammad ʿAlī al-, *Mawsūʿa Kashāf Iṣṭilāḥāt al-Funūn wal-ʿUlūm*, ed. ʿAlī Daḥrūj. Beirut, Lebanon: Maktaba Lubnān Nāshirūn, 1417/1996.

140. Tirmidhī, Muḥammad b. ʿĪsā al-, *Sunan al-Tirmidhī*, 5 vols., ed. Aḥmad Muḥammad Shākir, Muḥammad Fuʾād ʿAbd al-Bāqī & Ibrāhīm ʿIwaḍ. Cairo, Egypt: Muṣṭafā al-Bābī al-Ḥalabī, 1395/1975.

141. Ṭūsī, Nāṣir al-Dīn al-, *Talkhīṣ al-Muḥaṣṣil*. Cairo, Egypt: Maṭbaʿa al-Ḥusayniyya al-Miṣriyya, n.d.

142. Ūshī, Sirāj al-Dīn ʿAlī b, ʿUthmān al-, *Badʾ al-Amālī*, ed. ʿAbd al-Ḥamīd al-Turkmānī. Amman, Jordan: Dār al-Fatḥ, 1436/2015.

143. ʿUqaylī, Muḥammad b. ʿAmrū al-, *Al-Ḍuʿafāʾ al-Kabīr*, ed. ʿAbd al-Muʿṭī Amīn Qalʿajī. Beirut, Lebanon: Dār al-Maktaba al-ʿIlmiyya, 1404/1984.

144. Wafā al-Qurashī, ʿAbd al-Qādir b. Muḥammad b. Abī al-, *Al-Jawāhir al-Muḍiyya fī Ṭabaqāt al-Ḥanafiyya*, ed. ʿAbd al-Fattāḥ al-Ḥilū. Beirut, Lebanon: Muʾassasa al-Risāla, 1426/2005.

145. Zabīdī, Muḥammad b. Muḥammad al-Ḥusaynī, better known as, Murtaḍā al-, *Tāj al-ʿArūs min Jawāhir al-Qāmūs*. Dār al-Hidāya, n.d.

146. Zabīdī, Muḥammad b. Muḥammad al-Ḥusaynī, better known as, Murtaḍā al-, *Itḥāf al-Sāda al-Muttaqīn bi-Sharḥ Iḥyāʾ ʿUlūm al-Dīn,* 10 vols. Beirut, Lebanon, Muʾassasa al-Tārīkh al-ʿArabī, 1415/1994.

147. Zarkalī, Khayr al-Dīn b. Maḥmūd al-, *Al-Aʿlām,* 8 vols. Beirut, Lebanon: Dār al-ʿIlm lil-Malāyīn, 1399/1979.

148. Zarrūq, Aḥmad b. Muḥammad al-, *Sharḥ Asmāʾ Allah al-Ḥusnā*, ed. Aḥmad al-Ṭaḥṭāwī. Cairo, Egypt: Dār al-Faḍīla, 1430/2009.

149. Zuḥaylī, Wahba al-, *Al-Tafsīr al-Munīr*, 30 vols. Damascus, Syria: Dār al-Fikr, 1418/1998.

INDEX

The Foundational Proofs of Imam al-Sanusi is one of the foundational works in Islamic theology and is considered historically as an elemental text in traditional Islamic education. Studied for centuries and memorized by children throughout the Islamic world, *The Foundational Proofs* offers readers a methodical outline of Islamic doctrine that satisfies the mind and the heart alike. In this age of mass confusion and intellectual malaise, where fundamental Islamic beliefs are misunderstood and credulity is championed as faith, *The Foundational Proofs* explains the tenets of faith and supports them both rationally and textually.

Further enhancing the value of this work is the engaging and relevant additions of Shaykh Saʿid Foudah, one of the world's leading Islamic theologians today, who presents Imam al-Sanusi's work with the interlineal commentary of Imam Ahmad b. ʿIsa al-Ansari and engaging and detailed footnotes collated from a variety of famous commentaries, such as those by Imam al-Bajuri, Imam al-Battawi, Imam al-Sawi, Imam al-Marghani, and others, as well as his own insightful comments.

> One of the most important tasks for a person to engage in is earnest research into the doctrines of the Islamic faith. That is because the religion of Islam is based upon proofs and sound evidence; it does not contradict science or violate the fundamentals of rationality. Fundamentally, the religion of Islam is based upon rationality, and while it is true that it does not ignore the emotional aspect of religion, faith that is not grounded in the intellect is not considered perfect faith, nor is it capable of withstanding or confronting false beliefs, specious arguments, or the doubts that are spread in each age. Here Shaykh Saʿid Foudah has taken it upon himself to explicate the foundational beliefs of Islam and tenets of faith as based on the intellect, and to demonstrate their congruity with and non-contradiction to logic and science.
>
> —*Shaykh Galal al-Jihani*

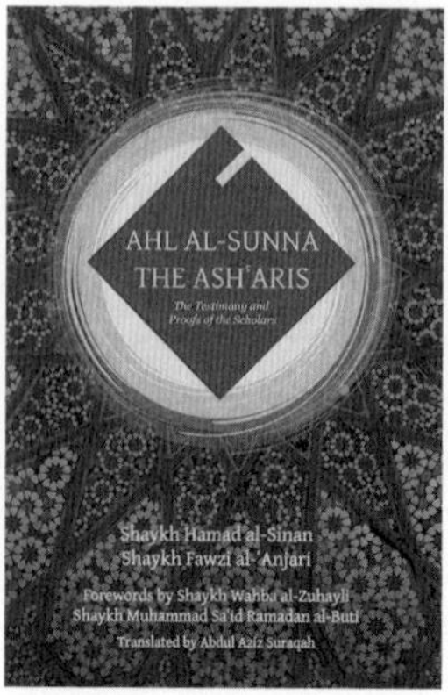

In an age in which intra-Muslim religious argumentation dominates, heterodox groups have tried and had great success in presenting their beliefs as normative Islam to the average lay Muslim. Unfortunately many of these beliefs are largely at odds with the classical articulations of Sunni orthodoxy throughout the ages.

This work, *Ahl al-Sunna: The Ashʿaris*, aims to remedy this problem. Drawing from the works of Islam's greatest scholars through the centuries, Shaykh Hamad al-Sinan and Shaykh Fawzi al-ʿAnjari detail the genesis, rise, beliefs, and contributions of the Ashʿari school of theology, and address—in a refreshingly fair-minded and non-sectarian way—common misconceptions about the Ashʿari school and demonstrate how its rich religious discourse is firmly anchored in the Qurʾan, the Sunna, the way of the Companions, and sound reasoning.

> The book in front of us is a useful and blessed endeavour that clarifies what Shaykh al-Islam and Imam amongst the Imams, Abu al-Hasan al-Ashʿari, was upon: a creed free from anthropomorphism or negation of Allah's attributes. His was indeed the creed of the pious predecessors [*salaf*]. Through its compelling arguments, numerous scholarly quotes, and discussions by prominent scholars, *Ahl al-Sunna: The Ashʿaris* succeeds in its aim, and is added to the long list of works compiled by Hadith scholars and theologians who defended Imam Abu al-Hasan al-Ashʿari, such as Ibn ʿAsakir's *Tabyin Kadhib al-Muftari* (Clarifying the Lie of the Calumniator), al-Bayhaqi's declaration in the beginning of his compilation on belief entitled *al-Iʿtiqad*, and others... May Allah reward the two authors with goodness for their eagerness through this work to defend the tenets of faith upheld by the vast majority of Muslims.
>
> *—Shaykh Husayn ʿAbd al-ʿAli*

Man is not complete until he is acquainted with the sciences by which he is able to act. The best of these is the science of Divine Oneness. It is the greatest knowledge, the medicine of the hearts, the basis for righteous actions, and the foundation of spiritual wayfaring unto the Lord of the worlds.

—Shaykh Saʿid Foudah

The Differences between the Ashʿaris & Maturidis, Shaykh al-Islam of the Ottoman Empire, Imam Ibn Kamal Pasha identifies twelve areas where the Imams of Ahl al-Sunna—Abu al-Hasan al-Ashʿari and Abu Mansur al-Maturidi—have subtly differed in theology. Topics discussed include amongst others, the attributes and actions of Allah, the question of good and evil, the role of the human intellect, man's capabilities and his condition in the Hereafter. Invaluable in elaborating on these differences is the expert commentary of leading contemporary theologian Shaykh Saʿid Foudah in which he succinctly explains the causes of the disagreements and their levels, allowing the reader to benefit from the objective of the treatise.

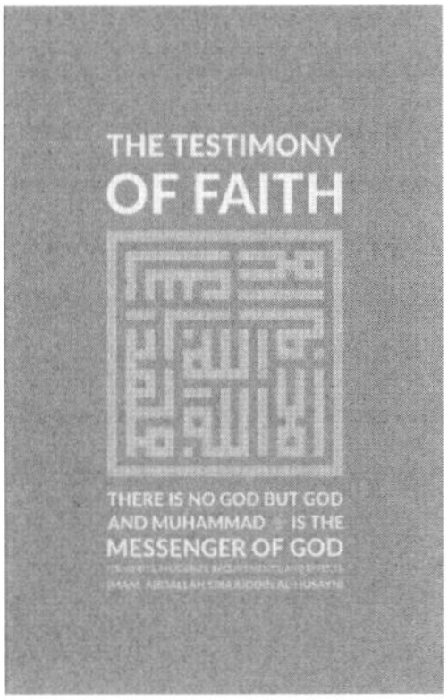

Written by the renowned scholar of Aleppo (Syria), Imam ʿAbdallah Sirajuddin al-Husayni, *The Testimony of Faith* elegantly portrays the beauty of the *shahada*, the Islamic testimony of faith: There is no god but God and Muhammad ﷺ is the Messenger of God. Going beyond cursory explanations, the author provides a precise explanation of its meanings and conditions, and presents an exhaustive discussion on its merits, virtues, and benefits in this life and the Hereafter.

How strange it is, how can God be disobeyed
And how can the obstinate disbeliever deny Him

When in every movement and stillness *There is always for Him a witness*
And in everything there is a sign *Showing that He is One*

How astounding are
Allah's affairs in creation
Each person finds facilitation
for what he was created to be

Perhaps one of the most controversial scholars of the classical era, Taqi al-Din Ibn Taymiyya's works in theology have been promoted by the modern day *Salafi* movement as an accurate representation of the creed of the predecessors [*salaf*]. In *The Palmyran Creed*, named after the ancient city of Palmyra (Tadmur, Syria), Ibn Taymiyya presents the foundations of his theology, expounds upon its principles and offers his arguments in support of it. At the heart of this lies his claim of affirming only what Allah and His Messenger ﷺ affirmed of the Divine attributes [*sifat*], "without inquiring into the modality [*takyif*], drawing likeness [*tamthil*], or engaging in alteration [*tahrif*] and denial [*ta'til*]," ostensibly purifying Divine Oneness [*tawhid*].

In his critique of the *Palmyran Creed*, renowned contemporary theologian Shaykh Sa'id Foudah clinically refutes Ibn Taymiyya's claim, demonstrating that it could not be further from the truth. The Taymiyyan theology of resemblance [*tashbih*] is deconstructed and the anthropomorphic premises [*tajsim*] for what Ibn Taymiyya considers to be the reality and attributes of Allah are revealed. Shaykh Sa'id establishes, rationally and textually, that ascriptions such as hands, eyes, face, shin, movement, direction, change, spatial contact, limits and boundaries are inconceivable with respect to Allah, and that nothing can possibly share in His reality. This ground breaking work elevates contemporary Muslim discourse beyond superficial polemics and into deeper realms of the rational sciences.

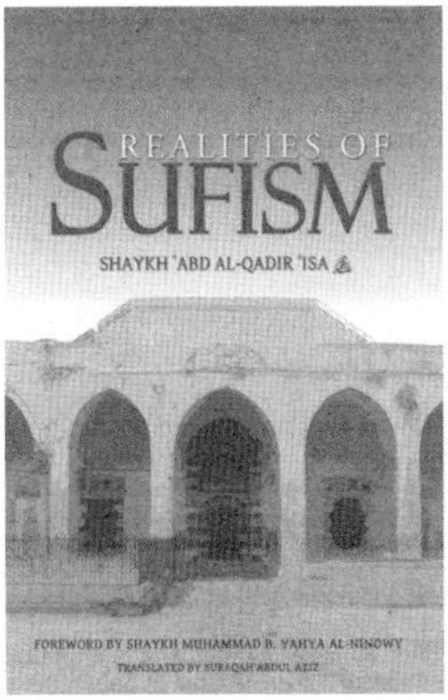

Sufism is good character
He who is ahead of you in good character
Is ahead of you in Sufism

The late Shaykh ʿAbd al-Qadir ʿIsa ؒ was one of the revivers of the Sufi tradition in the Levant. In a time of gross materialism and imported profane ideologies into the Arab world, Shaykh ʿAbd al-Qadir ʿIsa provided the keys for a reclamation of Islam's spiritual riches and revived the spiritual path, imparting guidance and instruction to scores of people from all strata of society.

Realities of Sufism, the Shaykh's only book, takes readers on a journey to the heart of Islam. Expositing on the foundations of Islam's spiritual path, Sufism, Shaykh ʿAbd al-Qadir simultaneously describes the workings of the path of excellence—*ihsan*—and answers the doubts of the orientalists, modernists, and would be Islamic revivalists. Some of the topics in this book include: the history and etymology of Sufism, the conditions of a true spiritual guide, the proper manners of a spiritual seeker, the outer manners of the path, the inner manners of the path, the deeds of the heart, spiritual unveiling, miracles, oneness of being, and historic testimonies to Sufism's key role and efficacy in purifying the souls and elevating the Sacred over the profane in the lives of man.

> Our Shaykh ؒ was a Sufi of the old persuasion: the Sufism or purification indicated in the Book of Allah Most High, and which the Messenger of Allah ﷺ was keen to teach. Our Shaykh used to say: 'The spiritual path has five pillars: remembrance, instruction, knowledge, struggle, and love.'
>
> —*Shaykh Muhammad b. Yahya al-Ninowy*

A Commentary upon the Creed of Imam al-Dardīr

Translation & Commentary
by Siddiq Adam Mitha

Forewords *by*
Shaykh Walead Mosaad &
Shaykh ʿAbd al-Raḥmān al-Shaʿʿār

Sunni Publications